# THE COMMERCIALIZATION OF MICROFINANCE

## Balancing Business and Development

*Edited by*
**Deborah Drake and Elisabeth Rhyne**
**ACCION International**

Kumarian
**Press, Inc.**

*The Commercialization of Microfinance: Balancing Business and Development*
Published 2002 in the United States of America by Kumarian Press, Inc.,
1294 Blue Hills Avenue, Bloomfield, CT 06002 USA

Copyedit, design, and production by Joan Weber Laflamme, jml ediset, Vienna, Va.
Index by Robert Swanson
Proofread by Philip J. N. Trahan/Sarov Press

The text of this book is set in 10.5/13 Times.
Printed in Canada on acid-free paper by Transcontinental Printing.
Text printed with vegetable oil-based ink.

♾ The paper used in this publication meets the minimum requirements of the American National Standard for Information Sciences—Permanence of Paper for Printed Library Materials, ANSI Z39.48–1984.

**Library of Congress Cataloging-in-Publication Data**

The commercialization of microfinance : balancing business and development / edited by Deborah Drake, Elisabeth Rhyne.
    p. cm.
"For ACCION."
Includes bibliographical references and index.
  ISBN 1-56549-153-X (pbk. : alk. paper) — ISBN 1-56549-154-8 (hardback : alk. paper)
  1. Microfinance. I. Drake, Deborah. II. Rhyne, Elisabeth. III. ACCION International (Organization)
HG178.3 .C65 2002
332—dc21

                              2002007897

11 10 09 08 07 06          10 9 8 7 6 5 4 3 2    First Printing 2002

# Contents

## Part III
### Commercial Entrants into Microfinance

## Part IV
### Challenges to Commercial Microfinance

# Illustrations

# Tables

# Preface

### by Anicca Jansen

This book builds on work completed under the United States Agency for International Development (USAID) project Microenterprise Best Practices, or simply, MBP. MBP began in 1996 shortly after the publication of *The New World of Microenterprise Finance* (Otero and Rhyne 1994) and ended in 2001 with the production of the manuscript for this book.

During this time period, *microenterprise finance* evolved into the shortened term *microfinance.* This is not simply a grammatical shortcut but rather a change in thinking and perspective. The focus shifted from making the microenterprise viable to making the microfinance provider viable. As Christen and Drake point out, this focus on profitability of microfinance providers is the heart of commercialization, and it is the heart of this book.

This book approaches commercialization both from the standpoint of nongovernmental organizations (NGOs) transforming into regulated financial institutions (see the chapters by White and Campion, and Otero and Chu) as well as exploring the for-profit sector delving into a "market" normally served by NGOs (Mommartz and Schor, and Valenzuela). Meanwhile, Lennon and Richardson discuss a shifting from within as credit unions renovate and upgrade methodologies and standards of practice keeping pace with, and in some cases, out-distancing, the professionalization of the sector.

The following chapters draw heavily on the commercialization experiences in Latin America. This is by choice. Latin America is sometimes said to be a generation ahead of other regions with respect to the development of the microfinance sector. Therefore, it was felt that these experiences (many of which had been documented by MBP research) should be shared in order to provide road markers so others might follow the same path or, in other cases, to post signs warning of potholes, barriers, and collapsed bridges. The cases of Corposol (Lee) and FASSIL (Curran), go a long way toward charting the difficulties, challenges, and rewards encountered in day-to-day operations. The analysis of one of the most mature markets, Bolivia (Rhyne), provides a glimpse down the road and raises serious issues about the capacity of microfinance institutions to withstand the impact of competition and economic shocks.

It is important to keep in mind that, with all our experiences to date, the microfinance industry as a commercial venture is still very, very young. Technologies, both "hard" (management information systems, credit bureaus) and "soft" (e.g., ownership structures), are still being developed, still being refined. As we speed down the highway, we are still developing the tools of the trade, still inventing the wheel.

Anicca Jansen is USAID's Microenterprise Development Regional Technical Advisor for West Africa, based in Dakar, Senegal. Dr. Jansen directed MBP from 1998 until 2001. The Microenterprise Best Practices project was managed by Development Alternatives, Inc. (DAI), and this book represents years of behind-the-scenes work by DAI managers (in chronological order): Jeff Poyo, Joan Parker, Robin Young, Paul Bundick, Jimmy Harris, and Ira Singh. All of the MBP documents that were used in this book are in the public domain and can be downloaded from USAID's microenterprise website, http://www.mip.org.

# Acknowledgments

This book was made possible through the Microenterprise Best Practices project (MBP), funded by the United States Agency for International Development (USAID) with the objective of expanding the knowledge base of microenterprise practices in developing countries through research and publications, a grant facility, and information sharing. The editors wish to express their appreciation to USAID and to Development Alternatives, Inc. (DAI), which managed the MBP project. In particular, we want to thank Anicca Jansen, who in her role as director of MBP first recognized the importance of sharing commercialization experiences and challenges through the publication of this book. We also are appreciative of Katherine McKee, director of Office of Microenterprise Development, USAID, for her enthusiastic support of the project.

Special thanks go to Jimmy Harris, formerly our MBP counterpart at DAI and currently at the SEEP Network, whose guidance, good humor, and equanimity kept the project moving forward. We also want to thank Ira Singh, Paul Bundick, and Mary Miller of DAI for their close collaboration and thoughtful advice during this process.

The editors wish to thank the following individuals at USAID who reviewed various drafts of the book and gave valuable comments: John Berry, Geoff Chalmers, Elizabeth Hunt, Barry Lennon, Liza Valenzuela, and Lilly Villeda. Monique Cohen provided helpful guidance on key contents of the book.

We are greatly appreciative of the efforts of María Otero of ACCION International, who supported and guided this project from the very beginning. She was instrumental in shaping the original conceptual framework for the book.

Special recognition and gratitude go to Lynne Curran and Patricia Lee of ACCION International, who spent countless hours researching, writing, and editing chapters for this book; without their efforts and creative input, this book would not be a reality.

Our thanks go to Sahra Halpern, formerly of the Microfinance Network, who provided great input and whose coordination of the "Challenges to Microfinance Commercialization" conference convened by the Microfinance Network and ACCION International in June 2001 helped further discussions on the entire topic of commercialization of microfinance.

We truly appreciate the thoughtful contributions of all of the authors whose deep commitment to the microfinance industry is evidenced in the pages of this book. However, the opinions expressed in this book are the sole responsibility of each writer and are not necessarily those of the editors or any organization.

Our special recognition and admiration go to the microfinance institutions across Asia, Latin America, Europe, and Africa who graciously shared their experiences and knowledge with the authors. It is through their efforts that we are witnessing the commercialization of microfinance.

An expression of gratitude goes to Guy Bentham and his team at Kumarian Press, who provided important guidance and support throughout the process.

The contributors also wish to acknowledge particular individuals and organizations, though regretfully we cannot include all the people whose assistance was appreciated.

Anita Campion thanks the members of the MicroFinance Network who shared their information and knowledge, bringing practical lessons and experiences to her chapters.

Robert Christen would like to thank Lynne Curran for her thoughtful editing and input to Chapter 1, "Commercialization: The New Reality of Microfinance."

Lynne Curran would like to thank Claudia Ordoñez of FFP FASSIL for her interest and willingness to provide valuable information, as well as the time she dedicated to ensuring the accuracy of the data. Members of the management of Banco Económico also took important time out of their busy schedules to provide an update of the bank's recent history. Finally, she would like to recognize Jeffrey Poyo and Robin Young for all the thoughtful hard work they put into the creation of the original publication: *Commercialization of Microfinance: The Cases of Banco Economico and Fondo Financiero Privado FA$$IL, Bolivia.*

Elizabeth Dunn and J. Gordon Arbuckle would like to thank the general manager and staff of Mibanco, colleagues on the AIMS team, USAID's Office of Microenterprise Development, USAID/Peru, and the entrepreneurs who participated in the study. This research was sponsored by USAID's Microenterprise Impact Project (PCE-0406-C-00-5036-00).

Patricia Lee thanks Deborah Drake and Lynne Curran of ACCION International for their continued feedback and guidance. She also wishes to thank the communications department of ACCION International for its continued support and Sonia Saltzman for her invaluable review of the chapter. Finally, she would like to thank Jean Steege for the research and thoughtful analysis she put into the original document, *The Rise and Fall of Corposol: Lessons Learned from the Challenges of Managing Growth.*

María Otero thanks Rachel Rock and Sonia Saltzman for their contributions to the original document, *Principles and Practices of Microfinance Governance.*

Elisabeth Rhyne would like to thank Elizabeth Dunn for her contributions to Chapter 10, "Microfinance Institutions in Competitive Conditions."

Dave Richardson and Barry Lennon wish to thank all of our colleagues and friends within the international credit union movement who helped provide us with all of the financial and statistical data used in our chapter. They have proven beyond any doubt that older dogs are definitely a man's best friend!

Leslie Théodore would like to thank Julio Cesar Hebras of BancoSol, Endara Ximena of Banco Solidario, Enriqueta Claramunt de Rodríguez of Calpia, Pedro Arriola of Caja los Andes, Carlos Labarthe of Compartamos, Francisco Madrid Reyes of FINSOL, and Manuel Montoya of Mibanco for sharing their institutions' experiences. She would also like to thank Victoria White, Elisabeth Rhyne, and María Otero of ACCION International for their guidance and input.

Liza Valenzuela would like to thank all of the bankers who kindly took time from their busy days to respond to the bank survey that informs Chapter 3, "Getting the Recipe Right." Special thanks to the staffs at Banco Agrícola and Interfisa Financiera for their willingness to give us a glimpse of their journey into microfinance.

Victoria White and Anita Campion would like to thank the board, management, and staff of the three institutions that represent the primary case studies for Chapter 2: K-Rep Bank, CARD Rural Bank, and Mibanco, for being willing to share so openly their experiences with institutional transformation.

*Deborah Drake dedicates this book to*
*Joe, Philip, Patrick, and William.*

# Abbreviations

| | |
|---|---|
| ACP | Acción Comunitaria del Perú |
| ACTUAR | Corporación Acción |
| ADEMI | Asociación para el Desarrollo de la Microempresa, Inc. |
| AIMS | Assessing the Impact of Microenterprise Services |
| ASOFIN | Asociación de Entidades Financieras Especializadas en Microfinanzas/Association of Financial Entities Specialized in Microfinance (Bolivia) |
| ASA | Association for Social Advancement (Bangladesh) |
| ATM | Automated Teller Machine |
| BAAC | Bank for Agriculture and Agricultural Cooperatives (Thailand) |
| BancoSol | Banco Solidario (Bolivia) |
| BRAC | Bangladesh Rural Advancement Committee |
| BRI | Bank Rakyat Indonesia |
| CAF | Corporación Andina de Fomento |
| CAMEL | Capital Adequacy, Asset Quality, Management, Efficiency and Liquidity |
| CARD | Center for Agricultural Development (Philippines) |
| CBK | Central Bank of Kenya |
| CEO | Chief Executive Officer |
| CFC | Commercial Finance Company, Colombia |
| CGAP | Consultative Group to Assist the Poorest |
| CIPAME | Corporación de Instituciones Privadas de Apoyo Empresarial/Corporation of Private Business Support Institutions (Bolivia) |
| COFIDE | Corporación Financiera de Desarrollo/Development Financial Corporation (Peruvian development bank) |
| DAI | Development Alternatives, Inc. |

| | |
|---|---|
| DEG | Deutsche Investitionsund Entwicklungsgesellschaft (German development finance company) |
| DFID | Department for International Development (UK) |
| EBRD | European Bank for Reconstruction and Development |
| EDPYME | Entidades de Desarrollo para la Pequeña y Micro-empresa (Small Business and Microenterprise Development Institutions), Peru |
| ESOP | Employee Stock Ownership Plan |
| FFP | Fondo Financiero Privado (Private Finance Fund), Bolivia |
| FIE | Centro de Fomento a Iniciativas Económicas (Bolivia) |
| FINRURAL | Asociación de Instituciones Financieras para el Desarrollo Rural/Association of Financial Institutions for Rural Development (Bolivia) |
| FMO | Dutch Development Finance Company |
| GEMINI | Growth and Equity through Microenterprise Investments and Institutions |
| GTZ | Gesellschaft für Technische Zuzammenarbeit (German technical assistance agency) |
| IDB | Inter-American Development Bank |
| IFC | International Finance Corporation |
| IFI | Instituto de Fomento Industrial/Institute for Industrial Development (Colombian development bank) |
| IFI | International Financial Institution (multilateral or bilateral institutions) |
| IIC | Inter-American Investment Corporation |
| IMI AG | *Internationale Micro Investitionen AG* |
| IPC | Internationale Projekt Consult |
| KfW | Kreditanstalt für Wiederaufban |
| K-Rep | Kenya Rural Enterprise Program |
| LIBOR | London InterBank Offering Rate |
| MFI | Microfinance institution |

| | |
|---|---|
| MIF | Multilateral Investment Fund of the Inter-American Development Bank |
| MIS | Management Information System |
| MSEs | Micro and Small Enterprises |
| | |
| NBD | National Bank for Development (Egypt) |
| NGO | Non-governmental organization |
| | |
| OECD | Organisation for Economic Co-operation and Development |
| | |
| PEARLS | Protection, Effective Financial Structure, Asset Quality, Rates of Return and Costs, Liquidity, Signs of Growth |
| Prodem | Fundación para la Promoción y Desarrollo de la Microempresa (Bolivia) |
| | |
| ROA | Return on assets |
| ROAA | Return on average assets |
| ROE | Return on Equity |
| | |
| SBEF | Superintendencia de Bancos y Entidades Financieras (Superintendency of Banks and Financial Entities) |
| SBS | Superintendency of Banking Supervision |
| SDRs | Special Drawing Rights |
| SEEP | Small Enterprise Education and Promotion (Network) |
| SIDI | Société D'Investissement et de Développement International |
| SOFOL | Sociedad Financiera de Objeto Limitado (limited liability financial company) (Mexico) |
| | |
| TA | Technical Assistance |
| | |
| USAID | United States Agency for International Development |
| | |
| WOCCU | World Council of Credit Unions |

## Part I

# A Framework for Understanding
# the Commercialization
# of Microfinance

# 1.

# Commercialization
## The New Reality of Microfinance

### Robert Peck Christen with Deborah Drake

## OVERALL FRAMEWORK

### What Does the Commercialization of Microfinance Mean?

To put it simply, microfinance is becoming more commercial. Not only are traditional nongovernmental organizations (NGOs) dedicated to microfinance transforming into licensed banks and non-bank financial intermediaries in order to access public funds or small savings deposits, but some banks and finance companies are noticing the potential of microcredit to enhance their product mix and bottom line. At the same time, credit unions are reviving themselves and seeking to regain their leading role as suppliers of a full range of financial services to the poor. Central bankers and finance ministries are examining whether microfinance represents a viable option for rescuing troubled state-owned development, agricultural, savings, postal, and commercial banks. All of these organizations regard microfinance as a potentially viable business, regardless of whether they are constituted as profit-maximizing entities.

An important number of people in the field regard commercialization as a necessary step to provide high quality financial services to the poor. Others feel that the introduction of the profit motive into microfinance necessarily degrades an organization's commitment to the very poor, who will be crowded out by less poor clients. This debate gets to the heart of whether the process of commercialization is "good" for the industry.

This introductory chapter, and ultimately the remainder of this book, explores many of the issues derived from the increased commercialization of microfinance. The process of commercialization has become closely linked to increasing degrees of competition in local markets among providers of banking services for the very poor. In some regions competition has increased to the point that we see real (and expected) effects, from improvements in the quality of client service, to diversification in lending products, to a broadened definition of target group, to decreases in the interest rates charged on loans. There are some negative effects of this competition, including over-indebtedness on the part of clients and systemic risk for microfinance institutions (MFIs).[1] Additionally, MFIs have a much smaller window of opportunity in which to exploit innovations before they are copied by competitors.

## Commercialization

The apparent *commercialization* of microfinance leaves no one in the field untouched. In its most basic incarnation, Merriam Webster defines *commercialize* as "to develop commerce in" or "to manage on a business basis." Many promoters and managers of microfinance NGOs readily embrace this notion of commercialization as one that reflects their commitment to a "market approach" to microcredit. In their minds, a "market approach" implies principles such as sustainability, professionalism, and efficiency in the provision of financial services. In some areas of the world, most notably Latin America, the commercialization of microfinance has been heartily embraced by industry pioneers and, indeed, sought after as a prime objective. Perhaps the most important driver of the commercialization process in Latin America has been the desire of MFIs to grow exponentially, on the basis of borrowed funds.

### Mission Drift?
Early pioneers who sought to bring microcredit closer to the formal banking sector in Latin America recognized that the vast amounts of funding required to reach the region's poor with credit could only come from the banking sector itself. They also recognized the importance of generating verifiably high levels of repayment and overall financial performance as an important pre-condition for accessing commercial sources of funding.

At the other end of the spectrum from those who see commercialization as the only option lie those who see commercialization as the introduction of a profit motive into microfinance, a process they see as intrinsically debasing the quality of service (manifested in a commitment to helping the poor) in order to maximize financial returns. This squares with Webster's third definition of *commercialization* as a process of something that "loses quality to gain profit," as in the commercialization of Christmas (where gift giving has for many families replaced the original spiritual or religious nature of this holiday).

Promoters and managers of MFIs who see commercialization from this viewpoint fear that a profit motive necessarily detracts from service quality in a sort of zero-sum game: more profit = less service and, implicitly, fewer benefits to clients. These individuals are most concerned about a *mission drift* that would be associated with a commercial approach to microfinance. They are convinced that a commitment to sustainability (profit) virtually guarantees that an MFI will move up market, abandoning poorer clients. In fact, critics of commercialization frequently note that the average loan size of commercialized microfinance institutions is significantly higher than that of nonprofit MFIs that target the poorest clients.[2] While many in this group have come to recognize that sustainability represents a pre-condition for extensive outreach, they are uncomfortable with the notion that a commercial banking institution could ever become committed to the types of clients they serve.

In this book the term *commercialization* is used to refer to the movement of microfinance out of the heavily donor-dependent arena of subsidized operations into one in which microfinance institutions "manage on a business basis" as part of the regulated financial system. These institutions may be nonprofit institutions that have become integrated into the financial system in their countries as regulated, for-profit entities, traditional financial institutions, or other specially created entities that offer microfinance services. It is understood that the process of *commercialization* is predicated on a commitment to financial performance and sustainability. In addition, most of the authors in this book would express a general enthusiasm for the notion that microfinance institutions embracing a profit motive work harder at becoming more efficient and sustainable and at achieving greater outreach than those institutions that distrust a profit motive. On the other hand, most would also be concerned about the effect that an unbridled profit motive could have on the social mission of MFIs.

### Who's Driving the Commercialization of Microfinance?

At its most basic level, the process of commercialization of microfinance has been driven by the success of industry pioneers in creating a market for microcredit. Leading organizations have demonstrated that they can build a substantial portfolio of very small loans to poor families, with high repayment rates, and do so on a sustainable basis. While millions of relatively poor families continue to be served by heavily subsidized, government-sponsored credit schemes, a small yet varied group of MFIs are slowly demonstrating that these families can be served with loans at interest rates that allow full cost recovery.

Two types of institutions are currently leading the commercialization of microfinance: (1) microfinance NGOs that have transformed into licensed non-bank financial intermediaries or banks; and (2) large retail banks (including state-owned institutions). Microfinance NGOs probably pioneered lending technologies for reaching a poorer population than that generally reached by any of these other types of institutions. However, in any given country, any one of these more commercially minded institutions might well represent a far more powerful alternative for achieving exponential growth.

Arguably, the commercialization of microfinance is most advanced in Latin America, where pioneers realized early on that funds for their growth would necessarily come from the financial sector, as opposed to donor agencies or governments. Additionally, early loan portfolios in Latin America were based on microenterprises that grow and generate employment, rather than on poorer, marginalized women, as was the case in South Asia, particularly in Bangladesh. As a result, the boards of directors of Latin American microfinance NGOs tended to be formed by individuals from the business and banking communities as opposed to social work or community development. As such, the leaders of these organizations saw the road to sustainability as commercialization, through financial sector funding provided to efficient financial institutions.

According to a recent review of Latin American microfinance published by CGAP, commercial (regulated) banking institutions currently serve over half (53 percent) of all clients and provide 74 percent of the funds for microcredit (Christen 2000).[3] This represents a dramatic shift from a decade ago when microcredit in the region was totally dominated by microfinance NGOs. Even more striking is the fact that traditional commercial banks provide 29 percent of the loan volume. So, while specialized microfinance institutions continue to dominate, traditional banks are fast becoming very important players in the provision of financial services to the poor in Latin America. These traditional commercial institutions include state-owned institutions (Banco del Estado in Chile, Banco do Nordeste in Brazil), large, private retail banks (Banco Santander in Chile, Banco de Pichincha in Ecuador), smaller private banks focusing on small and medium business lending (Banco Solidario in Ecuador and Banco de Desarrollo in Chile), and non-bank financial intermediaries (Financieras Familiar and Vision in Paraguay). Liza Valenzuela describes the increasing involvement of the commercial banking sector in microfinance in Chapter 3, "Getting the Recipe Right: The Experience and Challenges of Commercial Bank Downscalers."

Similarly, the growing commercialization of microfinance in Latin America is evident from a review of statistics and financial indicators included in the *MicroBanking Bulletin.*[4] In 2001, 124 MFIs were reporting to the *Bulletin,* of which sixty-four were fully sustainable institutions. About thirty-five of the sixty-four sustainable institutions operate in Latin America. Thirteen of the thirty-five operate in countries that have developed special non-bank financial intermediary licenses, eight are credit unions, and another eight have bank licenses.[5] *Thus, a total of twenty-nine out of thirty-five profitable Latin American MFIs are regulated banking institutions.* Many others are actively pursuing plans to purchase finance company licenses or in some other way become part of the formal financial sector. Although Latin America is more advanced in terms of the development of a commercialized microfinance industry than other regions of the world, it is expected that the demonstration effect will allow commercialized markets to develop much more rapidly now in other regions of the world.

### Transformed Microfinance NGOs

As described by Elisabeth Rhyne in Chapter 6, "Commercialization and Crisis in Bolivian Microfinance," the transformation model was introduced over a decade ago in Bolivia when PRODEM, the leading microfinance NGO in the country, sought and obtained a bank license. The early success of that bank, BancoSol, considered from its inception to be one of the best performing banks in Bolivia, gave credibility to the notion that microfinance NGOs could become part of the regulated financial landscape. As Victoria White and Anita Campion note in Chapter 2, "Transformation: Journey from NGO to Regulated MFI," the desire to join the financial system is a reflection of many microfinance NGOs' twin goals of reducing donor dependence and exponentially increasing the number of clients with access to microfinance.

The Bolivian success has led to a great deal of interest among practitioners, donors, and other supporters in the potential of microfinance

NGOs to grow and become part of the regulated financial sector. This enthusiasm has propelled legislators and regulators in various countries to create new legislation that will facilitate the transformation of microfinance NGOs and generate a whole new class of financial intermediaries dedicated to serving the poor. Leslie Théodore and Jacques Trigo explain in Chapter 12, "The Experience of Microfinance Institutions with Regulation and Supervision: Perspectives from Practitioners and a Supervisor," that special regulatory windows have been established in some countries within the agency, which supervises financial institutions to oversee specifically these new regulated MFIs. In Bolivia, the Superintendency of Banks introduced legislation creating *Fondos Financieros Privados* (Private Financial Funds), or FFPs, in the mid 1990s. The FFP structure was created specifically to provide an adequate legal structure for institutions offering financial services to micro and small enterprises. The experience of one FFP is included in Chapter 7, "The FFP Experience: FASSIL Case Study."

In Chapter 9, "Creating a Microfinance Bank in Peru: ACP's Transformation to Mibanco," Anita Campion, Elizabeth Dunn, and J. Gordon Arbuckle Jr. provide a case study of an NGO that transformed into a full-fledged commercial bank with the explicit support of the Peruvian government. Interestingly enough, in contrast to the argument of those who believe that the commercialization of microfinance necessarily brings a mission drift, Dunn analyzes ACP client data collected before and immediately after the transformation, and concludes that there is actually some evidence of a shift in the client profile toward poorer clients during the transition period.

Given the push toward transformation engendered by the Bolivian experience and that of other successful transformations, such as ACP/Mibanco, we can expect transformed MFIs to play an important role in the future of an ever more commercialized microfinance industry. Whether the opening of a regulatory framework leads to the development of a microfinance industry, or whether it is the visionary and competent microfinance NGOs that lead the way, operating as regulated entities will inevitably sharpen the microfinance institutions' focus on financial performance and, ultimately, make them more commercial in their outlook.

### Large Retail Banks

As Liza Valenzuela points out in Chapter 3, the number of "other" commercial institutions, meaning institutions that did not begin as NGOs, that have entered the market is increasing. In particular, large retail banks have competitive advantages that arise primarily from (1) extensive branch networks offering immediate channels for market penetration; (2) experience in offering savings and payment services; and (3) access to resources needed to establish a microcredit program, possibly including loan capital, funds for capital improvements, and administrative infrastructure. In the survey of commercial banks reviewed in Chapter 3, Valenzuela reports that forty-three of the forty-five institutions with microcredit programs use their own funds for the microcredit program.

Virtually every country in the world has examples of banks with these inherent advantages. Often they are state owned, with mandates to carry out agriculture and rural development. Typically, these banks were established to provide subsidized credit to farmers, through extensive branch networks reaching deeper into rural areas than other banks. Moreover, most developing countries have savings banks that were established during colonial times to provide payments and savings services. As a result of poor performance and the withdrawal of government subsidies, many of these banks are now bankrupt or moribund. Many governments are actively seeking to transform these institutions, due in part to the need to stem ongoing losses that require outlays from government budgets, but also to the recognition that rural areas remain vastly underserved by financial institutions.

When contemplating the transformation of a poorly performing state-owned development bank, governments face several options for dealing with money-losing branch networks: to close down those parts of the bank that are losing money (typically branches in small towns and rural centers); to allow the bank to become largely a savings bank, with rural branches serving as collection points for deposits channeled to urban areas; or to restructure the bank using a microfinance model such as that of Bank Rakyat Indonesia (BRI). Each of these options could be carried out with or without financial restructuring (that is, new capital infusion) or privatization. Although the microfinance option is the most difficult, it also potentially offers the greatest rewards, offering the prospect of both profitability and outreach into rural areas.

For many years BRI stood alone as the only successfully transformed rural-development bank providing microfinance services. Its Micro-Banking Division (also known commonly as Unit Desa, or local banking system) is still the largest sustainable microfinance bank in the world, with an estimated 24 million depositors and 2.4 million borrowers

(Robinson 2001). Although the savings reforms that led to this situation are only fifteen years old, already one in three Indonesian families has an account at the BRI Unit Desa. BRI has demonstrated the profitability of microfinance with returns on assets of over 5 percent for years. During the Asian crisis, BRI fared relatively well, especially when compared to the commercial banks that were collapsing all around it. It faced a relatively small and temporary increase in its loan default rate, with portfolio at risk rates peaking at 6.08 percent at the height of the crisis in 1999 (Rulianti 2001). While critics within the industry have complained that BRI does not reach the poorest end of the market, its average loan balance of US$356 (34 percent of GNP per capita) compares well to the mainstream of the microenterprise lending industry.

In the past few years other large state-owned commercial banks have also initiated microfinance operations. These include Banco do Nordeste in Brazil, Banco del Estado in Chile, and the Bank for Agriculture and Agricultural Cooperatives (BAAC) in Thailand. Banco do Nordeste in Brazil has become one of the largest programs in Latin America, with fifty-five thousand borrowers (Schonberger and Christen 2001). Having only started its microcredit program in January 1999, Banco do Nordeste has built up its portfolio in one-third the time it took programs of a similar size to reach similar portfolio sizes.

In Chile, Banco del Estado's microfinance program, known as Banestado MicroEmpresas, has been able to grow faster than all other microfinance programs in the country over the past four years on the strength of lending to its existing client base of savers. It is now one of the two largest microfinance programs in Chile. It uses a sophisticated individual lending technique that has precursor elements of credit scoring and very carefully designed systems that allow it to operate in a highly decentralized manner. In Thailand, BAAC, the country's massive agricultural bank, has just finished a significant microenterprise lending pilot and is poised to roll this product out through its entire branch-office network.

But state-owned banks are not the only class of large retail banks that are getting into microfinance. Private retail banks have also gotten into the market. Few included in Valenzuela's study have "massified" yet, but the study does show that private retail banks, particularly those with a large branch network, also have the potential to reach large numbers of clients. Most notable among private retail banks that have created successful microfinance programs is the National Bank for Development

(NBD) in Egypt, which has the largest microfinance program in the Middle East with over twenty thousand clients served through sixty-six branch offices. One unique feature of the NBD program is that regular bank employees carry out the microlending activities after hours and are paid according to a performance-based incentive system. Profit margins in the program currently run at about 15 percent (Dhumale, Sapcanin, and Tucker 1998).

In Chile, Banco Santander bought a finance company that had already established a strong microenterprise credit program within its consumer-loan portfolio. The finance company became the consumer division of Banco Santander in Chile, and today Banefe, as it is called, is the leading microcredit program in Chile in terms of the number of clients (forty thousand). Banco de Pichincha, a large retail bank in Ecuador, is currently in the pilot phase of its microenterprise credit program, called Credifé, but has been hampered by the severe economic crisis that has affected the entire Ecuadorian financial sector. Although the Credifé program was serving approximately nine thousand clients at year-end 2001, Banco de Pichincha has the infrastructure and potential to grow the program to scale very quickly.

If they can get it right, these large retail banks will be formidable competitors, not only for microfinance NGOs, but also for other formal financial institutions. However, "getting it right" is not easy. Valenzuela illustrates that, thus far, large banks have encountered difficulties in expanding their microenterprise clientele due to the challenge of assimilating a microfinance product into a corporate bank structure. Transforming these banks involves overcoming an entrenched corporate culture that is usually antithetical to microfinance—including lack of incentives and accountability for performance—and a lack of understanding of informal sector borrowers. Larger, older banks may lack the flexibility to adapt policies and procedures to handle hundreds of small loans efficiently and profitably. In some cases, thorough management change is needed, and most of the time major staff retraining is required. Such processes cost significant amounts of money and time, and success is far from assured. However, as Liza Valenzuela describes in Chapter 3, several large retail banks have been able to overcome these obstacles and put in place successful microfinance programs. These bank-based programs are no longer anomalies; rather, they have gained a substantial place in the microfinance industry, and they usually dominate microlending in the markets in which they operate.

## Small Commercial Banks and Finance Companies

An increasing number of small commercial banks and finance companies are developing microfinance services, generally on a relatively modest scale. As Valenzuela points out, because of their size these small commercial banks and finance companies are more flexible than large banks and, in many cases, are highly motivated by a need to survive in a competitive banking world. At the same time, many small, private commercial banks see low-end clients as their natural market niche.

As Rochus Mommartz and Gabriel Schor explain in Chapter 4, "The Role of Specialized Investors in Commercialization," IPC has found that the approach of starting a small, regulated institution from scratch works quite well, especially in countries of Eastern Europe. Other small banks dedicated to microfinance include BanGente in Venezuela, the Commercial Bank of Zimbabwe, and Centenary Bank of Uganda.

## Credit Unions

For a variety of reasons, credit unions are not normally considered when we refer to MFIs. Unfortunately, even when statistics of credit unions are included in publications or studies that consider the "entire" microfinance industry, the number

> **Box 1.1: Consumer Credit—
> A Challenge to Microfinance?**
> Consumer credit is a close cousin of microfinance, and it is quickly moving closer. In fact, many microenterprises may be able to access credit more simply through consumer finance companies that lend to salaried family members than through the often cumbersome procedures of the MFIs. As more and more small banks and finance companies get into the business of microlending, it would not be surprising to find that such institutions are already serving many potential clients of microfinance through their consumer-lending activities. The extent of the "crossover" between microfinance and consumer credit has not yet been researched in-depth, nor was there the space or the resources to explore it in this book (although the important impact of consumer-credit institutions on microfinance is recognized throughout the book, especially in Chapter 6, "Commercialization and Crisis in Bolivian Microfinance").

of credit unions included in the study is usually quite small and therefore not representative of the participation of credit unions in the industry. Of the 124 MFIs included in the spring 2001 edition of the *MicroBanking Bulletin,* only sixteen are credit unions. Credit unions were not even included in the previously mentioned CGAP survey of Latin American MFIs, and related credit union statistics are usually not mentioned in discussions on clients served and amounts lent. Instead, such totals represent clients of the "microenterprise credit" and "village banking" community of targeted lending programs. In Chapter 5, "Teaching Old Dogs New Tricks: The Commercialization of Credit Unions," Barry Lennon and David Richardson describe the commercialization experience of credit unions, as these institutions have also recognized the need to commercialize in order to expand outreach.

Credit unions in many parts of the world have a significant number of members who could be classified as microenterprise clients or, at least, are members of the same low-income communities microcredit programs seek to reach. Credit unions dominate the microfinance industry in West Africa, as evidenced by the highest concentration of credit union lending to low-income, unsalaried microentrepreneurs in Africa.

Exactly how much overlap exists between "traditional" MFIs and credit unions the world over is not clear. Yet, credit unions unquestionably operate in poor areas and reach many poor clients. It has been estimated that in Latin America, credit union lending to firms represents 40 percent of their total loans (Westley and Shaffer 1999). Survey work in Nicaragua, El Salvador, and Ecuador found that virtually all credit union loans to enterprises could be classified as microenterprise on the basis of number of employees (fewer than five).

It is possible to estimate the total volume that credit unions may be lending to microenterprise clients by taking a highly conservative approach. The World Council of Credit Unions (WOCCU) estimates that total lending in 1998 by credit unions in Latin America amounted to US$6.5 billion. While WOCCU member institutions do not constitute the totality of credit union lending in the region, this total is probably representative in the same way the CGAP MFI survey is representative of the total microcredit for the region. One might assume that 25 percent of this total corresponds to the non-agricultural enterprise lending and that only one-third of this volume corresponds to "poor" microenterprises. This means that credit unions lend US$516 million to microenterprises and another US$323 million to very small farmers for a total of US$840 million, an amount quite similar to the total for the "microfinance" community (Christen 2000).

It is hard to ignore the fact that the performance of credit unions is far better than the aggregate of microfinance NGOs in most countries.

Informal estimates in many countries put the number of bankrupt credit unions at between 25 to 40 percent. Still, this means that many years after their founding as many as 60 to 75 percent of the entities are still viable commercial enterprises. While microlenders have certainly discovered how to reach clients that are even poorer than the typical member of many credit unions, credit unions do represent legitimate platforms for extending financial services to the poor on a commercial basis.

### Consequences of Commercialization

#### Transformation in Ownership

While many of the new actors getting into microfinance are traditional commercial banking institutions, most MFIs began as microfinance NGOs. Victoria White and Anita Campion discuss in Chapter 2 that as NGOs seek exponential growth, they find that transformation into a regulated financial entity is necessary in order to increase access to diversified funding sources. In most countries an NGO is not legally permitted to be the sole shareholder of a licensed financial entity; therefore, additional partners must be identified. These partners typically own an important number of voting shares and change the governance structure of the resulting organization. María Otero and Michael Chu discuss the implications of this broader board composition in Chapter 11, "Governance and Ownership of Microfinance Institutions."

The transformation in ownership is not only a consequence of the transformation of microfinance NGOs to regulated institutions, but also a consequence of the transformation of the entire industry and its move toward commercialization. This transformation in ownership through the incorporation of investors from international organizations, multi- and bilateral agencies, specialized investment funds, and the private sector has brought broader competencies to microfinance. At the same time, balancing shareholders' demands for client outreach and profitability can stress the traditional MFI structure so greatly that many of its core staff, including the founders, frequently find themselves marginalized in the reformed institution. One of the most telling differences between the pioneering NGOs and bank-based programs is that while NGOs seem to revolve essentially around the personality of their founder, banks can experience wholesale changes in top management without serious impediment to the program. Chapter 8, "Corposol and Finansol: Institutional Crisis and Survival," illustrates how the dependence on the charismatic personality of one MFI's leader contributed to serious challenges and problems at two Colombian institutions.

Whether they are getting involved in transformed institutions or represent retail banks getting into microfinance, the fact is that a wider variety of owners and stakeholders are being drawn to microfinance. They bring with them a variety of motivations for entering this field. Public development agencies and nonprofit organizations remain the largest investors in most transformed MFIs. However, as Chapter 4 illustrates, more and more specialized investor groups and multilateral organizations are taking ownership positions in transformed MFIs. These two groups offer a combination of reputation, capital, technical expertise, and a long-term investment perspective that has so far made them indispensable as co-owners of MFIs.

Regardless of their motives for investing, these new shareholders bring with them a sharper focus on financial performance and accountability. Victoria White and Anita Campion note that a benefit of private investors is that since they have a financial stake in the MFI, it is presumed that their participation should bring a heightened interest in detecting early signs of problems and identifying potential opportunities. However, a continued concern voiced by some players in the microfinance industry is that private ownership may bring about a reduced concern with reaching down as far as possible into poor segments of the economy.

## The Ultimate Irony?

Commercial financial institutions are able to provide many more financial services to the microfinance client than microfinance NGOs. Services that are valuable to this target clientele include savings, insurance, payments systems, and remittances. Experience has shown that such services should probably only be developed by large institutions with extensive infrastructure and financial strength.

Regardless of legal structure, achieving scale is critical to success; from an institutional perspective, the key to developing a wide variety of services for a large number of clients lies in reducing the average transaction cost. One way to decrease the average transaction cost is to increase dramatically the number of transactions that flow through each teller window. To reduce transaction costs and increase scale, it will be necessary for MFIs to expand financial services offered and to strive to reach all possible persons within a geographical area.

Another way to decrease average transaction costs is to place microcredit operations within infrastructures that have been developed for other purposes. For example, post offices in many parts of the world are developing a wide variety of payments services to capitalize on their investment in a huge teller-window network. In Brazil, Banco do Nordeste has an agreement in place to receive loan payments through the post office network in certain states.

For the reasons cited above, *the ultimate irony of microfinance may be that the best way to reach a large number of the truly poor with financial services will be through commercial banking institutions, not microfinance NGOs*. Nevertheless, given the highly specialized nature of microfinance, relatively few banking institutions will or should ever take it on as a core banking business. In this sense microfinance will also ultimately be a niche banking activity. Having said this, increased commercialization will broaden the range of clients, products, delivery mechanisms, and institutional structures involved in the provision of financial services for the poor.

### The Making of a Market and the Competitive Response

In Chapter 10, "Microfinance Institutions in Competitive Conditions," Elisabeth Rhyne points out that until the late 1990s most MFIs did not have to worry about competition. Ultimately, if an institution is effective in lending out small amounts sustainably, others will want to do the same, and competition will be generated, regardless of whether the original MFI supports the notion of building a commercial market. Today, in a few countries around the world, especially in the most densely populated areas of those countries, a large number of MFIs operate in competitive environments that they themselves helped to create. Clients in several Latin American countries, the city of Kampala in Uganda, the District of Tangail in Bangladesh, and the Island of Java in Indonesia now may choose to borrow from any one (or more) of several MFIs. MFIs must respond to such market forces in much the same way as any business, as their institutional survival depends on their ability to compete in an increasingly commercialized environment. In these areas MFIs have begun to compete among themselves to attract staff, retain clients, and draw in donor subsidies.

The competitive behavior of microfinance institutions is consistent with what would be expected from any commercial firm operating in a competitive environment. In fact, many of the recent changes in microfinance in these markets can best be understood as a response to competitive pressure and an attempt both to gain and to retain clients through improved service. Two of these key changes are described below.

*A shift toward individual loans:* Most people would generally prefer not to join groups in order to receive a loan. Microfinance institutions, however, have traditionally required clients to join solidarity groups as a way to reduce risk by enhancing their borrower selection capability and creating social pressure to repay. Early in the development of microenterprise loan products, it seemed necessary and prudent to break the paradigm of "the poor cannot or will not pay" with lending technologies that erred far to the side of risk management. The result has been an industry characterized by very good repayment performance among leading microfinance institutions. Over time, in mature markets, the group lending methodology may begin to break down as borrowers with a strong repayment record prefer to borrow directly using an individual credit product. As Rhyne points out, client preference for individual loans over group loans is being noted in competitive environments. She describes how, in Bolivia, several competent individual lenders, led by Caja Los Andes, are lending in direct competition to solidarity group and village bank lenders. Their success has created a trend toward individual lending, as seen in the rapidly increasing proportion of individual loans in Bolivia's total microfinance portfolio.

*Technological advances:* As part of their efforts to position themselves favorably in competitive markets, microfinance institutions are developing and implementing innovative techniques for making these loans available in an attempt to position themselves favorably in products and techniques. MFIs around the world are experimenting with credit cards, smart cards, ATMs, credit scoring, pawn loans, payments through post offices or retail outlets of chain stores, hand-held personal computers, biometrics for identifying individuals, and satellite based communications (see Campion and Halpern 2001). Most of these innovative techniques seek to drive down transaction costs for both clients and MFIs in an attempt to make services more accessible and more responsive to clients' needs. Many would argue that it has become evident that commercial MFIs are in a far better position to experiment with many of these capital-intensive innovations than their NGO counterparts.

## Regulation and Supervision

Most of the leading MFIs that have evolved up to this point did so in the absence of any guiding regulatory framework. One might best describe the environment in which many of them have operated as "legal limbo." In most countries, borrowing funds to on-lend would be considered financial intermediation and should fall under the supervision of the banking authorities. Technically, then, most microfinance NGOs would be operating outside of the legal framework. But, just as banking authorities are reluctant to supervise department-store credit cards, they have traditionally felt that microfinance NGOs are just not worth the effort from a prudential standpoint. As former superintendent of banks in Bolivia Jacques Trigo states in Chapter 12, "Supervisors can afford to ignore the microfinance sector without jeopardizing the health of the financial system they are entrusted to protect."

Today, however, there are a great number of countries that have become convinced that microfinance must be carried out by regulated institutions. Many countries are now engaged in the process of developing regulatory frameworks for a new category of licensed MFIs. NGOs and multilateral agencies are pressuring governments in many African and South Asian countries to write regulations that would encourage the transformation of microfinance NGOs into regulated non-bank financial entities. Laws have been written or are being actively considered in many countries that would bring microfinance NGOs under the regulators' umbrella in order to facilitate access to funds from apex organizations, secondary financial markets, and savings deposits from the general public.

One might argue that this "rush to regulate" obeys the needs of multilateral banks

---

**Box 1.2: Credit Bureaus**

It is easy to see why the first and most important piece of industry-wide infrastructure that must be built once markets develop for microcredit is a client information system, or a *credit bureau*. Only the existence of a well-functioning credit bureau offers the means to cut defaulting clients off from future credit relationships—the very essence of character-based lending. As Jacques Trigo explains in Chapter 12, it does not matter whether a credit bureau is maintained by the public or private sector, as long as it functions well and includes all of the information necessary to evaluate credit risk.

Anita Campion and Liza Valenzuela explore the usefulness of credit bureaus in microfinance in Chapter 13, "Credit Bureaus: A Necessity for Microfinance?" Although microfinance loans are just beginning to be incorporated into credit bureaus in some countries, Campion and Valenzuela argue that as microfinance markets develop, credit bureaus will play an increasingly important role in stabilizing the market and discouraging client over-indebtedness.

and local governments to set up mechanisms to channel funds through regulated entities and a misguided push by the MFIs themselves to access public savings (see Christen and Rosenberg 2000). In either case, there is movement to incorporate the microfinance NGOs into the regulated financial sector. Even though many of the regulatory schemes proposed do not suggest that relatively small microfinance NGOs become subjected to heavy prudential supervision, history supports that there will be a natural tendency of regulators to overreach once regulatory mechanisms are put in place.

As Leslie Théodore and Jacques Trigo discuss in Chapter 12, regulated MFIs clearly consider supervision to be a challenging consequence of commercialization. Along with the accepted benefits of regulation, there are many costs that MFIs might not always recognize before deciding to establish a regulated institution. Such costs include adding and training staff, modifying or replacing management information systems in order to conform to information requirements, as well as supervisor fees. However, Théodore and Trigo also note that all of the MFIs surveyed for the chapter believe that the benefits of being regulated outweigh the costs. In addition to benefits such as increased access to diversified funding sources, MFIs also attribute other benefits to their status as regulated entities. These other benefits include increased profitability and the ability to be more innovative in product offerings.

### Concluding Comments

The commercialization of microfinance is a process that has its own inexorable logic. Financial self-sustainability is a necessary pre-condition for achieving exponential growth. Without it, no amount of subsidy is sufficient to preserve the long-term access of a large number of very poor clients to basic financial services. Donor organizations are simply unwilling, as well they should be, to heavily subsidize microfinance operations once an MFI clearly demonstrates that it can operate on a sustainable basis with a prescribed target group. Irrespective of whether an MFI is profit oriented, the desire to reach a large number of low-income clients should drive it to build a sustainable model. The fact that some leading programs are still subsidy dependent has more to do with their denial of the effects of inflation on the value of their equity, even in low inflationary environments, or their commitment to passing on to the borrower the subsidies they receive.

Once a basic operational model has been worked out locally by microfinance NGOs, it appears to be the replicators that have made other policy choices to ensure their programs move to the next level. This is the fundamental lesson of the past few years. Movement in the industry usually comes from successive waves of new and innovating MFIs rather than from within the pioneering cohort. Thus, the very success of the NGO pioneer in establishing a viable working model for institutional microfinance virtually ensures its ultimate commercialization.

That the commercialization of microfinance is inevitable is not to say that this is either good or bad. Without doubt, MFIs that seek to grow exponentially and reach hundreds of thousands of poor clients will find that taking a businesslike approach to building a profitable program is a pre-condition to fulfilling that mission. At each and every level of target client, poor or not as poor, MFIs that take a more businesslike approach dominate in local markets. The scant evidence we have to date suggests that more commercially oriented entrants into microfinance tend to come into the market at the same level and with the same general target groups as their nonprofit precursors.

On the other hand, Mohammed Yunus of Grameen Bank and others have a very powerful point—less poor clients crowd out poorer clients in any credit scheme, regardless of the general level of poverty of the participating client group. Numerous studies of development credit schemes have demonstrated this behavior, especially in subsidized credit programs. New research is demonstrating the further truth that many of the poorer potential clients of microfinance are self-excluding from current MFIs because their loan products simply do not meet these potential clients' cash flow patterns.

If we put these two truths together, we conclude the following: commercialization is a process to be sought after in microfinance. In it lies the potential for truly exponential growth and, ultimately, vastly improved financial service to the poor. Competition for microenterprise clients will improve product design, delivery systems, and, perhaps even outreach. However, commercialization does not necessarily drive MFIs further down market, out market, or in any other way—into more marginalized target groups. It remains up to the "development finance" community to continue to innovate in the areas of targeting tools, product and service delivery design, and the organization of operations in order to reach the full range of low-income families in any given market with effective, institutionally based, microfinance services. This, in addition to the deployment of required industry-wide infrastructure, will require substantial industry support from governments and the donor community for years to come. The fact that the industry is becoming more commercial, and that we would wish for microfinance NGOs to be committed to building sustainable demonstration models, does not take away the need to continue to subsidize innovative models for deepening and broadening the outreach of MFIs.

There are many topics not included in this introductory chapter that are included in the book itself. For example, although here there is little mention of the value of commercial institutions being able to provide savings services to microclients, White and Campion discuss this important topic in Chapter 2. Additionally, we recognize that there are undoubtedly many other areas of interest and importance that due to lack of space were not included in the book. Although this is unfortunate, we look forward to lively discussions and future publications that will address new and evolving issues in the commercialization of microfinance.

## NOTES

1. The term *microfinance institution*, or MFI, describes all institutions that provide microfinance services, whether or not the initial drive behind the establishment of the institution was to serve microentrepreneurs. Although the term has been used previously to refer only to regulated institutions providing microfinance services, or rather, regulated non-bank financial intermediaries, for the purposes of this book MFIs include commercial banks, state banks, not-for-profit organizations, non-bank regulated financial intermediaries, finance companies, and credit unions.

2. This phenomenon is noted in "Commercialization and Mission Drift, The Transformation of Microfinance in Latin America" (CGAP Occasional Paper No. 5 [December 2000]), through comparative average loan balances in Latin America. It is also noted in the paper, however, that the two groups of MFIs started out with very different views of their target group and these differences may have less to do with mission drift than the fact that the early pioneers were seeking to serve microbusinesses and later entrants sought to serve very poor women in village-banking-style programs.

3. Christen addresses these and other important issues on the basis of recent information from Latin America, attempting to provide a sense of the state of the industry in the region and the challenges it faces. *Microcredit* was defined in the study as loans equal to less than 200 percent of GNP per capita. Credit unions were not included in the study.

4. The *MicroBanking Bulletin* is a semi-annual publication that gathers the financial results of MFIs around the world, puts them on common ground, and compares the results to set benchmarks.

5. *MicroBanking Bulletin* 6 (April 2001).

## Part II

# Approaches to a Commercialized Microfinance Industry

# Transformation
## *Journey from NGO to Regulated MFI*

**Victoria White and Anita Campion**

## NGO TRANSFORMATION

With the creation of BancoSol in 1992, the microfinance industry witnessed the birth of a new trend in institutional development: the transformation of NGOs into regulated financial institutions. While not embraced by all, institutional transformation has become the strategic end-objective of a large number of microlending NGOs. The concept was born over a decade ago out of the twin goals of exponentially increasing the number of clients with access to microfinance and reducing donor dependence.

The term *transformation* is used generically here to reflect the institutional process of change that occurs when microfinance NGOs create or spin off regulated MFIs. This chapter summarizes the findings and preliminary lessons learned from microfinance NGOs that have created privately owned, regulated MFIs.[1] It begins by looking at the institutional characteristics of these pioneering NGOs and outlines the reasons why a nonprofit NGO would consider transforming into a for-profit, regulated financial institution. Through a close examination of the transformation process among organizations from Asia, Africa, and Latin America, the chapter highlights key issues associated with transformation.

### *The Transformation Landscape—Who Is Transforming?*

Of the seven thousand NGOs providing microfinance services to poor entrepreneurs throughout the world, only a minute percentage has initiated transformation into privately owned, regulated MFIs. Table 2.1 captures basic information on seven transformed MFIs. As evident from the table, NGO transformation is not limited to a certain type of lending methodology or determined by a certain outreach level or portfolio size. It is, however, initiated by institutions that have achieved cost recovery in their operations and have made a commitment to expand outreach.

### Objectives in Transformation—Why Transform?

Common objectives of NGOs that have created privately owned MFIs to date include access to commercial capital, the ability to mobilize local savings, improved customer service, and expanded outreach. In general, the institutions have thus far shown success in meeting their principal objectives, although not to the extent previously expected.

### The Institutional Perspective

For MFIs that adhere to the financial systems approach to microenterprise development, transformation into a formal financial institution is a natural progression, as it is viewed as the only means to attain self-sustainability and profitability. MFIs that began more as international development projects may see transformation as a way to increase development impact. Regardless of the origins of the microfinance institution, given an amenable regulatory environment, transformation into a formal financial institution can offer many benefits not available to unregulated NGOs.

### Access to Commercial Capital

Few microfinance NGOs are able to access capital markets as needed for loan portfolio expansion at a reasonable cost. Benefits of access to commercial capital include the ability to source capital more rapidly and increased leverage.

*Reduction in capital shortage risk:* While donor funds may be sufficient for initial startup capitalization needs, MFIs tend to grow quickly and require greater and more rapid access to sources of loan capital. An MFI's ability to quickly access capital from diversified funding sources, including the discount window at the central bank, can reduce the risk of a liquidity shortfall.

**Table 2.1: Statistics for MFIs at the Time of Transformation**

| NGO name | Prodem | AMPES | ProCrédito |
|---|---|---|---|
| New financial institution | BancoSol | Financiera Calpiá | Caja Los Andes |
| Date of transformation* | Feb '92 | Jul '95 | Jul '95 |
| Country | Bolivia | El Salvador | Bolivia |
| Transformed institutional structure | Commercial bank | Non-bank financial institution | Non-bank financial institution |
| Lending methodology | Solidarity groups | Individual loans | Individual loans |
| No. of active borrowers of NGO at transformation | 22,743 (12/31/91) | 7,769 | 12,662 |
| Value of outstanding loan book at transformation | $4.5 million (12/31/91) | $4.4 million | $4.2 million |

**Table 2.1—***Continued*

| CARD | ADEMI | ACP | K-Rep |
|------|-------|-----|-------|
| CARD Rural Bank | BancoADEMI | Mibanco | K-Rep Bank |
| Sept '97 | Jan '98 | May '98 | Sept '99 |
| Philippines | Dominican Republic | Peru | Kenya |
| Rural bank | Development bank | Commercial bank | Commercial bank |
| Village banking | Individual loans | Individual loans & solidarity groups | Solidarity groups |
| 10,868 | 18,000 | 32,000 | 13,201 (12/31/98) |
| $1.7 million | $30.3 million | $14 million | $3.3 million (12/31/98) |

*Refers to date of official opening as a formal financial institution.
Sources: Prodem: Drake and Otero 1992; AMPES: Financiera Calpiá (1999); ProCrédito:
Los Andes (1999); CARD: CARD (1998); ADEMI: ADEMI (1998); ACP: ACP (1998); K-Rep:
K-Rep (1999).

*Leverage:* As unregulated microfinance institutions, NGOs in general have not been successful at leveraging their equity base. Without some form of guaranty facility, commercial banks are reluctant to lend amounts much greater than the net worth of the unregulated MFI. As a regulated financial institution, however, the MFI is subject to ongoing supervision by a regulatory authority, providing depositors, commercial investors, and other banks a greater sense of security. As such, the MFI has the potential to leverage its equity up to eleven times, the limit prescribed by the Basle Convention, the international capital adequacy standard for regulated financial institutions.[2] However, most regulated MFIs have not obtained such high leverage due to the higher risks typically associated with a microloan portfolio. BancoSol, which obtained its banking license in 1992, has maintained its leverage ratio between 5:1 and 6:1 since 1994.

### Ability to Attract Savers

Regulatory policies in most countries prevent nonprofit, unregulated organizations from collecting savings, because there is no way to insure deposits placed at an unregulated institution. In such cases, only by becoming registered as a formal financial institution can an MFI gain access to this most stable capital base, voluntary local savings deposits. By mobilizing savings, an MFI can increase the number of clients served, improve customer satisfaction, improve loan repayment, stabilize sources of funds, and improve governance of the MFI.

*More clients served:* Experience has demonstrated that low-income people can and do save, and that they will entrust their savings to formal financial institutions if they are provided security, convenience, liquidity, and positive rates of return (Robinson 1994b). Transforming MFIs have the benefit of a base of loan clients from which to begin marketing savings services. Furthermore, many people dislike or fear becoming indebted and prefer self-financing, which can be facilitated by access to savings services.

*Customer satisfaction:* MFIs can better serve clients by offering savings products specifically designed to suit their needs. Potential benefits to clients include (1) liquidity; (2) savings for investment and interest earnings; (3) savings for consumption purposes not usually eligible for loans by MFIs; (4) lower transaction costs by increasing geographical access and convenience to savings products; (5) replacement or supplement to credit; (6) increased access to credit through use of savings as security or down payment on a loan; and (7) confidence that their savings are secure.

*Improved loan repayment:* Loan repayment can improve when clients use their accumulated savings to make loan payments as necessary to cover periods of low income. In addition, clients can use their deposits to secure loans, allowing them to leverage their assets and increasing their level of commitment to repayment.

*Stabilize sources of funds:* Over the long term, mobilizing savings can build a more dependable source of capital funds for MFIs, reducing the need for external funds and offering stability in times of crisis. In fact, low-income earners tend to increase savings in sound financial institutions in times of crisis to guard against potential future income shortages. During the recent financial crisis in Asia, Bank Rakyat Indonesia's (BRI's) rural Unit Desa clients continued to save. Between 1996 and 1999, the number of savings accounts at BRI increased by 50 percent from 16.1 million to 24.1 million (Robinson 2001, 248).

*Improved governance:* Savings mobilization can improve the governance of an MFI since it heightens the board and management's client orientation and requires a higher level of supervision and oversight.

Unfortunately, savings mobilized by regulated MFIs continue to be rather low. There are many cases of regulated microfinance institutions that have transformed into non-bank financial intermediaries and still cannot capture savings. This depends on the regulatory framework of the country in which they are operating, as many countries do not allow such regulated finance companies, which usually have lower minimum capital requirements than banks, to capture savings. At the same time, some transformed MFIs that are legally able to capture savings do not take advantage of their ability to mobilize savings. One reason for this is the dominating influence of the NGO's original lending culture; any cultural shift requires MFI managers and staff to become more familiar with local markets and to shift from the social service perspective typical of an NGO to a customer-service orientation appropriate for a financial intermediary.

Transforming MFIs must weigh the benefits of savings mobilization against the costs. The development of savings products is expensive and complex, requiring high levels of liquidity and risk-management skills, as well as an understanding of the local economy. The addition of savings products is often more difficult than the addition of loan products. It is often more efficient for microfinance institutions to mobilize savings only after achieving a scale sufficient to offer savings products cost effectively.

The impact of savings mobilization on an MFI cannot be overstated. The addition of savings products usually leads to an increase in loan sizes, as borrowers leverage their savings to access larger loans. While there are relatively few MFIs that mobilize savings currently, those that do often serve far more clients through their savings products than their loan products. The most impressive example is BRI's MicroBanking Division, which serves almost ten times as many clients with its savings services as with its lending operations.[3]

## Improved Customer Service

As markets become more competitive, as in Bolivia and Bangladesh, MFIs must pay more attention to their customers' needs and desires in order to retain their market share. Otherwise, MFIs risk losing customers to the competition. MFIs can encourage customer loyalty by offering competitive interest rates and by providing quality products and services. Transformation allows MFIs to offer the widest array of products and services to meet customer needs at one convenient location. Over the long term, keeping existing customers satisfied is far less expensive to the MFI than identifying new customers to replace them (Churchill and Halpern 2001).

## Expanded Outreach

With increased access to cheaper sources of funds, transformation enables the MFI to increase market penetration, open new branches, and increase its loan portfolio. Additionally, by offering new products the transformed MFI can expand its client base and more fully serve its existing clientele. Between its creation in 1998 and December 2000, Mibanco increased its active client base to fifty-eight thousand from thirty-two thousand, and its outstanding loan portfolio to US$40 million from US$14 million.

## The Industry Perspective

Leading microfinance visionaries, practitioners, donors, technical assistance providers, and researchers have espoused beliefs that transformation would lead to increased commercialization and integration of MFIs into the formal financial sector. This vision implies not only increased access to capital markets but also the transfer of ownership to private investors with strong vested interests.

## Private-Sector Ownership

To date, transformation has only attracted a small amount of private-sector ownership in MFIs. While all of the transformed NGOs in this study involve some form of private-sector investment, this has typically represented only a small part of the overall ownership structure of the transformed institutions. However, public development agencies and nonprofit organizations remain the largest investors in most transformed MFIs.

Specialized equity funds, such as ProFund, the ACCION Gateway Fund, and Internationale Micro Investitionen AG (IMI AG) are not pure private investors, yet they play an important role in the transition toward increased commercial investment in microfinance.[4] While primarily capitalized by the public sector, these funds are managed and treated as private commercial money. If successful, these funds will demonstrate that investing in MFIs is viable and will divest their holdings to pure private investors.

## Improved Governance and Accountability

With the involvement of new owners/investors, transformation requires a revision of the governance structure. This revision allows the MFI to renew the board's commitment to the institutional mission and to reinforce its long-term strategic plans, while keeping in mind both social and commercial objectives. Regulatory requirements can also influence the strength of the governance and internal control structures.

The specialized equity funds help compensate for the lack of private-sector representation on MFI boards, as they tend to have a strong interest in overseeing both the commercial and social objectives. Despite holding minority ownership positions, these funds make an important contribution to the governance of microfinance institutions by linking technical expertise with ownership.

NGO investors tend to place a heavier emphasis on the fulfillment of the social mission than the commercial objective, in line with their original reason for engaging in microfinance. The Corposol/Finansol crisis in Colombia offers one example of the governance limitations of controlling ownership by the founding NGO, particularly when the NGO is a majority shareholder and there remains a strong operational link between the NGO and the new bank.[5] NGOs can fulfill their governance role only if they apply high professional standards and technical expertise to analyze and interpret the MFI's evolution.

## Key Issues in Transformation

The creation of privately owned, regulated MFIs is technically defined by two distinct events: the granting of a license by the central bank and the introduction of ownership through stock issuance. A third, more evolutionary phase of the transformation process is characterized by a multitude of organizational development changes.

### Integration into the Formal Financial System

The licensing process and integration of an MFI into the formal financial system typically proceeds in one of two ways. MFIs either select an appropriate institutional structure from current banking legislation or work with the supervisory agency to enact special regulatory legislation, such as defining a category of non-bank financial institutions. An MFI must begin the process of entering the formal financial system with a review of the country's political and economic environment, as well as an in-depth understanding of the regulatory framework.

### Political and Economic Environment

Contextual considerations of the country's political and economic environment play a determinant role in the implementation and timing of the transformation process. MFIs must determine whether the anticipated benefits associated with transformation can in fact be achieved in the current political and economic environment. In addition, a transforming MFI should be aware of the long-term implications of integration into the formal financial system.

#### Key Contextual Considerations

Key political and economic issues MFIs need to consider as they assess the options and timing of their transformation include:

- *Stability of the political climate*: A country's overall political stability can significantly influence a transforming MFI's ability to attract and maintain access to investment capital. Political instability can lead to arbitrary changes in monetary policy, such as statutory reserve requirements, foreign-exchange holding policies, or directed lending mandates. Unstable political environments may also magnify competing political agendas among government officials, including bank regulators, creating significant delays in license processing.

- *Macroeconomic trends:* MFIs looking to transform into regulated financial institutions consider general macroeconomic trends in both their country and their region. Such trends would include the level of inflation, currency stability, unemployment, and the general health of the financial sector and the economy.
- *Characteristics of the financial system:* As a regulated financial institution, an MFI enters into a new competitive environment. Transforming MFIs need to be aware of the full range of players in their country's financial system. In addition, the banking laws and regulatory environment play a key role in attracting investors, particularly as they affect the rights of shareholders.
- *Current policy environment for microfinance*: The government's support for and understanding of microfinance play a significant role in determining the timing of transformation. For example, in a country where interest rates are limited by usury laws or where government-directed credit programs are prevalent, an MFI's ability to charge adequate interest rates to cover costs and provide a return for investors may be limited. The extent to which legal contracts are enforceable and sanctions for default, fraud, or theft are applied also influence a microfinance institution's ability to manage its loan portfolio quality.
- *Political nature of the superintendent*: While the independence of bank regulators is often cited as a critical ingredient of a stable financial system, the political nature of the superintendent's position can limit the level of independence. In countries where the government specifically targets the microenterprise sector in its plans to promote economic growth, the bank superintendent often acts as the link between the government's political agenda and the regulators' work. This was the case in Peru with Mibanco, where the approval process was relatively short because the bank superintendent was aware that the country's president was interested in the establishment of a Peruvian microfinance bank.[6]

### Implications of Integration into the Formal Financial System

While some countries have begun to include provisions for microfinance NGOs in their regulatory frameworks (Uganda, Ghana,

South Africa, Ethiopia), most NGOs have evolved outside of any regulatory restrictions, allowing them to operate with relatively few constraints in terms of geographic location, methodology, cost structure, and growth rate. By transforming into regulated financial institutions, however, MFIs could lose this independence as their operations become closely linked to the overall stability of the banking system.

## Regulatory Framework

Transforming MFIs need to examine carefully the pros and cons of each regulatory category before selecting the institutional type best suited to their operations. This process represents the beginning of a long-term relationship that must be carefully built with regulators through a variety of exchanges.

### Examining Options

Before deciding on their institutional structure, transforming MFIs must first research all available alternatives. While many transforming NGOs seek to establish a regulated financial intermediary within the country's existing regulatory framework, some lobby regulators to create a new financial institution category.

### Exchanges with Regulators

For the first NGO transformation in a country, an MFI usually has to assume responsibility for orienting the local banking superintendency about the particular characteristics of microfinance and its role in the larger financial sector. This orientation ranges from extensive one-on-one dialogues, to the hosting of local policy workshops, to inviting and accompanying regulators to examine field operations of successful MFIs both nationally and internationally. While both CARD and Mibanco experienced a relatively short time delay (approximately six months) between the submission of their banking license application and its approval, both organizations dedicated many years to regulatory dialogue and education prior to submitting the application.

In many cases the standard regulatory framework for financial institutions is not appropriate for the supervision of microfinance institutions. From a traditional bank examiner's perspective, many of the characteristics of microfinance (including unsecured loans and limited financial statement analysis) are considered unsound. The transforming MFI is tasked with convincing the regulators of the soundness of their practices or making the necessary changes to comply with regulatory requirements. For example, the security of the proposed bank's location was just one of the many issues raised by the Central Bank of Kenya (CBK) that K-Rep had to overcome to secure its bank license. K-Rep successfully convinced the regulators of the importance of conducting operations in low-income areas for proximity to its clients but still has to comply with the CBK's higher physical security standards.

## Ownership and Governance

Once the MFI decides to transform into a privately owned institution, it must determine the desired composition of its new board. In most cases the NGO board will develop the proposed institution's mission and use it as a guide in seeking potential owners and board members. Potential owners review the capitalization and asset-liability transfer strategies before reaching their investment decision. For a description of the ownership structures of the seven MFIs from this study, see Table 2.2.

### Institutional Mission

Transforming NGOs attempt to strike the desired balance between commercial and social objectives in the development of the new board. A well-defined mission statement can help guide the board through the selection process. Boards can also add clauses to the new institution's bylaws that ensure a commitment to the target sector, for example, by requiring that the MFI's borrowers represent the microenterprise sector, measured by loan size or by clients' profits or accumulated assets.

### Board Formation

A transforming NGO should not assume that its current board has the necessary skills and financial backing to guide it through the transformation process or to lead it as a regulated financial institution. While there is no formula for board formation, ideally the board consists of members with a diverse set of skills, including private business, financial sector and legal or regulatory expertise.

*Board member selection:* Board members of NGOs are usually selected for their community connections or respected technical expertise. While these attributes are certainly relevant for a regulated financial institution, a bank board also typically includes representatives of the

**Table 2.2: Ownership of Transformed MFIs**
**At transformation (left column) and in 1999 (right column)**

|  | BancoSol | | Financiera Calpiá | | Caja Los Andes | |
|---|---|---|---|---|---|---|
| **Country** | *Bolivia* | | *El Salvador* | | *Bolivia* | |
|  | 1992 | 1999 | 1995 | 1999 | 1995 | 1999 |
| % founding NGO | 29 | 20 | 30.0 | 30.0 | 37.5 | 39.1 |
| % other NGOs | 19 | 14 | 19.8 | 19.8 | 0 | 0 |
| % public development agency | 0 | 22 | 50.0 | 50.0 | 43.7 | 39.3 |
| % specilaized equity fund | 0 | 34 | 0 | 0 | 0 | 13.9 |
| % foreign private investor | 27 | 0 | 0 | 0 | 0 | 0 |
| % local private investor | 25 | 10 | 0.3 | 0.3 | 18.7 | 7.7 |
| % ESOP | 0 | 0 | 0 | 0 | 0 | 0 |
| Minimum capital requirement at transformation | $3.2 million (commercial bank) | | $1 million (financiera)[4] | | $1 million (private financial fund, PFF) | |

**Table 2.2—Continued**

| CARD | | Banco-ADEMI | | Mibanco | | K-Rep | |
|---|---|---|---|---|---|---|---|
| Philippines | | Dominican Republic | | Peru | | Kenya | |
| 1998 | 1999 | 1998 | 1999 | 1998 | 1999 | 1998 | 1999 |
| 27 | 44.2 | 24.0 | 24.0 | 60.0 | 60.0 | 32.5 | 32.5[1] |
| 0 | 0 | 0 | 0 | 0 | 0 | 0 | 0 |
| 0 | 0 | 0 | 0 | 0 | 0 | 30.7 | 30.7 |
| 0 | 0 | 0 | 0 | 26.0 | 26.0 | 0 | 0 |
| 0 | 0 | 0 | 0 | 0 | 0 | 26.8 | 26.8 |
| 73[2] | 33.1[3] | 39.0 | 39.0 | 13.2 | 13.2 | 0 | 0 |
| 0 | 22.7 | 20.0 | 20.0 | 0 | 0 | 10 | 10 |
| $116,279 (rural bank) | | $2.2 million (development bank) | | $5.6 million (commercial bank) | | $6.8 million (commercial bank) | |

[1] *K-Rep Holdings Ltd., a newly established holding company, will own 32.5 percent of K-Rep Bank rather than the NGO.*

[2] *Represents selected senior management.*

[3] *Represents client ownership.*

[4] *Financiera Calpiá is currently considering transforming into a commercial bank.*

institution's key investors—individuals who have a financial stake in the future of the organization. Additionally, the banking superintendency will often require that a certain number of board members have formal financial-management experience.

*NGO board member overlap:* The prevalence of former NGO board members in transformed MFIs typically reflects the percent of NGO ownership of the new MFI. For example, in the case of CARD Rural Bank, three of its seven board members are from the former NGO board, which corresponds with the NGO's 44 percent ownership.

*Client representation:* Clients are rarely represented on the boards of regulated MFI. As board members, clients' ability to balance their own interests as net borrowers against the institution's larger interests of outreach and sustainability is inevitably tested. A central bank might limit this potential conflict of interest through restrictions on loans to directors, officers, shareholders, and related interests, as in the case of the Central Bank of the Philippines and CARD Rural Bank.

*Employee representation:* In many cases the new board includes the managing director/president as a member. However, due to concerns regarding the sensitivity of information discussed at board meetings, rarely are other employees allowed to participate in board meetings. This also helps ensure that the three organs of the bank—the board, management, and staff—function semi-independently of each other.

## Ownership Options

### NGO Ownership

The dominance of NGO ownership and control raises questions about the nature of transformation. Since NGOs by definition have no owners, their ownership in the transformed financial institution does not represent personal equity. Regulators, however, typically want to see a group of individuals or firms (not donors) who have put funds at risk. A dominance of NGO ownership can reduce the intended benefits from private ownership of increased accountability and access to additional sources of capital.

In all the cases of transformation included in this chapter, the NGO, through various mechanisms, capitalized a sizable portion of the new financial institution. In each of these transformations NGO ownership was considered vital to carrying on the founding vision to the regulated financial institution. Among these newly regulated financial institutions, the initial level of NGO ownership ranged from 27 percent at CARD to 60 percent at Mibanco.

The NGO's management of its new ownership stake in a commercial MFI is a critical issue. The new bank charter should clearly define the NGO's intentions for disposing of this investment in the future, and this issue should be addressed within the framework of the NGO's plans for future income generation and asset accumulation. If the NGO plans to continue as some form of operating entity, it needs to have a clear funding strategy, independent from the new bank.

### Limited Local Private Ownership

The initial amount of local private ownership in these new formal financial institutions is quite limited. K-Rep initially sought local banks as investors, but the Kenyan banks were not interested because they were unfamiliar with microfinance. Only later, as the process advanced and K-Rep received support from reputable international entities and positive media attention, did local banks express an interest. Unfortunately, at that point it was too late for their participation. Mibanco's local private ownership comprises two private commercial banks, Banco de Crédito and Banco Wiese, each of which owns 6.6 percent of the bank. There was interest by other banks and insurance companies, but with the NGO taking 60 percent of the shares, the potential for private ownership was minimal.

Private investors have not necessarily been convinced that investment in an MFI makes sense, for a number of reasons. First, except in a few isolated cases, returns within the microfinance industry have not yet been realized. Second, in most cases, there is no liquid market for the shares, limiting the investor to dividend returns and hindering exit strategy. Third, when the founding NGO maintains majority

> **Box 2.1: BancoSol Lists on the Bolivian Stock Exchange**
>
> In September 1997 BancoSol became the first microfinance institution to be listed on a national stock exchange and one of only twelve publicly traded companies on the Bolivian stock exchange. While there is very little liquidity in the Bolivian market, the listing represents a significant step in commercializing microfinance. BancoSol first began preparing the market for public offering in 1997, when it issued its first dividends of $162,857 or $0.45 per share on 1996 earnings of $1.1 million.

ownership, private investors are led to question both their own abilities to shape the long-term vision of the organization and the NGO's commitment to prioritizing profitability.

*Employee Stock Ownership Programs (ESOPs)*

ESOPs provide a mechanism for aligning employees' goals with the goals of the company. In general, these programs offer employees the ability to benefit from the increased value of the company, either directly as shareowners or indirectly through incentives tied to profitability.

In three of these seven cases, an ESOP was designed to reward and acknowledge the contribution of staff and management's service to the organization, ranging from 10 percent at K-Rep Bank to 22.7 percent at CARD Rural Bank.[7] In both CARD and K-Rep, nonvoting shares are made available to staff based on a combination of seniority and professional status.

In K-Rep's case, staff that have been employed by K-Rep for three years or more are eligible to participate in the ESOP. Participation is voluntary, and 90 percent of staff hold stock options. Eligible members must agree to purchase one right for every right awarded as a bonus. To facilitate this process, employees can borrow money to purchase shares at 9 percent per annum for five years, although in case of payment default, all shares are lost. With initial funding from CGAP, the Kwa Multipurpose Cooperative Society, a credit and savings cooperative for K-Rep staff, purchased and assigned these initial rights to members.[8]

Transforming MFIs need to be aware that there is an element of risk in ESOPS and ensure that there is a balance between individual risk and salary stability. There is usually a great deal of pressure to participate in the program, yet no proven stream of earnings to aid staff in making informed decisions as the ESOP is typically launched in conjunction with the opening of the newly formed bank. CARD and BancoADEMI both awarded shares to staff as a special bonus, essentially eliminating individual risk. Since 1998, BancoADEMI, where employees own 20 percent of the bank, has paid out US$1,286,620 in dividends on employee shares.

*Client Ownership*

CARD Rural Bank is the only institution among those examined to incorporate client ownership into its initial share structure. CARD now offers preferred stock to individual members who meet certain eligibility criteria and allows clients to use their center fund contributions (composed primarily of clients' compulsory savings) or cash to purchase the shares. As of June 2001, client member ownership represented 29 percent of the total CARD capital structure.

*Capitalization*

The initial capitalization of a regulated financial institution is typically determined by two factors: the regulatory requirements in the country and the institution's business plan. In this review, minimum capital requirements ranged from US$161,000 (CARD Rural Bank) to US$6.8 million (K-Rep Bank). In addition, diverse growth plans led to different capitalization strategies.

In NGO-to-bank transformations, the net assets of the NGO are typically transferred to the new regulated financial institution in exchange for some combination of debt and equity in the new institution. The transaction can be either a direct swap, as in the case of Prodem/BancoSol, whereby the assets of the NGO were directly sold to the bank in exchange for shares,[9] or as a cash capitalization, as in the case of ACP/Mibanco and CARD, in which the NGOs provided the paid-up capital in cash.

## Asset and Liability Transfer Issues

The transfer of assets and liabilities from an NGO to a regulated financial institution raises a number of key issues. These include the following:

- *Debt/equity split:* The proportion of debt to equity is influenced by five primary factors: (1) the minimum capital requirements in the country; (2) the maximum leverage ratio allowed by bank regulators; (3) the value of the NGO's net assets; (4) regulatory limits to ownership; and (5) to a certain degree, the NGO's ownership ambitions.
- *Valuation exercise:* While the net value of the new institution can be determined internally, it is typically done through a formal valuation of assets and liabilities by a reputable accounting firm.
- *Premiums:* In transformation, the new financial institution gains instant access to the NGO's client base. As compensation, some NGO-to-bank transfer strategies are structured to include a premium payment from the bank to the NGO. For example, Mibanco agreed to administer ACP's existing loan book at no cost for the first year, and to pass on interest revenue on all pre-existing loans until they came due. In addition, Mibanco paid ACP a premium of US$1 million in cash for access to ACP's clients. The agreement

between CARD Rural Bank and the NGO required that the bank pay 8 percent of the total value of the portfolio as a premium and all recorded development costs related to building up that portfolio.

- *Lender negotiations:* NGOs that have sourced funds from commercial or other lenders need to negotiate carefully either a transfer of this liability to the regulated institution or some other arrangement that will allow the NGO to continue to pay off the debt with resources from the regulated institution.

- *Donor negotiations:* Funded by taxpayers, development agency resources are typically restricted to nonprofit organizations with social objectives. When the NGO creates a for-profit financial institution, the transfer of assets funded by donations from these institutions can raise concern among donors. In Bolivia, for example, only after complex negotiations did USAID approve the transfer of a significant portion of Prodem's loan book, largely funded by USAID, to BancoSol in exchange for shares. This decision was based on the notion that the funds were no longer classified as U.S. government funds since they had been lent once and repaid. Despite many donors' support for commercialization of MFIs, most donor agencies do not yet have formal policies and procedures to address the issue.

- *Capital transfer to private individuals:* In a number of NGO transformations, donor funds have been used to capitalize individual shareholdings. While in some cases shares in the new financial institution were sold to private individuals, in others the shares were simply transferred to board members, managers, or staff of the NGO. Donors that have supported the subsidized transfer of shares to private individuals argue that funding individual share ownership helps foster enhanced levels of governance and accountability. CGAP, for example, provided funds to facilitate the creation of an ESOP for K-Rep employees. CGAP views this support as an important contribution to moving microfinance forward and hopes that K-Rep's ESOP will encourage higher levels of staff commitment and productivity, while providing a demonstration model to other MFIs.

## *Organizational Development*

A range of organizational development changes must be addressed in any transformation process, and these changes represent an evolutionary process. A new mission must be identified for the founding NGO, and the leadership of the new institution must communicate its vision to employees and clients, generating enthusiasm without creating unrealistic expectations. Systems must be put in place, and new staff hired and trained.

## Organizational Culture

Organizational culture is a system of shared beliefs and values that develops within an organization and guides the behavior of its stakeholders. It is created by the leadership of the organization, often articulated in the organization's mission statement, and shaped and sustained by the organizational structure, policies, and procedures, and the relationships among staff and between staff and management. When a nonprofit NGO transforms into a privately owned, regulated financial institution, each of these influential factors can change, thereby altering the MFI's organizational culture.

The degree to which transformation affects the organizational culture of an institution is largely influenced by changes in management and communication styles. In Mibanco's case, the strategic plan called for a blend of NGO and bank managers in the management hierarchy. The addition of traditional banking professionals with strong personalities in key management positions led to changes in communication patterns among staff (more hierarchical and formal) and in methodology (more traditional banking methods). These changes temporarily lowered employee morale and customer satisfaction. The board quickly recognized and corrected the imbalance by shifting management positions so that former NGO staff would hold positions involving close contact with branch staff and clients.

In contrast, CARD has not experienced a significant change in organizational culture. From both an accounting and organizational chart perspective, CARD is composed of two distinct entities, a bank and an NGO. However, when viewed from an operational perspective, CARD is one organization. This distinction is important because it underlays CARD's ability to implement successfully a phased approach to transformation. Bank and NGO staff do not see themselves as working for two separate organizations. In addition, CARD did not hire a cadre of traditional bankers when launching CARD Rural Bank, opting instead to train current staff in their new responsibilities.

Effective leadership and management are essential to the transformation process. Because transformation can take a long time, both what is communicated about the change and how it is communicated to staff are critical. The challenge for a leader is to keep staff informed of anticipated changes and to generate enthusiasm for these changes without excessively raising expectations or causing fear among staff. This is a delicate balancing act. If change is oversold, unmet staff expectations may lead to low employee morale in the future. On the other hand, if not enough information is communicated to staff, unfounded fears about job stability may mount.

## Human Resources

The set of skills required of staff changes as NGOs transform into regulated financial institutions. Whether an organization chooses to hire traditional bankers, to initiate an intensive training program for its own staff, or to apply a combination of the two, MFIs need to be aware of the significant amount of time and money required to prepare staff for the transformation. At Prodem, for example, the executive director prioritized building staff capacity, invested heavily in preparing the NGO's employees for the transition, and determined that NGO staff would fill as many bank positions as possible. Seminars and training sessions, which focused on the technical aspects of banking as well as on the cultural differences between an NGO and a bank, were held for all staff levels. BancoSol's early success is largely attributed to this emphasis on cultural integration and to the effectiveness of training in smoothing the transition. At Mibanco, over US$180,000 was spent on training in one year, preparing employees for the transformation. Both K-Rep and CARD contracted outside service providers to conduct introductory courses on traditional banking for their staff.

### From Credit Officers to Financial Service Marketers

In a microfinance NGO most field staff focus only on the provision of loans to clients. For those MFIs that become deposit-taking institutions, the MFI must also sell clients on its financial strength and build their trust in its ability to manage their savings. Transforming NGOs need to train employees to handle this level of financial service marketing. Employees will need to understand the typical concerns clients have about saving in a formal financial institution and how to address them. In addition, as new loan products are introduced, such as individual loans, loan officers may require a different set of tools to analyze the creditworthiness of their borrowers. For example, loan officers may need to be trained in basic cash-flow and balance-sheet analysis.

### Importance of Grooming Middle Management

Transformed microfinance institutions tend to expand rapidly, leading to an increase in new branch openings and therefore increased demand for branch managers—many of whom are chosen from the pool of loan officers. One of the key challenges faced by transforming microfinance institutions is to develop a management training program that will adequately supply a quickly expanding middle-management team.

### Increased Responsibilities of Senior Management

The responsibilities of senior management increase significantly with transformation to a regulated financial institution. A newly regulated MFI needs to create an institutional culture with the right mix of cultures, adequate to provide the security of a formal bank while catering to the microenterprise market. Traditional bankers are appropriate for new positions that require traditional banking expertise, such as investment or treasury officer. Existing staff, however, are often better suited for positions that require an in-depth understanding of microfinance and that directly oversee branch level personnel, such as operations or business manager.

## Client Transitioning

While the benefits to clients of an MFI's transformation to a regulated institution may be clear to management and staff of the organization itself, the clients' perception of the transformation process will depend on the organization's ability to market these changes effectively. For instance, the word *bank* often has negative connotations for people who have been excluded from the formal financial system due to lack of traditional collateral requirements or insufficient minimum balances. An NGO's announcement that it plans to create a bank may fuel concerns that the organization will shift target markets or that customer service will deteriorate.

MFIs considering transformation need to involve their clients in the transformation process from the beginning. This involvement may include focus groups to collect input on the transformation process or workshops to explain the potential impact of transformation. In CARD's case, for example, clients were informed from their initial membership with CARD about CARD's intention to become a bank. Mibanco officially communicated the transformation to clients through a written letter mailed to each customer, verbally by employees, and through posters that described Mibanco's mission statement and commitment to serve microentrepreneurs. In addition, radio and newspaper advertisements announced the transformation publicly.

Finally, clients need to see tangible benefits of the transformation soon after the bank is opened. Clients often expect to see immediate greater efficiency, a broader selection of products, and improved customer service. The more well-prepared an institution is for the operational side of transformation, the more easily it will meet its clients' expectations.

### Summary

Transformation is just one component of a broader movement toward the commercialization and integration of microfinance into the formal financial sector. The transformation phase of the microfinance industry's evolution has been essential to this movement because it has allowed MFIs to reach critical mass in terms of business operations and outreach, and to demonstrate financial viability and profitability. The transformation phenomenon has already attracted attention from the commercial world and caused donors to change policies in preparation for a burgeoning microfinance industry based on market principles. Transformation has been closing the gap in the provision of services to microentrepreneurs and opening access to financial services that had long been denied to the poor. Competition from transformed MFIs has caused banks to attempt to reach further down to lower income sectors and microenterprises. If transformed MFIs demonstrate the levels of success and profitability to which they aspire, access to commercial sources of funds, including equity from private investors, will likely increase.

## NOTES

1. This chapter summarizes findings from Anita Campion and Victoria White, "Institutional Metamorphosis: Transformation of Microfinance NGOs into Regulated Financial Institutions," Occasional Paper No. 4 (Washington, D.C.: The Microfinance Network, 2000).

2. The Basle Convention requires an institution's equity be no less than 8 percent of its risk-weighted assets.

3. BRI reported 24.2 million savings clients and 2.5 million loan clients as of December 31, 1999.

4. ProFund is an investment fund created in 1995 to support the growth of regulated, efficient financial intermediaries that serve the small and microenterprise market in Latin America and the Caribbean. The ACCION Gateway Fund was created in 1997 to support MFIs through debt or equity investments. Internationale Micro Investitionen AG (IMI AG) was initiated with 51 percent ownership by the German private consulting firm IPC. In 1999, however, IPC owned less than 20 percent of IMI, following subsequent investments by other public sector entities.

5. Corposol/Finansol is not included in this chapter because the major crisis experienced by the institution in 1995–1996 and the subsequent restructuring into FINAMERICA, S.A. make it difficult to compare it with the other MFIs included here. For further information on the Finansol crisis, see Chapter 8 herein.

6. See Chapter 9 herein for more detail on the Mibanco transformation.

7. As of June 2001 the ESOP portion of employees holding stock options at CARD had decreased to 5 percent, as the number of CARD members increased.

8. Kimanthi Matua, Microfinance Network ACCION Commercialization Conference, Washington, D.C. (June 2001).

9. BancoSol exchanged shares based on the value of Prodem's loan book plus a 10 percent premium.

**3.**

# Getting the Recipe Right

## The Experience and Challenges of Commercial Bank Downscalers

**Liza Valenzuela**

Commercial banks and other regulated actors continue to enter the microfinance world. In Latin America alone over seventy commercial institutions have entered the market in a process called *downscaling,* motivated by the potential profits of a new niche or, in some cases, by the fact that large numbers of people still lack access to formal financial services. The experience of these new entrants in microfinance has been mixed; a few commercial actors are succeeding, others are struggling, and some have simply given up. However, looking at the range of downscaling experiences, there are at least four reasons to be cautiously optimistic.

- More commercial banks are using "microfinance best practices" than ever before.
- Some commercial actors have been able to reach tens of thousands of clients quickly, at minimal cost to donors.
- There is no single downscaler profile; commercial institutions of all shapes, sizes, and orientations have entered the market.
- Some commercial actors are showing important profits in their microlending operations (sometimes exceeding those of other bank departments).

This chapter draws from the experience of fifty-three bank downscalers that have entered the microfinance world since the mid 1990s. It derives lessons from two sources: a quick update of the experience of eighteen bankers featured in the 1997 report entitled "Commercial Banks in Microfinance: New Institutional Actors in the Microfinance World" (Baydas, Graham, and Valenzuela 1997) and a new survey of forty-two commercial banks conducted in early 2001.[1] With the exception of a brief mention of BancoSol and Caja Los Andes in Bolivia, transformed NGOs, credit unions (many of which are also downscaling), and specialized micro-banks that are emerging in Eastern Europe and in a few other countries are not included.

It should be emphasized that any conclusions expressed here are preliminary or in some cases notional based on anecdotal evidence and the small survey sample. Further research, observation, and time will be necessary before a final verdict can be declared on the success or failure of the downscaling approach.

## WHAT HAPPENED TO THE EIGHTEEN PIONEERING BANKS?

"Commercial Banks in Microfinance" recorded data on eighteen institutions that participated in an international bankers conference in November 1996. They included twelve commercial banks, two transformed NGOs, one finance company, one building society, one rural bank, and one state bank. Four were from Africa, three from Asia, and eleven from Latin America and the Caribbean. Excluding Bank Rakyat Indonesia (BRI), which had 2.4 million borrowers and some 12 million savers in 1996, the remaining seventeen institutions had 173,002 active microloans with US$179 million in loans outstanding. Most were at an incipient stage, experimenting with methodologies and organizational structures.

Since the 1996 conference, the aggregate experience of the eighteen institutions has been only satisfactory. External factors, such as economic downturns and increased competition among microcredit providers have had a constraining effect on many of the programs. Internal factors have also contributed, as some institutions have had difficulty adjusting systems and procedures to serve the lower end of the market.

As illustrated in Table 3.1, seven of the original eighteen institutions showed strong performance. Four institutions experienced very high levels of growth in borrowers or depositors. Three additional institutions experienced moderate growth, doubling the number of borrowers in four

*Liza Valenzuela*

**Table 3.1: Downscaling Bankers from the 1996 Survey: Then and Now (1996 and 2001)**

| | |
|---|---|
| High growth (> 200%) in microcredit borrowers or depositors | **Borrowers:**<br>Centenary Bank: 3,900 to 16,640 (326%)<br>Panabo Rural Bank: 1,600 to 7,000 (337%)<br>**Depositors:**<br>BRI: 12 to 24 million (100%)<br>Standard Bank: 287,786 to 2.4 million (734%) |
| Moderate growth (100% - 200%) in microcredit borrowers | **Borrowers:**<br>*Caja Los Andes:* 17,800 to 42,000 (136%)<br>Family Finance: 6,000 to 12,000 (100%)<br>MultiCredit Bank: 1,450 to 3,776 (160%) |
| Low growth (< 100%) in microcredit borrowers and depositors | **Borrowers:**<br>*BancoSol:* 57,700 to 67,000 (16%)<br>Financiera Familiar: 4,600 to 7,300 (59%)<br>National Development Bank: 20,852 to 21,476 (3%)<br>Banco Agrícola, 8,000 to 9,500<br>**Depositors:**<br>Bank Dagang Bali: 344,619 to 384,000 (11%) |
| Decline in microcredit borrowers | Banco del Desarrollo: 17,500 to 14,000<br>Bank of Nova Scotia: 9,000 to 1,200 |
| Banks that closed | Banco Empresarial<br>Worker's Bank<br>Banco del Pacífico |
| Banks that withdrew from microcredit | Banco Wiese, Peru |

Data for 1996 are drawn Mayada Baydas, Douglas Graham, and Liza Valenzuela, "Commercial Banks in Microfinance: New Actors in the Microfinance World" (Bethesda, Md.: Development Alternatives, Microenterprise Best Practices Project, 1997). Data for 2001 correspond to December 2000 and are drawn from the author's 2001 survey and telephone interviews. Data for Bank Dagang Bali are from *WWB Global Directory of Banking Innovation in Microfinance*, sections on Asia (September 2000).

Institutions in italics are transformed NGOs, not downscalers.

years. The remaining eleven experienced limited growth, exited the microfinance market, or failed as banking institutions.

Since 1996, four of the eighteen banks exited microcredit. Banco Wiese pulled out of the Peruvian microcredit wholesale market when it invested in Mibanco, a transformed NGO. Three other banks discontinued microcredit because the overall bank failed after a period of severe economic crisis in their respective countries.[2]

## 2001 SURVEY RESULTS

The 2001 survey consisted of a four-page questionnaire (based on the original 1996 survey) sent to over 100 banks engaged in microfinance around the world. Forty-two banks responded to the survey—twenty-nine from Latin America, six from Europe and Eurasia, six from Africa, and one from Asia. Of the forty-two respondents, 44 percent started their microlending program during or before 1996, 29 percent during 1997 or 1998, and 27 percent during 1999 or 2000. For reasons of confidentiality, most of the data are presented only in the aggregate or as part of a peer group. While the fit in the peer groups is not perfect and the sample is small, this approach does offer some interesting comparisons that shed light on the experience of the banking sector in microcredit.

### Types of Commercial Actors

In late 1996 the largest group of commercial actors in microfinance was the traditional banks, many of which were receiving assistance from various international donors. By 2001 the commercial microfinance institutional landscape had become more complex, with finance companies and specialized microbanks growing in importance.

### The Peer Groups

Table 3.2 lists the survey respondents and categorizes them into four types based on institutional structure and size.

Table 3.3 provides a snapshot of basic data of the institutions responding to the survey by their peer groups.

**Table 3.2: List of Respondents by Institutional Type (surveys of 1996 and 2001)**

| Type of Institution | 1996 Survey (18) | 2001 Survey (42) |
|---|---|---|
| Large, private, multipurpose commercial banks Full-service intermediaries; the majority offer a diverse array of products | Banco Agrícola, El Salvador<br>Banco del Desarrollo, Chile<br>Banco del Pacífico, Ecuador<br>Bank of Nova Scotia, Guyana<br>Banco Wiese, Peru<br>MultiCredit Bank, Panama<br>National Development Bank, Egypt<br>Standard Bank, South Africa<br>Worker's Bank, Jamaica | Banhcafe, Honduras<br>*Banco Agrícola*, El Salvador<br>Banco Balcarce, Argentina<br>Banco de Pichincha, Ecuador<br>Bancafé, Guatemala<br>Banco del Comercio, Honduras<br>*Banco del Desarrollo*, Chile<br>Banco del Trabajo, Peru<br>Banco Multibanco, Paraguay<br>Banco Salvadoreño, El Salvador<br>Banco Santander, Chile<br>Bank de l'Union Haitienne, Haiti<br>*Bank of Nova Scotia*, Guyana<br>*MultiCredit Bank*, Panama<br>Sogebank/Sogesol, Haiti<br>*National Development Bank*, Egypt<br>CBAO, Senegal<br>Commercial Bank of Zimbabwe<br>Kenya Commercial Bank<br>Almaty Merchant Bank, Kazakhstan<br>Bank CenterCredit, Kazakhstan<br>Bank TuranAlem, Kazakhstan<br>Kazkommertsbankt, Kazakhstan<br>Narodny Savings Bank, Kazakhstan<br>Eurobank, Bulgaria |

**Table 3.2 (continued): List of Respondents by Institutional Type (surveys of 1996 and 2001)**

| Type of Institution | 1996 Survey (18) | 2001 Survey (42) |
|---|---|---|
| Small commercial banks<br>Full-service intermediaries with a small volume of assets (less than US$50 million). | Banco Empresarial, Guatemala<br>Bank Dagang Bali, Indonesia<br>Centenary Bank, Uganda<br>Panabo Rural Bank, Philippines | Akiba Commercial Bank, Tanzania<br>Banco de Desarrollo Unificado, DR<br>Banco Solidario, Ecuador<br>Mi Banco, Panama<br>*Panabo Rural Bank*, Philippines |
| State banks<br>Full-service intermediaries; generally large numbers of small savings accounts. | Bank Rakyat Indonesia | Banco del Estado, Chile<br>Banco Nacional de Costa Rica<br>BanRural, Guatemala<br>Kenya Postal Office Savings Bank |
| Finance companies/consumer lenders/credit card companies<br>Regulated non-bank institutions, usually active in consumer lending; some also capture deposits. | Family Finance Building Society, Kenya<br>Financiera Familiar, Paraguay | Aval-Card, Honduras<br>Crédito Familiar, Mexico<br>El Comercio Financiera, Paraguay<br>FASSIL, Bolivia<br>*Financiera Familiar*, Paraguay<br>Financiera Compartir, Colombia<br>Financiera Solución, Peru<br>Visión de Finanzas, Paraguay |
| Transformed NGOs—not covered in this chapter | BancoSol, Bolivia<br>Caja Los Andes, Bolivia | n/a |

Banks in italics also participated in the 1996 survey.

**Table 3.3: 2001 Survey Respondents by Peer Group**

| | Average Age of Program (years) | Number of Active Loans | Average Number of Loans | Number of Loans, Range | Loan Volume (US$) | Average Balance (US$) |
|---|---|---|---|---|---|---|
| Large commercial banks (25) | 4.9 | 146,275 | 5,851 | 159–35,912 | 215,023,145 | 1,512 |
| Small commercial banks (5) | 2.9 | 21,402 | 4,280 | 620–10,845 | 10,562,111 | 494 |
| State banks (3)* | 3.0 | 59,400 | 19,800 | 3,875–32,525 | 86,234,026 | 1,452 |
| Finance companies (8) | 3.6 | 76,851 | 9,606 | 959–26,200 | 69,216,187 | 901 |
| Total (41)* | | 303,928 | 7,413 | 159–35,912 | 381,035,469 | 1,253 |

Numbers in parenthesis in the first column indicate the number of respondents in each peer group.
* Excludes Kenya Post Office Savings Bank, which had no loans outstanding in December 2000.

### Why Downscale?

The 1997 report speculated that profitability (for most) and image (for a few) were the driving forces behind downscaling. In 2001, however, the most common response among the large commercial banks was that there was a market opportunity—most likely reflecting the fact that they were seeking to diversify. The smaller banks, on the other hand, generally listed market opportunity and social responsibility, and the four state banks listed social responsibility as their primary goal. Finance companies were evenly divided among those that were pursuing financial benefits and those that felt a sense of social responsibility.

The 2001 survey and follow-up interviews offer a more complex understanding of the motivating factors. Profitability *in and of itself* does not explain the entry of the traditional banks. Commercial bank entry appears to be principally associated with the fact that financial margins are being squeezed, and as a result, they are seeking new profitable market niches. The fact that microcredit can be profitable is a necessary but not sufficient condition to motivate bank entry. However, demonstrated profitability is necessary for the expansion and permanence of microfinance operations within a commercial institution.

### Institutional Outreach and Profitability

#### Outreach

Outreach (measured by the number of active loans) is generally modest among most of the forty-two banks surveyed. As of December 2000, ten banks had over ten thousand active loans. Of these, six had over twenty thousand active loans, of which three had over thirty thousand active loans.

Based on the survey data, the most important determinant of outreach appears to be the type of institution.[3] Eight of the ten banks with over ten thousand loans were either state banks or predominantly consumer lenders. Of the institutions with over thirty thousand loans, two were consumer lenders that had initiated operations only three years earlier, and the third was a state bank. For the consumer lenders, anecdotal evidence suggests that they can increase outreach quickly (albeit often with arrears problems). For the state banks, rapid growth is clearly facilitated by an ample, accessible, and well-established branch structure.

It could be circumstantial that the large private banks are *not* present among the ten institutions with the largest outreach. But the survey and interviews suggest that large corporate bank downscalers have the most difficulty expanding their microenterprise program. It is speculated that this is due to difficulties in assimilating a microfinance product into a corporate bank structure.

## Growth Projections

The survey asked the institutions to project the number of microenterprise clients they planned to have in 2005. The intent was to understand whether banks saw themselves as large-scale providers or microcredit as a side activity. The ten institutions with the most aggressive targets generally fell into three categories: bank subsidiaries, consumer lenders (either as large banks or as finance companies), and state banks. Bank subsidiaries are created specifically to serve microentrepreneurs and are generally in tune with the outreach goals of the larger microfinance industry. Three of the five subsidiaries had plans to reach between 70,000 and 100,000 clients. The social motivation behind state banks also leads them to share outreach goals. Three of the four state banks in the sample (one is also a subsidiary) also had high growth projections, in the 90,000 to 100,000 range. Finally, four consumer lenders (two operating as finance companies and two as large banks) also had aggressive targets, ranging from 60,000 to 75,000. There was only one bank that did not fit into the above categories—a small bank that also projected growth targets above 60,000 loans.

## Profitability

The 2001 survey did not request data on profitability, anticipating that most banks would be unwilling or unable to share such information. Instead, the survey asked the banks whether they *thought* their microcredit product was profitable. Almost 78 percent of the banks responded that it was. Nine banks indicated that the product hadn't reached the break-even point, a reasonable answer since they had introduced microcredit only within the last three years. Another two respondents, both large commercial bank downscalers that had recently started microcredit operations, indicated they didn't know if the product would be profitable.

While the majority of banks surveyed believe that their microcredit product is profitable, it is unclear how they can be certain of this, as most appear to lack a product-accounting system that allows them track its costs. A number of the banks listed this as an area of concern. Some of the banks cited high interest rates and good repayment rates as evidence of likely profitability.

## Organizational Structure and Funding

The 1996 survey found that it was difficult to accommodate the idiosyncrasies of a microcredit product in a large corporate structure. The evidence from the 2001 survey appears to confirm this finding. Of the twenty-two large commercial banks (excluding those heavily engaged in consumer lending), only three had over five thousand loans—an indication that they have experienced slow growth. By and large, however, some microfinance best practices lessons appear to have filtered into most of these institutions. For example, in the 1997 report four institutions had *minimum* loan terms above six months. In the 2001 study only one institution had minimum loan terms above six months, suggesting an improved understanding of the short-term nature of microcredit for working capital.

Both the 1996 and 2001 surveys found that small banks generally integrate microfinance better than large banks. This may be because microcredit is a more significant part of their portfolio and garners more resources and attention. Little was said in 1996 about the integration of the product into a consumer-lending setting, given that this was not yet a phenomenon of major significance. Based on the 2001 data, however, it appears that microcredit can adapt fairly well, as some consumer finance companies have experienced explosive growth.

## Subsidiaries

The 1997 report identified the subsidiary as a model that could provide needed independence for the microcredit program in large commercial institutions. Among the banks attending the 1996 conference there were three subsidiaries: Bank Rakyat Indonesia, Banco del Desarrollo, and Bank of Nova Scotia (Scotia Enterprises). By 2001, only five of the twenty-nine large private commercial and state banks surveyed had established subsidiaries.[4] Most continued to integrate the microcredit program into the small/medium enterprise department or the consumer-lending department. This may just reflect caution—banks may prefer to "test" a new product by inserting it into the existing bank structure, rather than making the bold, long-term commitment of a separate subsidiary. It could also reflect the fact that these banks generally received less technical advice than those that did form a subsidiary. Three of the five subsidiaries

received technical assistance specifically focused on organizational structure issues. Four of the five were performing better than the average as
measured by outreach and general lending practices.

### Funding

Forty institutions reported using their own funds for the microcredit
program. Some also access international funds, such as rediscount lines
from the IDB or funds from the European Bank for Reconstruction and
Development. In addition, a few use guarantee programs through USAID
or Britain's Department for International Development (DFID). Contrary
to common wisdom of the past, the availability of loan funds is not a
requirement for establishing a microlending program within a commercial institution. The greater constraint appears to be obtaining operating
resources needed to grow the program—for setting up branches, hiring
and training staff, and developing interface systems.

## Products and Loan Methodology

### Individual and Group Lending

Individual lending is the predominant methodology used by the banks.
However, fourteen institutions (mostly among the large commercial banks,
curiously) offer group loans. Of the fourteen, twelve offer solidarity group
and individual loan products, while the other two, Bancafé in Guatemala
and Commercial Bank of Zimbabwe, offer group products only.[5] Two of
the commercial banks that started with solidarity group loans only (Banco
del Desarrollo and Bank of Nova Scotia) have now introduced individual
lending in response to a more competitive environment and/or client demand. Most of the fourteen banks received specialized technical assistance that influenced their choice of lending methodology.

#### Minimum Loan Size and Term Offered

The minimum loan offered by the surveyed banks ranged from US$13
and US$22 to the more common cases between US$200 and US$300.
There was only one bank in the sample with a minimum loan requirement over US$500. If one accepts the notion of loan size as a proxy for
the poverty level of the client, then this would suggest that the loan products are accessible to poorer microentrepreneurs.

Minimum loan terms averaged 2.9 months among the 2001 survey respondents and were shorter than for the eighteen banks surveyed in 1996 (4.5 months). Five of the seven banks that participated in both surveys shortened loan terms, most dramatically from twelve months to one month.

## Savings

Savings mobilization was important for all large private and state banks with over 100 branches. Four commercial banks had more than 400,000 savings accounts, and two had more than 100,000. All four of the state banks had large numbers of savings accounts, with very small balances. Small banks and finance companies generally had very small numbers of savings accounts. Only two (both small banks) had numbers that could be called significant, at 20,000 and 30,000, while most others had numbers less than 5,000. Over one-third of the respondents failed to answer the question on savings, a likely indication that they are not mobilizing savings. With one or two exceptions, none of the respondents appeared to have a program geared toward capturing savings of poor or low-income households, which is surely a missed opportunity.

## Loan Stratification

Are commercial bank downscalers really reaching poor microentrepreneurs? The general stereotype is that commercial actors have average loan sizes much above those of NGOs and that they do not reach the poor. The data from the survey confirms that average loans are generally higher than those of NGOs and transformed NGOs listed in the *MicroBanking Bulletin*. However, average loan size is a less than perfect indicator, particularly to assess the depth of outreach of institutions that offer a wide range of loan products. It is clear from the survey that commercial actors can offer very small loans to microclients while offering larger loans to clients with larger credit needs.

To understand how average loan size corresponds with institution type, the survey requested that respondents categorize their outstanding microloans into six loan ranges, as shown in Table 3.4. One of the interesting findings is that small commercial banks and finance companies have the most loans under US$300. Small commercial banks also have the least number of loans over US$5,000 (only 1 percent). Similarly, the small commercial banks group has 85 percent of its loans under US$1,000

*Liza Valenzuela*

**Table 3.4: Microloan Sizes by Peer Group (US$)**

| | $0–$300 | $301–$500 | $501–$1,000 | $1,001–$2,500 | $2,501–$5,000 | $5,001 and Up | % Loans <$1,000 | Average Loan Balances |
|---|---|---|---|---|---|---|---|---|
| Large commercial banks (17) | 8% | 11% | 25% | 41% | 10% | 4% | 44% | $1,512 |
| Small commercial banks (5) | 17% | 22% | 46% | 11% | 2% | 1% | 85% | $494 |
| State banks (3) | 10% | 13% | 31% | 29% | 13% | 4% | 54% | $1,452 |
| Finance companies (7) | 20% | 12% | 14% | 35% | 14% | 5% | 46% | $901 |

and the smallest average outstanding loan size of all of the institutional types.

### Use of Technology

Surprisingly, few of the banks and finance companies surveyed use high-end technology or information databases. The Automated Teller Machine (ATM) is the most common of the technologies among the sample, though there is no data on whether microentrepreneurs themselves have access to them or use them. Only 40 percent of survey respondents consult a credit bureau. This might reflect the unavailability of credit bureaus in a particular country, or simply the fact that the banks do not view consultation as useful for the microloan clients.

### Technical Assistance and Areas of Concern

Seventy-eight percent of the institutions surveyed in 2001 had received or were currently receiving some form of technical assistance for their microfinance product line, as compared to 50 percent in 1996. No information was gathered on the quality or length of the technical assistance. With one exception, all of the institutions expressed interest in receiving technical assistance in the future. Areas of interest included new products, credit methodology, collections, organizational structure, human resources, product accounting, training, MIS, credit scoring, technology, rural finance, and service delivery. Twenty-seven respondents indicated they would be willing to pay for at least half of the costs of technical assistance. Eight said they would be unwilling to pay, and five said it depended on the cost.

## HURDLES OF DOWNSCALING: WHY BANKS SUCCEED OR FAIL

The 1996 and the 2001 samples present an interesting and evolving experience, yet downscaling as an approach is far from showing signs of vigorous growth and long-term stability. What are the problems that have been plaguing downscalers? Why do banks fail at microcredit? Can downscaling be successful over the long term? What are some of the ingredients for that success?

## External Factors: Economic Crisis

As banking industries suffer crises and are forced to consolidate, weeding out weaker players through mergers, buy-outs, or outright liquidations, two common effects have been observed. First, financial crises keep new entrants out of the microfinance market; it is unusual to develop new initiatives or embark on less familiar territory in a time of crisis. Second, when banks fail, their microcredit programs usually die with them.

It is ironic that in this period of financial liberalization and increased banking-sector competition, the very forces that attract many small banks to microlending are the same forces that shut them down when a crisis hits. By and large the small banks most attracted to the microenterprise segment are those in a weaker position, seeking a new niche to help them regain profitability in light of heavy competition.

Finance companies that live primarily off consumer loans also tend to do poorly in times of economic crisis. Many of the consumer goods that clients seek are imported appliances whose prices will become unaffordable. Also, new consumer purchases, such as housing improvements, new educational opportunities, a new car, and vacations are less of a priority during crisis. In Chile, only one of close to a dozen finance companies survived after a consumer spending frenzy dwindled during a recent recession.

Crises that seriously affect clients and client demand have been fewer. However, natural disasters, such as floods, hurricanes, or even severe economic recessions that affect the economic activities of microentrepreneurs, do take a toll on microfinance institutions. Banco Económico's (Bolivia) exit from microcredit was largely a result of a worsening situation of the clients themselves, triggered by changes in customs policies and the general over-indebtedness of the sector (see Box 3.1). Although Económico didn't participate in the study, its experience shows that devastating blows to clients will make the financial institution vulnerable as well. Commercial actors with multiple options will tend to withdraw when they see potential losses lurking.

## Internal Factors

Although the economic crises that closed the microcredit programs of many banks received much attention among members of the microfinance community, it appears that the biggest "killers" of downscaling efforts are internal. Many Latin American banks entered the market and exited soon thereafter, mainly due to organizational factors that constrained the microcredit program from quickly becoming a major product line.

Internal problems are generally worse for banks that integrate the microcredit product into existing operations. Given that microcredit is a new product line, it generally becomes a division or unit under a larger department. In many cases department heads do not understand microcredit, and the product is doomed from the start. Anecdotal evidence suggests that banks handling medium and large business loans often apply a very centralized approach to the microcredit program. Other banks, lacking adequate pricing and methodology, find that the endeavor is not profitable enough to merit continuation and simply exit the market.

### Responding to the Challenge

Despite a relatively fragile industry, there are a number of downscaling efforts that are showing promise. What are some of the ingredients or approaches that have helped these banks succeed? Three are worth mentioning: the operational champion, the subsidiary, and technical assistance in credit methodologies.

### The Operational Champion

When microcredit was a foreign concept to many bankers, the need for strong commitment to microcredit from high levels of the bank was key. Without such a champion (usually on the board of directors), the 1997 study hypothesized, the likelihood of success was minimal. Over the last few years, however, it has become evident that many Latin American banks are exploring this market, not only because they have a visionary champion on the board, but because they need to find new markets in response to competitive pressures. As countries in the region went through processes of liberalization and as banking became more competitive, older banks and small, new entrants in particular encountered market pressure to downscale. In developing countries with large numbers of poor entrepreneurs and households, the strategic decision to explore a large new market niche made sense. Moreover, other actors were publicizing their successes at lending to the poor. It was no longer a foreign concept that was triggered by the authoritative voice of a lone visionary.

At this stage, champions *within* the institution are most valuable— champions that can achieve the integration that seemed so elusive before. Asked why his bank's microcredit program succeeded, one board

## Box 3.1: Banco Económico: Last In, First Out

Económico was established as a commercial bank in 1990 in Santa Cruz de la Sierra, Bolivia. It entered and then quickly exited the micro-lending market when it appeared that the product would not produce the bottom-line results that are so necessary to a commercial bank. The target population of Banco Económico, since its creation, has been the small- and medium-sized enterprise sectors of Santa Cruz. In its early years of existence Banco Económico was very profitable, generating an average annual rate of return on equity of 26.2 percent between 1993 and 1997. The bank continues to be an important player in the Bolivian financial system as the eighth largest bank in Bolivia in terms of loan portfolio at year-end 2000.

Banco Económico's venture into microfinance consisted of the creation of a specialized division called Presto in early 1998. Presto was dedicated to serving Santa Cruz–based micro-entrepreneurs with both microcredit and consumer credit. Through this segmentation, Banco Económico was able to differentiate prices, charging higher interest rates for smaller loans to reflect higher risk and transaction costs, expecting that this would allow the bank to further increase overall profitability.

During the first year of Presto's operations, the quality of the loan portfolio was very good; however, the past-due portfolio increased rapidly in 1999. The declining portfolio quality was due not only to the economic recession and client over-indebtedness, which were affecting all Bolivian microfinance institutions, but also to changes in tax requirements aimed at reducing the amount of contraband goods arriving into Bolivia at the borders, especially the borders with Brazil and Argentina. Many of Banco Económico's clients relied on the sale of such goods, and thus the increased taxes greatly damaged their repayment capacity, which directly affected Banco Económico's portfolio quality. Instead of developing new ways to serve the microenterprise client niche, the management and board of Banco Económico made the decision to exit the market well before any other Bolivian lender. By October 1999 the Presto division was closed down, and all outstanding operations were consolidated within the bank at large. Along with this decision, the bank decided to stop disbursing loans to microenterprises; such loans were seen as very risky, given the increasing problems many microfinance institutions throughout Bolivia were encountering.

In management's own words, the bank was able to minimize losses by being the last to enter the microfinance market and the first to exit the market, before the crisis really hit large scale.

> **Box 3.1—*Continued***
>
> Today, Banco Económico has returned to focus on its original niche "just above micro," the small- and medium-enterprise segments. Although there are still a few loans within the portfolio that the bank classifies as microloans, those loans are between US$8,000 and US$10,000 and have full (actually 2:1) mortgage guarantees.
>
> Text written by Lynne Curran and drawn from interviews with Banco Económico management (January 2001); see also Jeffrey Poyo and Robin Young, "Commercialization of Microfinance: The Cases of Banco Económico and Fondo Financiero Privado FASSIL" (Bethesda, Md.: Development Alternatives, Microenterprise Best Practices Project, 1999).

champion said he had selected one of his finest managers to lead the microcredit unit. The manager was an enthusiastic, younger man with an excellent understanding of bank products as well as back-office operations. He came from a rural area and understood rural and lower-income clients. He was an *operational champion*, someone who knew what it takes to develop a new product line within the bank and could oversee its service delivery. This is a refreshing story, since in many other cases managers have lacked the qualities needed to lead a microcredit program. In fact, many viewed the microcredit job as a demotion.

The emergence of an operational champion or champions is a positive trend. Such champions are better able to garner internal resources needed to facilitate implementation than a board-level champion, who is more removed from daily operations. Anecdotal evidence points to strong internal leadership as an ingredient of success.

## Subsidiaries

To date, the experience of subsidiaries has been quite positive. As suggested in the 1997 study, a subsidiary can separate the microlending program from the organizational culture of the larger bank. If the subsidiary has its own staff, infrastructure, and systems, however, the parent bank is less able to cross-sell other bank products to the microentrepreneur. Hybrids—in which staff and systems belong to the subsidiary, and infrastructure and portfolio belong to the bank—appear to be a good compromise. The points of contact of the subsidiary with the parent bank (such as accounting, management information systems, payments) are carefully linked to facilitate integration. A smart, resourceful manager who has the authority to innovate and adapt without being constrained by bureaucratic rules of the larger bank can lead a microcredit subsidiary to rapid and effective growth.

**Box 3.2: Interfisa Financiera**
**From a Centralized Corporate Culture to a Microfinance Bank**

Interfisa Financiera was established in 1978 as a small corporate-lending finance company. While other finance companies focused on consumer lending, Interfisa positioned itself early on as a financier for medium- to large-scale Paraguayan corporations. In the early to mid 1990s, as a result of the entry of foreign banks, Interfisa began to feel squeezed out of its core corporate business. In 1996 the Central Bank's IDB-funded Micro Global program offered Interfisa technical assistance from the German firm IPC and with it the opportunity to explore a new market niche.

The first microenterprise loans made in 1996 were medium/large enterprise look-alike loans processed by a special unit at headquarters. Each loan (and client) was handled by various departments as it made its way through the loan-approval process. The initial evaluation was conducted by the bank officer who received the application. It was then sent to a second officer, who handled the fieldwork. The loan then moved to a credit-analysis department and finally to the department that prepared the loan contract. The general manager approved the loan. At the initial stages Interfisa processed loans at headquarters and in one pilot agency. When a loan became delinquent, the collections department would recover the loan.

To transform fully from a corporate to a microfinance institution and reach increasing numbers of clients, Interfisa decided to re-engineer its institutional culture, processes, and infrastructure. A resistant upper and middle management needed to be convinced of the potential of this market segment and the effectiveness of a new credit technology. Managers and other staff underwent an extensive training program, and loan processes were improved to better conform to a more decentralized structure. Interfisa began to expand its branch network to be closer to its clients, increasing its agencies from two in 1995 to fourteen by mid 2001. The number of staff also increased by 400 percent. The credit technology received a major overhaul with IPC technical assistance. Most important, the loan officer took on a central role between institution and client, assuming responsibility for identifying new clients, analyzing loan applications, recommending approvals, and recovering loans. A new incentive system was put in place, rewarding loan officers for high productivity and portfolio quality. Active clients increased to 7,173 by December 2000. It is noteworthy that at this time the Paraguayan financial system was registering delinquency levels averaging 18 percent, while Interfisa's

**Box 3.2—*Continued***

overall delinquency was below 10 percent and its microcredit portfolio at less than 4 percent. This was a confirmation of the effectiveness of the new methodology.

Today Interfisa faces new challenges, such as strong competition coupled with a serious national recession, and hopes to explore new market niches among Paraguay's underserved rural population. With its new decentralized organizational culture, Interfisa may be well positioned for this expansion.

In general, most subsidiaries have common elements in relation to the parent bank (see Table 3.5). Variations among subsidiaries arise in four main areas:

• *Role of Loan Officer:* In most cases loan officers of the subsidiary participate in the entire loan cycle, from client identification, to credit analysis and recommendation, to loan repayment monitoring and recovery. In other cases the process is more compartmentalized, with a sales force that transfers the loans to a loan officer within the subsidiary.

• *Bank Infrastructure:* In most cases the subsidiary uses bank branches located in lower-income areas of urban centers or towns near potential clients. This approach can be observed among banks with a large regional or national branch network, and among consumer lenders, which tend to have offices with the most basic staffing and equipment requirements. In a few cases the subsidiary creates its own infrastructure, with a friendlier, accessible space that will attract a lower-income clientele. In other cases, such as Banco del Desarrollo in Chile, a hybrid of the two

**Table 3.5: Characteristics of Subsidiaries and Parent Banks**

| Subsidiary | Parent Bank |
|---|---|
| • Recruits and pays loan officers | • Provides loan funds |
| • Manages staff incentive system based on productivity and quality of portfolio | • Bank teller windows handle loan disbursement and payment transactions |
| • Has its own information system for loan tracking that can be linked into the parent bank's system | • Pays a fee to the subsidiary, usually on a per loan basis |
| • Turns over the most serious of collection problems to bank | • Includes the financial statements of the subsidiary in its consolidated statements |

approaches is used, wherein the subsidiary utilizes some bank branches but also opens new specialized branches. In most cases the administrative offices of the subsidiary are not located within bank headquarters, but database linkages connect the two.

- *Ownership:* In most cases the parent bank owns the subsidiary. In a few, more recent cases, there is equity participation by technical assistance providers or interested international investors.
- *Loan Funds:* In all cases the funds used for lending are provided by the bank. In at least one case the bank lends to the subsidiary, and the loans appear as a liability on the subsidiary's balance sheet. In most cases, however, the bank itself assumes the credit risk and provides the loan funds through its own bank windows. Here, the subsidiary is a loan facilitator, not a retailer.

## ROLE OF DONORS

Donors will often avoid supporting for-profit companies, believing that public subsidies should not be used to benefit individual owners. The argument makes sense if the benefits go only to the bank's shareholders. But there is a greater public good from activities such as financial services geared toward lower-income individuals and households. The question for donors is not *whether* to support commercial downscalers but *how* to support them.

As donors consider support for commercial downscalers, there are two principal questions to be asked. First, to be most effective, what kinds of commercial institutions should donors support? And second, what kinds of interventions are most appropriate?

### Institutions

Drawing from the experience of the surveyed banks, the advantages and disadvantages of each peer group are briefly analyzed below. An additional approach, in which actors combine forces into strategic alliances, is also explored.

### Large Commercial Banks

For donors, the challenge of working with large commercial banks is substantial, yet the potential gains can be high. As shown by some in the sample, these banks are attractive because they can reach very low-income clients with a diverse array of products. Few in the sample have massive client outreach, but this group, particularly those with a large branch network, has the potential to reach large numbers of clients. Donors should be highly selective when engaging with these banks, choosing those with a high level of commitment to the target market derived preferably from their need to find a new market niche (versus their interest in improving their public image). Donors should look for domestic banks with a large, broad deposit base and branch network, and/or banks with a strong consumer-lending orientation. These banks may be in the best position to cover most of the expenses associated with developing a microcredit product.

## Small Banks

Small banks should be of interest to donors because they can also offer small loans, as shown by banks in the sample. Because of their small size, they are more flexible and adaptable than large banks and, in many cases, are highly motivated due to their need to go down-market to survive in a competitive banking world. With the right combination of leadership, financial strength, and donor support, small banks could become important retailers of microfinance. On the other hand, these banks are also often weak, poorly capitalized, and poorly equipped. Donors should be careful when engaging with them, as they are particularly vulnerable to changing economic circumstances.

## State Banks

Although state banks have generally under-performed, with at least five ingredients—strong, stable leadership; a commercial orientation; insulation from political dealings; strong community presence; and a good reputation—they might be partners of interest to donors. Their ability to grow programs rapidly through an extensive branch network, as shown by Banco del Estado, Banco do Nordeste, and BanRural, make them particularly attractive. Subsidiary arrangements would also appear to be an important option for state banks. Nevertheless, with state banks, or any institution associated with government, for that matter, there is always the underlying danger that political tides may shift.

## Finance Companies

Finance companies have received the least attention and support from donors, but they should not be overlooked. Some consumer lenders have

## Box 3.3: Banco Agrícola: Searching for the Right Recipe

Banco Agrícola, a private commercial bank founded in 1955, is the largest bank in El Salvador with 129 agencies and assets in excess of US$2.6 billion. Initiated in 1986, Agrícola's microenterprise lending program is an example of the many adjustments that large commercial banks must make to find the most appropriate institutional fit. The program started as a small unit under the Consumer Lending Division. By the end of 1996, despite its lack of an appropriate methodology, Agrícola had eight thousand active microenterprise loans.

Believing that methodological affinities would strengthen the program, in 1999 management merged it with small-business lending and transferred it to the Enterprises Division. Concerned that it was still not reaching its full potential, in 2000 management decided to elevate the program itself to the status of a division, sharing the same hierarchical status as the consumer-lending and enterprises divisions. The new division reports directly to the vice president for retail banking, who oversees products, services, and branching. This new structure has greatly facilitated internal coordination. Thanks to its new status, the program has also gained needed independence. Yet, as an operational unit, it must also prove itself as a profit center. Until the microfinance pilot proves itself, the bank continues to offer the traditional microenterprise products. A comparison between the old and new reflects a second search the bank has engaged in—the search for an appropriate methodology.

The old program, begun in 1986, is predominantly a bank loan lookalike with some elements of microfinance techniques. The client normally approaches the bank to request a loan. The loan officer visits the business to conduct a cash-flow analysis. Real estate, a salaried co-signer, a fixed asset, or a loan guarantee is used as collateral. The loan is presented to a loan committee at headquarters, and once the loan is approved, its monitoring is turned over to the Collections Division. If the loan becomes delinquent, collections staff respond with phone calls and letters. In tough cases the credit officer is called back to assist with locating the client. The responsibility for recovery, however, lies with the collections department. The loan is paid in monthly installments, and loan terms usually exceed one year, even those used for working capital. It takes the bank an average of eight days to issue a microenterprise loan, which is quite good for a large bank.

The new pilot program, begun in 2000, is a microfinance institution look-alike. Preliminary indications are that it has just broken even. Under the

---

**Box 3.3—*Continued***

pilot, the credit methodology is different.

The loan officer spends much of his or her time promoting the product in neighborhoods and talking to potential clients. The loan officer is responsible for the loan from its inception to recovery, including an analysis of the cash flow of the business as well as the home. The loan officer is also central in the approval process, along with the branch manager. The loan does not go the headquarters for approval. The product is also different: average loan sizes are much smaller and loan terms are much shorter. The loan can be repaid in weekly, bi-weekly or monthly installments over a three-month period. The analysis is quick, and the loan can be issued in three days. Nontraditional collateral is accepted, such as non-salaried co-signers or household items. Finally, the interest rate is higher in order to cover the higher costs and risks of the product and generate an acceptable return. So far, portfolio at risk stands at less than 3 percent. Client satisfaction appears to be high, and the bank is considering offering clients other products as well. The pilot is receiving technical assistance from a local USAID-funded project.

After sixteen years of trials and errors, it appears that Agrícola's microenterprise product is now firmly established within the bank with a solid methodology and the rank of a division. Coupled with strong organizational backing and leadership, the program promises to expand Banco Agrícola's services to microentrepreneurs as well as to generate attractive profits.

---

reached large numbers of microentrepreneurs while maintaining high quality portfolios. Many have cleverly adopted and adapted microfinance best practices. From this author's observation, what appears to be the most important factor distinguishing the good from the bad is the quality of leadership and vision.

## Strategic Alliances

Rather than a bank going through a long learning process, an alliance might be mutually beneficial. There are at least four such alliances that are worth considering.

- The bank as a wholesaler to a microcredit NGO. Banco Wiese in Peru, highlighted in the 1997 report, and BanRural in Guatemala both have had wholesaling programs for NGOs. State-owned Banco Nacional de Costa Rica has plans to become a second-tier lender as well.

- Commercial banks as partners in a new microfinance venture. These are ventures in which a local commercial bank has an important ownership stake along with socially motivated investors. In essence, they are subsidiaries of sorts, and can utilize bank infrastructure.
- An agreement with a reputable NGO to administer the bank's microenterprise loans. In such a situation, the NGO would handle credit identification and monitoring of the client, while the bank would handle all cash transactions (loan withdrawal, repayments, and savings). While no such cases exist, there has been talk of such arrangements in some Latin American countries.
- Commercial bank's purchase of the microcredit portfolio and expertise belonging to an NGO or another commercial actor. In Jamaica, the Jamaica National Building Society purchased the microcredit portfolio of the failed Worker's Bank. In Chile, Banco Santander bought out a small finance company, including its microcredit program.

### Appropriate Interventions

In the past, microenterprise donors have typically offered loan funds, guarantee funds, technical assistance, and operating expense support. What kind of support do downscalers need from donors? Are some forms of support more appropriate than others?

### Loan Funds

Over the years, loan funds have been donors' largest offering. Typically channeled through central banks, these are intended to "lure" banks into microlending. However, banks that are only willing to offer microloans funded by cheaper donor funds may be signaling that they do not see microcredit as a core business. With few exceptions, donors should not provide loan funds to banks to help start microcredit programs. All of the banks in the study used their own resources, and none mentioned lack of funds as a constraint. In some very specialized cases, however, liquidity shortages resulting from a banking crisis may limit ongoing microcredit programs, and funds in such special cases might be advisable.

### Guarantee Funds

Donors such as USAID and DFID have invested heavily in guarantee funds, yet few banks in the survey utilize them. These programs have intended to attract banks to microcredit by reducing credit-risk exposure, but in reality, they may simply reinforce the notion that microentrepreneurs don't have hard collateral. If guarantees are to play an important role in supporting downscaler efforts, new approaches will need to be devised.

### Technical Assistance

It is clear from both surveys that technical assistance has played a key role in helping orient and expand the programs of downscalers. Of all possible donor interventions, this appears to be the most fruitful (and perhaps the cheapest). In the 2001 survey there was a slight correlation between technical assistance and performance. Banks that had not received technical assistance were often those that used poor practices, resulting in poor performance.

### Special Operating Expenses

Support for operating expenses is an intervention that has been used rarely with commercial actors, though it is very prevalent with NGOs. An interesting approach is found in Chile, where the government subsidizes lenders with a fee per microloan. Lenders present bids for operating support funds to a government agency that allocates the funds through an auction. The system has helped spark the commercialization of microfinance in Chile. The banks take 100 percent of the credit risk, but the subsidy helps cover the high transaction costs associated with tiny loans.

## CONCLUDING REMARKS

One of the most important conclusions to be derived from this study is that the downscaler approach is highly diverse. The common stereotype of the downscaler is that it is a large corporate bank offering individual loans to upper-end microenterprises that some would call small businesses. It enters the market because it has received cheap donor funds, and as soon as it finds out that the market is not profitable enough, or when the donor funds run out, it will exit. In reality, however, downscalers cannot be stereotyped. Not only do the institutions hold different charters (full-service banks of all sizes, non-bank financial institutions, state banks), they are also motivated by different factors, operate in different product markets, approach microfinance differently, have different organizational structures to handle microfinance, and reach a wide range of clients, from poor to less poor.

While the downscaler experience so far is mixed, and includes cases of bank exits as well as many sluggish programs, there are a few banks that have been able to reach large numbers of people with a well-defined, well-integrated product. Some banks already have impressive track records, and some commercial microfinance providers are outpacing credit unions and microcredit NGOs. It is clear that downscalers are part of the microfinance landscape and will be present for the foreseeable future.

Adding a microcredit product to a public or private commercial bank or finance company is complex. It is analogous to experimenting with a recipe. Trial and error teaches the best combinations. From this research, some "ingredients" can be distilled as most important for success:

- A *champion,* not only at the board level, but perhaps more important, at the operational level. The board champion helps the institution decide to take the risk. The operational champion helps ensure a successful interface between the microcredit program and the various departments of the bank. This is necessary for all institutional types, but especially for large commercial and state banks with a wide range of product offerings.
- *Appropriate organizational fit.* While it cannot be said that subsidiaries are *the* model for large bank downscalers, it is true that in the short run they offer the independence needed to develop specialized microlending programs. The limited evidence from the survey suggests that subsidiaries may get off the ground faster than integrated models, which sometimes languish for years with internal structural issues. However, because subsidiaries tend to specialize in few products, more integrated models may ultimately be a preferred choice from the perspective of the consumer, as there will be wider access to the array of products and services offered by the bank. Hybrids, which combine the structural advantages of subsidiaries with the diverse product offerings of integrated models, may be the ideal option for many larger banks. More needs to be learned about the elements of successful subsidiary, hybrid, or integrated approaches and the ideal conditions for implementing each.
- *Openness to seek advice.* With a few important exceptions, the banks that have sought advice and participated in microfinance training

or observational visits have performed better than those with little or no external contacts. This outside advice has helped zero in on problem areas, such as delinquency control, methodology, staff training, and organizational issues. Banks surveyed are interested in receiving technical assistance, largely on new products and operational issues, and they indicate a willingness to pay for a portion of such assistance.

It is clear that there is a role for donors in advancing downscaling efforts. Technical assistance to help assimilate lessons from microfinance experience is probably the best intervention. This assistance, in most cases, should be discrete and highly focused. A number of institutions in the sample have developed strong programs at minimal cost to donors.

Is one institutional form better than the other for downscaling? Each of the peer groups reviewed has had successes and failures. If there is any lesson so far, it is that donors should be open to all institutional types and select opportunistically. The survey findings, however preliminary, do show that some institutional types may have a slight edge over others in terms of special developmental objectives. For example, large commercial banks may be able to reach the poorest clients for the least overall investment, given the infrastructure and systems they possess. Yet, they may also require the most patience from donors. The small banks appear to have been the most successful thus far in reaching the poorest clients and in adapting the product, yet they are also the most vulnerable. The state banks and finance companies reach the largest numbers of clients most quickly, though generally not the poorest clients.

With a few exceptions, banks are not targeting the poorest of the self-employed poor. By and large, they are reaching clients that are slightly better off than the average NGO client. However, banks, like credit unions, do not practice strict market segmentation and serve a diverse range of clients. In the sample, 26 percent of loans were under US$500; half of those were under US$300. While downscalers generally serve the more established microenterprises, they are also able to reach lower market segments.

Observers argue that private downscalers lack the sense of mission that motivates NGOs or credit unions, and that they may abandon the market segment at any time. This argument sounds logical, if one assumes that banks have many other profit-making options available. The reality is that in most developing countries in Latin America, Asia, and Africa, the largest segments of the population are at the lower end of the market, and if banks do learn to service this clientele, it will be in their economic self-interest to continue to serve them with an array of products.

## NOTES

1. Seven banks responding to the 2001 survey were also featured in the 1997 report, making a total number of fifty-three banks examined in this chapter.

2. Although Worker's Bank in Jamaica failed, its small but healthy microenterprise portfolio was purchased by the Jamaica National Building Society and is now managed by its subsidiary, the Jamaica National Microfinance Company.

3. The survey instrument was not an adequate mechanism to explore leadership or governance issues, which may in fact be the strongest determinants of success. Also, the survey did not explore the economic and policy environment in each of the countries, which may also influence outreach.

4. The five banks with subsidiaries in the sample were Banco del Estado, Chile; Bank of Nova Scotia, Guyana; Banco del Desarrollo, Chile; Banco Pichincha, Ecuador; and SOGEBANK, Haiti.

5. The fourteen banks offering group loans were Bancafé, Guatemala; Bank of Nova Scotia, Guyana; Banco del Café, Honduras; MultiCredit Bank, Panama; Narodny Savings Bank, and Center Credit, Kazakhstan; Commercial Bank of Zimbabwe; Banco del Desarrollo, Chile; Banrural, Guatemala; FASSIL, Bolivia; Banco de Desarrollo Unificado, Domincan Republic; Banco Solidario, Ecuador; Mibanco, Panama; and Akiba Commercial Bank, Tanzania.

# 4

# The Role of Specialized Investors in Commercialization

**Rochus Mommartz and Gabriel Schor**

## INTRODUCTION

Underlying this book is a relatively simple concept of commercialization. As Robert Christen and Deborah Drake write in Chapter 1, "In this book the term *commercialization* is used to refer to the movement of microfinance out of the heavily donor-dependent arena of subsidized operations into one in which microfinance institutions 'manage on a business basis' as part of the regulated financial system." This process has already been under way for over ten years, and today we can safely say that it represents an irreversible trend in the development of microfinance. To an increasing extent, *commercial* financial institutions are taking control of the business, which on balance is—at least, as we see it—a positive development from the point of view of the microenterprise target group.

Interventions in microfinance can be regarded as attempts to overcome market failure in the formal financial sector. Consequently, the policy strategies adopted must be designed to alleviate or eliminate the causes of this failure (Webster et al. 1996). But why did the market fail in the first place, and why is it still failing? Two sets of factors are to blame: (1) the characteristics of the microenterprise target group itself (the lack of documentation and formal accounts and the absence of the kind of collateral that banks usually require of their borrowers), and the nature of its credit demand (micro-borrowers demand relatively small loan amounts, which pushes up the intermediaries' administrative costs per unit); and (2) the difficulties that formal financial intermediaries encounter and their reluctance to try to come up with solutions to these problems. Given that the characteristics of the target group are an inherent part of their social and economic status and that it will not be possible to change them any time soon, it is necessary to change the market instead, that is, to identify the problems causing market failure and to find solutions to overcome them, thus enabling a market for financial services for microenterprises to develop.

The solutions must address three key areas: credit technology, institutional setting, and regulation. In other words, an appropriate credit technology has to be found, one which can overcome the lack of information and collateral and also alleviate the problem that making microloans is costly. Such a credit technology is a basic precondition for effective and efficient microlending. However, an appropriate credit technology can only be effective if it is used in an appropriate institutional setting (in terms of governance and ownership structure). And the advantages of both the technology and the institutional setting can be fully exploited only if the regulatory environment is adapted to meet the needs of microfinance institutions (MFIs). The regulatory regime must be designed to facilitate an ongoing process of market deepening, for without such a regulatory environment, financial institutions or private investors will be all the more reluctant to move into the mainly informal segment of the market. The evolution of microfinance can be interpreted as a series of attempts to provide solutions in each of these key areas.

It is fair to say that although the efforts throughout the years to promote microfinance can only be described as partially effective or efficient, it is at least clear now, looking back, that the goal of demonstrating that microfinance can be made to work has indeed been achieved and that considerable progress has been made toward overcoming market failure. Initially working primarily with NGOs, practitioners succeeded in showing how specially modified credit technologies make it possible to do business with microenterprises; later, the conversion of the best NGOs into regulated financial intermediaries (upgrading), as well as the establishment of microfinance operations at existing commercial banks (downscaling), proved that the microenterprise segment of the market can be reached efficiently and profitably using market-based approaches. These demonstration projects, in turn, had an impact on the regulation and supervision of microfinance, and this has—at least in some cases—generally helped to create a stimulating and enabling environment. All these developments taken together can be described as the successful commercialization of microfinance.

Nonetheless, it should be mentioned that not all of the original hopes have been fulfilled. At the outset, many proponents of microfinance hoped, either explicitly or implicitly, that if it could be successfully demonstrated that microfinance could be a profitable business, more private investors would be drawn toward microfinance and ultimately would become the driving force behind this market. This would be desirable because it would mean that substantially larger volumes of capital would be available for microfinance and hence for the development of local financial markets. Increased private-sector involvement in microfinance would also be desirable insofar as it could lead to substantial improvements to the ownership and governance structures of MFIs.

This optimistic vision of the future role of private investors in microfinance has yet to become a reality. There is no need to emphasize that it is still too early for a long-term assessment of the role of private investors, let alone a final verdict. Nonetheless, we believe there is now a relatively broad consensus that the reality has not lived up to the initial high hopes. For example, Victoria White and Anita Campion comment in Chapter 2 that "to date, transformation has only attracted a small amount of private-sector ownership in MFIs." And Bob Christen and Deborah Drake state in Chapter 1 that, "given the highly specialized nature of microfinance, relatively few banking institutions will or should ever take it on as a core banking business. In this sense microfinance will also ultimately be a niche banking activity."

This raises two fundamental questions. First, why have private investors (so far) been relatively reluctant to invest in microfinance? Or, to put it another way, what structural or other characteristics might be standing in the way of greater private-sector participation? The following section examines this question in more depth.

Second, why are specialized investors increasingly moving in to plug the gap that has not yet been filled by private investors? According to White and Campion, "Specialized equity funds, such as ProFund, the ACCION Gateway Fund, and Internationale Micro Investitionen AG (IMI AG), are not pure private investors, yet they play an important role in the transition toward increased commercial investment in microfinance." What are the specific comparative advantages of these specialized funds? Why is this group of investors less severely affected by the structural or specific problems of microfinance than the pure private investors? The third section of this chapter is devoted to answering these questions.

In the fourth section we briefly describe some of the experiences that one specialized investor in microfinance institutions, IMI AG, has gathered over the past few years. And in the final section we draw conclusions from those experiences that point toward the increased involvement of commercial investors in the future.

## UNDERSTANDING THE PERSISTENCE
## OF MICROFINANCE MARKET FAILURES

Why has the successful commercialization of microfinance not been sufficient, on its own, to motivate purely private investors to move into microfinance on a large scale? Are there specific features of microfinance, perhaps overlooked so far, that continue to make the commercialization of ownership difficult despite the successful completion of the demonstration phase?

To answer the latter question, we must begin by considering the criteria that constitute decisive factors for a private investor. These criteria should be fairly easy to define, given that, in this regard, microfinance is no different from any other segment of the financial services market. "Increasingly, microfinance will be driven by the twin concerns of the competitive marketplace: Market share and profits" (Rhyne and Christen 1999, 1). Profitability is undoubtedly a priority for private investors—there must be profitability, and it must compare favorably to other investment opportunities (that is, it must have a relatively high net present value). And profitability, in turn, is ultimately determined by expected growth and long-term risks.

Thus, it must be asked whether and to what extent these factors are sending signals to potential investors indicating that the profitability of an investment in the microfinance segment would be too low in comparison to alternative investment options. And it seems that there are some characteristics of investments in the microfinance segment which are seldom examined closely enough in the current discussions on this issue. These can be summarized in the following three points:

***The labor-intensive nature of microlending, which can be standardized only to a very limited degree, is a clear barrier to entry.***

To succeed in a significantly more competitive market and earn acceptable returns, an institution must grow rapidly. Only when the institution

has reached a sufficient operating volume can it achieve a
efficiency that will ensure its long-term survival in a comp
ronment. This poses a fundamental problem for new interm
tering the market. For, in microfinance, sufficient size is not
function of marketing, product design, and pricing; rather, it requires a
sufficient number of trained employees. Microfinance calls for the intensive use of human resources and, in addition, requires the staff to develop specialized skills that are not taught in standard training programs.
An insufficient number of trained staff over the short term is a genuine
obstacle to rapid expansion in the microfinance segment. Due to this
constraint, new intermediaries entering the market can build up a high
operating volume only very gradually if they wish to maintain appropriate standards with regard to risk. Thus, although, as Rhyne and Christen
state, "a bank can secure all the know-how needed to implement
microfinance by hiring one or two staff members from an experienced
institution," this does not necessarily mean, in our view, that the "entry
barriers to microfinance have fallen quite low," as the authors imply
(Rhyne and Christen 1999, 18).

New intermediaries entering the market thus face a choice. They can
adopt a risk-averse strategy through which they will operate with higher
average costs for a longer than usual period of time and, as a result, must
accept lower profitability even after the start-up phase. Clearly, this is
not a particularly attractive prospect for investors. Or, alternatively, they
can implement a credit technology based on the one used in consumer
lending, which will enable more rapid growth but which also entails much
higher risks. As experience in Bolivia has shown (see Chapter 6) this
prospect is also not particularly attractive in the long term.

**Due to the effects of demonstration projects, whether highly
successful or less so, private investors are confronted in many
of the most attractive markets with a very fragmented market
structure.**

The microfinance segment is often seen as an almost limitless market—a classic supplier's market with only limited competition, and a
market in which it is possible to earn considerable extra profits. Indeed,
there are numerous microfinance projects which have shown that, with
very little price elasticity on the demand side, even the most extreme
forms of inefficiency need not prevent an institution from earning profits

in this market. However, though this scenario may have been a fair description of the market for microfinance several years ago, it no longer applies today in most countries. It is farthest from being the case in precisely those countries where there have already been a great number of demonstration projects, successful or otherwise. These markets usually end up with a fragmented structure, characterized by one or two intermediaries with a very large market share, while the rest of the market is divided among a large number of smaller intermediaries. This does not make private investors' decisions any easier; on the contrary, many investors are put off by such a market structure, which tends to foster cutthroat competition. This is especially true of the segments within microfinance that are of interest to private investors, namely, enterprises in urban areas, particularly those which show potential for growth—in other words, precisely those enterprises that the existing intermediaries are already seeking to win as customers. Today's potential private investors, therefore, face a different initial situation from the intermediaries that sought to demonstrate the commercial viability of microfinance in the 1990s. For one thing, new private investors would be entering a market in which competition is already intense, not a point in favor of investment in microfinance compared to other investment opportunities available to investors. This is the downside of the large number of demonstration projects; that is, however much such projects may have contributed to widespread acceptance of the notion that microfinance can be a profitable business, they now constitute a major disincentive for bringing private investors into their local markets.[1]

This evolution of the market, in addition to the high degree of segmentation, which will inevitably result in the consolidation of the market, challenges all investors. In the case of purely private investors, it makes the market fairly unattractive both in the short term and in the long term. Although it goes without saying that the long-term aspect is a key factor in deciding whether to invest, and that long-term prospects are difficult to assess, it should also be repeated explicitly that microfinance is not suitable for short-term investments (for example, to absorb surplus liquidity). For one thing, it takes a long time to build up a microfinance institution to the point where it is on a sound, profitable footing. And even thereafter, the pace of growth will inevitably be very gradual, as microlending is very labor intensive and can be standardized only to a very limited degree. This is why it necessarily calls for a long-term perspective, which many private investors do not share.

*During recessions, micro and small enterprises (MSEs) can be just as vulnerable as other market segments. This is especially the case given the risk of the politicization of microfinance during economic crises.*

Apart from growth in the market share of a given institution, growth of the market as a whole is also relevant to long-term profitability. Even though MSEs account for a considerable share of overall economic output in many Latin American countries, the microfinance segment cannot be described as a particularly attractive growth market. There are two pertinent aspects here: (1) When the market segment grows in size, it is usually a reflection of a macroeconomic downturn in the country as a whole, which in turn means that the risks entailed in lending to these businesses increase. Thus, when the number of MSEs increases, the overall environment for investment can be perceived as generally unfavorable. And (2) the MSEs themselves do not really constitute a growth segment capable of making a favorable impression on investors. It must be kept in mind that MSEs that achieve significant growth are the exception rather than the rule. Most entrepreneurs in this segment run businesses that have little potential for expansion and merely allow the entrepreneurs' families to survive. Thus, judged by the criterion of growth, microfinance is not a particularly attractive investment.

For a long time private investors vastly overestimated the risks involved in lending to informal microenterprises. The successful demonstration projects, however, served to show that by using credit technologies appropriate to the target group, the risk of default could be kept to a minimum. The high degree of diversification due to the division of loan portfolios into small amounts distributed among large numbers of borrowers also helps to reduce risk. However, as the situation in Bolivia now demonstrates, MSEs can be as vulnerable during recessions as other enterprises, because they frequently lack financial reserves and do not have the option of turning to the export market to compensate partially for the poor domestic market. This ability to access the export market becomes particularly important when potential investors are assessing long-term investment prospects.

Another specific risk is the danger of the politicization of microfinance, which can make it a very unpredictable activity for private investors. As evidenced in many Latin American countries, governments tend to undertake drastic interventions in the market during periods of economic crisis (for example, by deferring debts). Even when carried out with the best intentions, such interventions undermine the development of the market and can be very damaging for the intermediaries and, in the medium term, harm the borrowers as well. As for private investors, it simply scares them off.

## A SPECIALIZED PUBLIC-PRIVATE PARTNERSHIP AS A SUSTAINABLE BASIS FOR MICROFINANCE

The developments we have observed in various microfinance markets and the structural difficulties characterizing the microfinance market in general, as discussed above, lead us to conclude that private investors are unlikely to become the dominant players in this segment. And precisely because the private sector, at least to date, has clearly failed to take the lead in these areas, specialized public-private partnerships have become the predominant force in commercial microfinance.

What exactly are public-private partnerships, and why do they appear to be more capable of solving the problems described above? On the one hand, many of the international financial institutions (IFIs) such as the multilateral and bilateral development institutions are increasingly changing their roles to become commercially oriented owners of MFIs. In the past IFIs have acted almost exclusively as providers of funds to MFIs, and have not been particularly interested in ensuring that those funds are repaid; their primary goal was to get the funds to the target group. With the commercialization of credit technologies and particularly with few private investors, both the attitude and the role of these sponsors have undergone a fundamental change. They have come to regard the provision of funds, whether in the form of credit or as an equity stake, from a much more commercial point of view. As noted above, many IFIs are increasingly playing the role of owners, which enables them to fill the void created by the continuing reluctance of private investors to enter the market.

Until recently, most of the IFIs chose not to take an active role in the MFIs in which they had become shareholders, preferring to act as silent partners. There may be several reasons for this passive relationship: they may be unwilling to bear the costs that active ownership inevitably entails; they may have taken a politically motivated decision not to intervene; they simply may not have a business strategy for the institutions concerned; or they may lack the technical know-how that would enable them to make an active contribution. For these or other reasons, many of these organizations would not take the step of investing in a microfinance intermediary if specialized private investors did not also acquire equity stakes in the institution alongside them. The emergence of these specialized investors and the commercialization of the donor institutions have been parallel developments. The new investment funds could best be described as conveyors of know-how. Generally, they play a very active role in the MFIs in which they acquire stakes, and their shareholders often take the view that inflows of capital into evolving target group–oriented financial institutions should be accompanied by an input of know-how and a set of values, and that the bulk of the capital for an investment fund of this kind should come from the private sector. In forming their various partnerships, these two groups of investors—on the one hand, public donor institutions operating on a commercial basis, on the other, specialized private investment companies—act as mutually complementary owners of MFIs and are thus playing a key role in creating a sustainable basis for the future of microfinance.

Naturally, the question arises as to what advantage the specialized investors have that "normal" private investors do not. In principle, the same problem of low relative profitability is a constraint for this group of specialized investors, just as it is for regular private investors. However, if we take a closer look at the above discussion of the difficulties encountered by a purely private investor who has no real previous experience of microfinance, it quickly becomes apparent where the specialized investors have an advantage. Specialized investors have extensive expertise in microfinance that enables them consistently to apply best practices, providing the MFI with a strategic competitive advantage, or at least a level of competitiveness equal to that of other MFIs. These investors can also use their network of contacts, their reputation, and their established names to obtain from the donor organizations not only technical support for the intermediaries during their start-up phase but also onlending funds, possibly on a long-term basis, allowing the intermediaries to achieve rapid growth, even while they are still in the process of building a broad-based deposit business. And not least of all, the specialized investors are under much less pressure than "normal" private investors to demand short-term profitability. Purely private investors, in contrast, do not have any specific advantages that would allow them to tap the potential of microfinance. Therefore, it is not surprising that most MFIs today, or at least the most advanced ones, have an ownership structure that features not only multilateral organizations (IFIs) and, to a certain degree, representatives of the local private sector, but also specialized strategic investors that act as catalysts, forcing the pace of the process when a new bank is established, actively intervening to ensure that best practices are implemented at the new intermediaries, and seeing to it that the intermediaries remain competitive over the long term.

## EXPERIENCES WITH A SPECIALIZED PUBLIC-PRIVATE PARTNERSHIP: THE EXAMPLE OF IMI AG

### *Some Background Information on IMI AG*

IMI AG was founded in Frankfurt in 1998 by the consulting firm IPC and a number of its employees (IPC Invest). They were soon joined by the DOEN Foundation (Netherlands), ProCrédito (a Bolivian foundation and founder of Caja Los Andes), Deutsche Investitionsund Entwicklungsgesellschaft (DEG), the German development finance company, and later by other institutional investors, the International Finance Corporation (IFC) and the Dutch Development Finance Company (FMO). IMI AG's equity is currently 52 percent private and 48 percent public. IMI AG's objective is to promote financial services targeted at MSEs and low-income groups. Its business strategy is to acquire equity stakes in financial institutions that have demonstrated willingness and ability to build a banking operation oriented toward this target group. This strategy may require setting up institutions "from scratch" (greenfield ventures)[2] or continuing to build upon an existing business catering to MSEs and other economically disadvantaged sections of the population.

IMI AG's owners share a number of beliefs: First and foremost, they are convinced that the provision of target group–oriented banking services is both possible and profitable. They also regard the strengthening of the institutions and their equity base as a precondition for the success of microbanking operations. They take the view that qualified providers of equity for commercially oriented development finance institutions that focus on the MSE target group should be active owners, and that not enough capital is being provided to financial institutions of this kind in developing countries and transition economies by competent, active, critical investors with a long-term orientation.

IMI AG is determined to close this gap. Alongside the specialized private investor IMI AG, the shareholders of all of the MFIs also include major investors such as the European Bank for Reconstruction and Development (EBRD), the German development bank Kreditanstalt für Wiederaufbau (KfW), the IFC, FMO, and the DOEN Foundation. In addition, local private investors hold small stakes in some of the MFIs, and recently the German commercial bank Commerzbank joined the group of investors.

During its first three years, its share capital has grown to €15 million, which is invested in seventeen different institutions. As a development-oriented investment company, IMI AG seeks to combine the pursuit of investor interests with the active provision of advice to, and participation in the control of, its partner MFIs. Thus, after the institutions have received an initial injection of funds to start their operations, they can continue to rely on IMI AG's support until such time as they are able to raise funds independently in the capital markets.

The results posted by the seventeen institutions in which IMI AG has invested to date are encouraging. In December 2001, that is, less than three years after IMI AG was founded, their combined loan portfolio amounted to €230 million, with a total of 141,000 loans outstanding and an average outstanding loan amount of €1,600. On the whole, the quality of the loan portfolios is very high (portfolio at risk averages 2 percent in Eastern European countries, 3 to 5 percent in Latin America), proving that small and micro loans are less risky than often claimed. Moreover, MFIs maintain a high level of loan loss reserves that cover twice the level of the portfolio at risk. The development of the institutions' deposit-taking business has also been encouraging, despite its relative youth. The €200 million combined volume of deposits, spread among 120,000 depositors, is a testament to the widespread trust placed in the MFIs. Results indicate that after three years of operation, they can achieve a sustainable return on equity (after tax) of 10 to 15 percent.[3] IMI AG itself is also a profitable company.

All of these developments—to the extent that one can judge at such an early stage—add up to a highly successful example of the commercialization of microfinance. It is therefore of interest to examine in more detail the specific conditions and circumstances that have contributed to this success—factors that go beyond the general advantages of the specialized public-private partnership in terms of governance of MFIs.

## Lessons from the Investment Approach and Consequences for the Commercialization of Microfinance

### Lesson 1

*In response to the specific circumstances in different financial markets, it has increasingly proved advantageous to set up new target group-*

*oriented financial intermediaries "from scratch." Good results have been achieved with these new MFIs, and many of the problems typically associated with upgrading and downscaling projects have been avoided.*

One of the main factors behind the success of specialized public-private partnerships is speed: it is essential that MFIs are built up quickly, that they rapidly accumulate a significant volume of total assets, and that they reach break-even within a calculable period (usually two to three years). IPC/IMI AG has found that building intermediaries from scratch is a very efficient way of accomplishing these goals. This approach, that is, deepening the financial sector by systematically founding new intermediaries, was first practiced by IPC/IMI AG in the transition countries of Eastern Europe, where de facto there was no other option, given that no real financial sector was in place. It is worth taking a closer look here at developments in the countries of Eastern Europe, since similar trends can currently be observed in some instances in the markets of Latin America, Africa, and Asia.

Since the sweeping political and economic changes that began between 1989 and 1991, Eastern Europe has seen the emergence of a broad new segment of MSEs which, in light of the generally poor and in some cases disastrous state of the local banking systems, face considerable problems in regard to financing. As in Latin America, both the downscaling approach (Wallace 1996; Neuhauss 2002) and the upgrading approach have been tried, the latter in the form of greenfield ventures.

By the end of 2001 microfinance banks were operating in Albania, Bosnia, Herzegovina, Georgia, Kosovo, Russia, Ukraine, and Yugoslavia, and finance companies specialized in lending to the target group had been founded in Moldova and Romania. It is surely no exaggeration to say that a similarly rapid expansion would not have been possible by means of the "traditional" approaches, upgrading in the classic sense (see Chapter 2) or through downscaling (see Chapter 3), even if NGOs or interested healthy commercial banks had existed in these transition economies. In our view, one of the main reasons for this is that the corporate culture that typifies an MFI is virtually incompatible with that of a traditional commercial bank, a conflict that considerably retards the downscaling process and in some cases causes it ultimately to fail.

Experience in Paraguay shows that private intermediaries can indeed be attracted to the microfinance segment. The development of microfinance in Paraguay is an example of the downscaling approach in which NGOs play only a subsidiary role. The existing private formal financial institutions, supported by the Micro-Global Program of the IDB, made a real contribution to the development of this market segment.[4] At the end of this project, carried out in two phases from 1994 to 2000, eight financial intermediaries were actively participating in the program and together were providing close to forty thousand microenterprises with an appropriate supply of credit. The combined portfolio of the participating intermediaries was US$33 million at the end of the project.

The Paraguayan experience also demonstrates that three conditions must be in place for private financial intermediaries to enter the market: competition, flexibility of financial institutions, and subsidies in the form of technical support. If there is sufficient competition, and if, as in Paraguay, there are flexible intermediaries operating in the market, then, with intensive support from external experts (accompanied by large-scale subsidies to cover the initial costs), private intermediaries will be willing to enter the microfinance market, and downscaling works. However, none of this serves to indicate whether these intermediaries will in general seek to enter the field of microfinance on their own initiative, even in the face of increasing competitive pressure. In any case, the experience of Paraguay should not be seen as proof that the commercialization of microfinance will inevitably take place, since, even in Paraguay, very specific conditions were required in order to make it possible to deepen the financial sector and the process of changing the corporate culture proved to be very time-consuming.

### Lesson 2

*It needs to be clearly emphasized that even where the relatively rapid approach of building a new intermediary is taken, technical assistance (TA) as well as funding is necessary and more efficient if provided by owners.*

Although experience to date indicates that building intermediaries from scratch takes less time than, say, an upgrading project, this new approach nonetheless also requires TA in order to minimize startup costs for the investors. Numerous examples of newly created banks in transition economies show that a two-year phase of active support is enough to turn a new bank into a profitable institution. Similarly, the rapid growth of a new bank is supported only rarely by principal financing through its deposit-taking business. Establishing a successful financial intermediary requires the provision of long-term onlending funds and technical assistance by IFIs. Since they are able to provide both support components, that is, both TA and funding, the participation of the IFIs in the ownership structures of the new intermediaries creates accountability and an incentive to provide oversight, particularly from the point of view of incentive compatibility.

### Lesson 3

*Given the specific situation and the level of unmet demand for financial services in the transition economies of Eastern Europe, the goal, right from the start of projects in these countries, is to establish full-fledged banks; in other regions, the same goal is also appropriate: to minimize risk, to broaden the range of products available, and to achieve an optimal scale of operations.*

As a consequence of the underdeveloped state of the Eastern European banking systems and also the geographical proximity of these countries to the markets of Western Europe, there is significant unmet demand in transition economies for non-credit financial services, such as current accounts, international and domestic money transfers, and various types of bank guarantees, not only among small enterprises but even among the larger microenterprises. Those nonfinancial services, together with the latitude in the range of loan products that MFIs in Eastern Europe can introduce at a very early stage, gives them greater scope than their counterparts in Latin America to implement the concept of "popular banking." Consequently, designers of microfinance projects are virtually obliged to apply, right from the outset, for a full banking license. This puts the commercialization of microfinance on a much broader footing and helps to increase the probability that, under these specific conditions, purely private investors will wish to get involved.

For different, though no less compelling reasons, the establishment of full-fledged commercial banks also makes sense in Latin America and other regions where financial markets are more developed. Admittedly, most MFIs in Latin America were not set up as banks and were focused almost exclusively on the microenterprise segment. Precisely because of this narrow focus on a single market segment, these institutions should diversify their risks during the growth phase. To this end, it can be beneficial for the MFIs to consider serving MSEs as well. Yet MSEs demand different financial services than microenterprises, such as funds transfers and current accounts. This fact alone obliges MFIs to transform themselves into universal commercial banks. In addition, conversion to a universal bank can enable an MFI to optimize the scale of its operations and thus capture economies of scale that in the long run are absolutely necessary to ensure that reasonably priced loans can be offered to microenterprises.

### Lesson 4

*Last but not least, the prominent participation of specialized investors improves the conditions for investment by purely private investors.*

Although experience to date in Eastern Europe and Latin America has shown that purely private investors are not generally interested in entering the microfinance market on their own initiative, they can be motivated if given the right incentive and opportunity to invest in an existing institution whose ownership structure is characterized by a specialized public-private partnership. One indication of the potential willingness on the part of the private sector to acquire equity participation in MFIs is the fact that the German bank Commerzbank AG has recently joined the group of investors that regularly collaborates with IMI AG.

To conclude, although considerable obstacles remain for the entry of purely private investors in MFIs, the prominent participation of specialized investors as described in this chapter is paving the way for their possible participation in the future. Private investors will be more willing to consider taking a stake in MFIs that have been established with strong IFI and specialized investor participation and that from the very beginning have targeted a broader market, not confining their activities exclusively to microfinance. This scenario has three key advantages from the point of view of private investors: First, the private investors do not need to cover the startup costs in full. Second, the crucially important know-how is available to the new institutions as a ready-made package. Third, precisely because the new institutions have a much broader business orientation, there are many possible synergies with private investors and private commercial banks in particular. For example, the shareholding commercial bank and its MFI can join forces to organize money transfer to and from various Eastern European countries. And in general, commercial banks have much greater affinity, in terms of both clientele and corporate culture, with microfinance banks than with narrowly defined microlending institutions.

## NOTES

1. Although this is indeed the case, it does not call into question the value of demonstration projects as such. It must be clearly understood that without demonstration projects, it is extremely likely that, due to the specific characteristics of microfinance, as described here, no market whatsoever would have developed for quite a long time.

2. The term *greenfield venture* means that, rather than founding and subsequently transforming a credit-granting NGO, a target group–oriented bank was founded from scratch. For more information, see C. P. Zeitinger, "Financial Institution Building: Only a Drop in the Ocean?" in *Banking and Monetary Policy in Eastern Europe: The First Ten Years*, ed. Adalbert Winkler (New York: Palgrave/ Macmillan, 2002; Reinhard Schmidt and C. P. Zeitinger, "Building New Development Finance Institutions Instead of Remodeling Existing Ones," *Small Business Development* No. 3 (2001).

3. See the IMI AG website: www.imi-ag.com.

4. The Micro-Global Program of the IDB is a downscaling program aimed at helping formal financial intermediaries enter the microfinance market by providing both onlending funds and technical assistance. In Paraguay, the primary incentive for the intermediaries to participate in the program was the technical assistance, that is, access to the specialized credit technology. All the leading intermediaries in the field of microfinance, with the exception of Financiera Familiar, work with technology that they implemented with the support of the project.

# 5

# Teaching Old Dogs New Tricks

## *The Commercialization of Credit Unions*

**Barry Lennon and David C. Richardson**

Credit unions operate in many different countries and environments around the world. They are community-based "financial cooperatives that are organized and operated according to basic cooperative principles: there are no external shareholders; the members are the owners of the institution, with each member having the right to one vote in the organization" (Ledgerwood 1999). They cater to a broad range of people of different social and economic strata, and they offer a wide range of financial services and products, such as savings, loans, and insurance. Most credit unions operate with the philosophy that by reaching out to diverse groups of people, they can meet most of these groups' financial needs through the principle of mutual self-help.

Generally, two types of credit unions operate in the world: open bond and closed bond. The bond, or field of membership, refers to the type of people who may join. An open-bond credit union typically operates in a community-based setting where anyone in the community may join. A closed-bond credit union is usually organized by a business employer and established exclusively for the employees of the business. In either setting, there should exist some type of affinity among the membership, even if it is only for satisfying financial needs. In the developing countries of the world the trend is toward the open-bond model, as credit unions need many members and a large volume of resources in order to be competitive and viable.

The microfinance industry often ignores the potential of credit unions as financial service intermediaries because they are seen as failed models, a legacy of subsidized production credit programs of the 1970s and 1980s, when international donors used credit unions as channels for credit to small farmers. The donor support severely weakened credit unions by creating an external dependency that was unsustainable. The potential for savings was ignored, because it was thought that the poor were unable to save, and lending policies were designed simply to transfer as much credit as possible to small farmers, while often ignoring capacity to pay and/or guarantees to ensure loan recovery.

As such, the credit unions were left with misguided operating policies and procedures, a belief that borrowers were more important than savers, and a dependence on external capital. When loan-delinquency rates increased and donor interest shifted, credit unions that relied on donor resources to finance lending were left illiquid (non-withdrawable), unprofitable, and insolvent. This image has remained frozen in the minds of many microfinance professionals, who have no apparent desire to revisit the credit union paradigm and find new ways to make these 150-year-old institutions relevant for poor people today.

The purpose of this chapter is to share a powerful new operating methodology that has revolutionized credit unions. This methodology has transformed them into commercially vibrant, highly efficient microfinance institutions that often reach more low- and middle-income clients with a broader mix of financial products and services at more favorable interest rates than many of the leading microfinance NGOs around the world. Even though these reformed credit unions are still a small minority in emerging nations, there are enough concrete examples in different cultural and economic settings to suggest they are worth a second look. Many of the new ideas and principles are relevant not only for credit unions but for NGOs as well, as they begin to operate on more market-based, commercial principles.

## CREDIT UNION COMMERCIALIZATION: WHAT IS IT?

In the late 1980s the World Council of Credit Unions (WOCCU) embarked on a new strategy to renovate and strengthen credit unions using a commercially oriented operating methodology.[1] WOCCU had come to realize that donor-funded lines of credit were not a panacea for poverty alleviation, and that donor funding did not provide a good framework around which to build sustainable institutions. Through trial and error, a new methodology emerged, with ten linked components:

1. Accounting and reporting transparency
2. Financial discipline and prudential standards
3. Operating efficiency
4. Financial restructuring
5. Physical-image enhancement
6. Savings mobilization
7. Product diversification
8. Aggressive market penetration and expansion of new market niches
9. PEARLS monitoring system[2]
10. Stakeholder equilibrium

When these ten components are part of an integrated development plan, they provide a sure way for any credit union to transform itself into a commercially viable microfinance institution. The term *commercialized credit union* applies to credit unions that have adopted this ten-point methodology.

Although there may be a sequential logic to the ten components, in practice, many need to be carried out simultaneously. The first five components are needed to "put the house in order," so that members/clients will have trust and confidence in the credit union. These components are manifested through quality services, professional image, and appropriate disclosure. The sixth component, savings mobilization, is mainly a function of attractive interest rates and trust. Excess liquidity is an interesting byproduct of successful savings mobilization, and product diversification, the seventh component, becomes an interesting and effective strategy to address the abundance of liquid resources. The eighth component, aggressive marketing and the expansion of new market niches, becomes possible with a broad and diverse selection of competitively priced products and services appropriate for different segments of the population. The PEARLS monitoring system, the ninth component, is a financial-performance monitoring tool to link financial discipline with expanded growth and outreach, as well as to the enforcement of prudential standards of safety and soundness. Finally, stakeholder equilibrium, the last component, cannot occur unless there is an effective and timely performance monitoring system, such as PEARLS, that ensures that the interests of each stakeholder are fully optimized without causing undue harm to the other stakeholders.

### Accounting and Reporting Transparency

Transparency is paramount to gaining credibility in the communities where credit unions operate. Transparency is achieved by replacing arcane accounting and reporting systems with clear, easy-to-understand accounts and reports that stimulate greater member confidence. Key financial information and ratios are made available through different media, the most common being the annual report and the annual general meeting. The final phase of transparency, which is already gaining momentum in Latin America, occurs when a professionally competent third party (such as the country's Superintendency of Banks or a rating agency) can verify and attest to the accuracy of the information.

### Financial Discipline and Prudential Standards

In order to provide a safe and sound place for members to deposit their savings, WOCCU has promoted eight core financial disciplines, accompanied by their corresponding prudential standards, defined below.

- Delinquency should be less than 10 percent of total loan portfolio over thirty days delinquent.
- Loan-loss provisions: 35 percent of all delinquent loans one to twelve months; 100 percent of all delinquent loans greater than 12 months.
- Loan charge-offs: 100 percent of all delinquent loans greater than twelve months.
- Institutional capital reserves should be greater than or equal to 10 percent of total assets.
- Liquidity reserves should be 15 percent to 20 percent of savings deposits.
- Nonearning-assets should be less than 10 percent of total assets.
- Operating-expense should be less than 10 percent of average total assets.
- Return-on-assets should be greater than 1 percent of average total assets.

### Operating Efficiency

As the commercialization process has created greater competition, the concept of operating efficiency has taken on greater significance. Competition has forced financial institutions, including credit unions, to look for ways to improve client satisfaction, including improvements to lending methodologies, product mix, and the cost of services, in order to retain their best clients.

Commercialized credit unions have proven to be some of the most efficient microfinance institutions now operating, as evident in Table 5.1.

**Table 5.1: Operating Efficiency of Commercialized Guatemalan and Ecuadorian Credit Unions**

| Ratio | Formula[1] | Eleven Credit Unions in Guatemala and Ecuador | Peer Group Latin America | All Latin America |
|---|---|---|---|---|
| Operating expense | Interest, loan-loss provision, and administrative expenses / average total assets | 25.6 | 40.2 | 36.7 |
| Administrative expense | Total admininistrative expense / average loan portfolio | 13.8 | 30.5 | 28.6 |
| Salary expense | Salary expense / average loan portfolio | 6.9 | 17.1 | 16.7 |

*Microbanking Bulletin* (February 2000).

[1] Formulas are those used and promoted by CGAP.

These numbers indicate that commercialized credit unions have been able to operate at about half the cost of other MFIs in Latin America. The same trends apply in Romania and the Philippines. Credit unions have historically used lower-cost, individual-based lending methodologies, an approach that most leading NGOs are now adopting in their search for greater efficiency and client satisfaction. Other important credit union strategies to maintain operating efficiency include the following:

- *Employee remuneration.* Credit union salaries are lower than NGO salaries because many of the credit unions are located in rural areas where salaries in general are lower.

- *Delinquency control.* Credit unions have found that as long as they can maintain their delinquency rate below 10 percent, they can still be profitable and ensure a safe and sound institution. Credit unions have found that the loan monitoring and collection expenses required to reach very low delinquency levels far exceed the cost of provisioning for delinquent loans.
- *Spreading fixed costs across larger volumes.* Because commercialized credit unions also offer large loans and seek large deposits from their members, they can offset the higher cost of making smaller loans to the poor by spreading out fixed costs.

### Financial Restructuring

The commercialization of credit unions implies significant structural changes to their financial statements. On the balance sheet, savings deposits are used to replace external bank credit, institutional capital replaces member shares, and liquidity reserves are set aside to meet normal withdrawal requests.[3] On the income statement, interest rates on loans are set to cover all related costs, while the interest rates on savings and shares are set to provide member-owners with a real return on their capital.

Of these structural financial changes, one of the most significant is the reduction of member shares. Historically, a person who wanted to borrow money from a credit union would purchase one share in order to become a member, and then, depending on the loan amount sought, would purchase additional shares. Shares were used to determine maximum loan amounts, with a 2:1 or 3:1 multiple usually being applied (for example, if a member wanted to borrow US$300, it was necessary to purchase US$100 worth of shares); donor funding was available to cover the US$200 gap between the loan amount and the amount of shares purchased. To the credit unions, shares were a form of risk capital to be used as collateral against loan defaults, and over time, shares grew to significant proportions. However, credit union members came to view their share investments with increasing disfavor because they were generally illiquid and rarely paid a real rate of return above inflation.

With the emphasis on savings mobilization in the late 1980s and 1990s, there was a push to sever the loan-to-share linkages of the past and replace member shares with institutional capital, a more permanent source of risk capital. This change in strategy allowed members to borrow money without having to purchase shares, but it created a new challenge—how to generate sufficient institutional capital to replace the shares that were eliminated. This challenge was overcome by pricing loans to cover costs and paying attractive rates on deposits.

For example, before WOCCU initiated a Credit Union Commercialization Project in Romania in 1996 with a small pilot group of twenty-four credit unions, the moribund Romanian credit unions relied on share capital as their main source of financing. They had very little institutional capital, and they paid their members minimal or no dividends on shares. In a country where the annual inflation rate was around 50 percent, shares lost their value, and net savers avoided the credit unions. The minimal cost of shares as a source of capital permitted a below-market loan interest rate of only 21 percent, but it also discouraged savings deposit mobilization because the credit unions couldn't afford to pay attractive yields to depositors. With the commercialization process, radical changes started to take place on the balance sheets of the credit unions, as shown in Table 5.2. If the trend continues, savings deposits will quickly overtake shares as the main source of financing for the credit unions.

**Table 5.2: Balance Sheet Accounts of Twenty-four Romanian Credit Unions, 1996 and 2000 (US Dollars)**

| Account | 12/31/96 | % | 12/31/00 | % | Change | Growth |
|---|---|---|---|---|---|---|
| Savings deposits | $0 | 0.0 | $3,591,676 | 30.5 | $3,591,676 | n/a |
| Member shares | $1,094,711 | 96.0 | $6,793,623 | 57.6 | $5,698,912 | 520.59 |
| Institutional capital | $41,216 | 3.6 | $1,229,169 | 10.4 | $1,187,953 | 2,882.26 |
| Total assets | $1,140,193 | 100.0 | $11,794,998 | 100.0 | $10,654,805 | 934.47 |

In order to pay attractive savings rates and build institutional capital through earnings, the credit unions also had to raise the subsidized interest rates on loans from 21 percent to a blended yield of more than 44 percent. The increased interest rates on loans have also increased the gross financial margin from 10.2 percent in 1996 to 18.75 percent in 2000.[4] As a result, net operating income dramatically increased from US$200,000 in 1996 to US$584,000 in 2000. Most of these earnings have been capitalized and explain the large surge in institutional capital from 1996 to 2000.

The Romanian credit unions are still a long way from becoming totally commercialized, but so far the response by members has been very
positive. With the new attractive rates on savings deposits, the total membership of the twenty-four Romanian credit unions has grown 49 percent, from 73,000 in 1996 to 109,000 in 2000.

### Physical-Image Enhancement

Credit unions that once depended on donor funding for the expansion
of their loan portfolios also faced major physical limitations. Because
many of these credit unions did not mobilize savings, there was no need
for spacious and comfortable facilities where members could deposit and
withdraw their savings without standing in long lines. In addition, there
was no space for strongboxes or safes, and the security systems were
totally inadequate. The successful attraction of new savers requires adequate space, safety, and a professional image. Therefore, concurrent
with the ongoing financial restructuring, significant remodeling and improvement of the physical facilities were also necessary. The attractive
public image of the physical infrastructure of an institution does much to
present an image of professionalism and soundness.

### Savings Mobilization

The success of credit union savings mobilization has shown that low-
income people will substantially increase savings deposits if provided
with convenient service, market returns, and security for their savings.
The most impressive result of savings mobilization is that it provides a
key solution to the outreach-versus-sustainability conundrum: like a gi-
ant magnet, it attracts large numbers of poor people seeking savings services, as well as depositors from different social and economic strata,
thereby attaining the liquidity and volume needed to ensure long-term
operating and financial sustainability. In other words, by serving a diverse group of people from different social and economic strata, credit
unions can help more poor people than if they only focused on the poorest of the poor.

The Guatemalan credit union movement was one of the first to dis-
cover this important principle. In 1987, the entire movement of more
than twenty credit unions had mobilized only US$2.8 million of savings
deposits and member share accounts. By offering convenient service,

market returns, and institutional security, eleven Guatemalan credit unions with a user base of 199,332 people, were servicing more than US$80 million in 345,000 accounts at year-end 2000, resulting in an average savings and share balance of just US$233.[5] Of that amount, almost 302,000 accounts had an average balance of only US$37. It is interesting to note that while the credit unions provided a very valuable service to the poorest of the poor, in terms of outreach and numbers of people served, they also provided a valuable service to other groups of poor and lower-middle-class people.[6] Even though the lower middle class accounted for only 16,064 accounts, they provided more than US$55 million, or 69 percent of the total volume of savings and share deposits. Were it not for this group of people, the Guatemalan credit unions would never have had the necessary liquidity for onlending purposes.

The Guatemalan example, as well as similar experiences in other countries such as Bolivia, demonstrates the power of savings mobilization and the outreach possible when institutions offer savings products with competitive interest rates, institutional security, and convenient services. Effective savings mobilization is one of the cornerstones of commercialization, because it requires strict adherence to market-based disciplines.

### Product Diversification

A significant benefit of savings mobilization is the remarkable surge in the volume of funds available for onlending. With liquidity to spare, a commercialized credit union can offer a broader selection of savings and loan products tailor-made to the needs of the membership. It has been shown that all human beings, whether rich or poor, have the following similar daily physical needs:

- Work
- Housing
- Health
- Education
- Transportation
- Security
- Savings

Virtually everyone experiences the same needs throughout his or her lifetime, but not everyone has the same needs at the same time. Hence, product diversification is necessary to meet the needs of a diverse membership such as one finds in credit unions.

At certain times during one's life, different needs emerge, such as small loans for school fees, unforeseen medical expenses, or working capital for a microenterprise. At other times a person may need larger loans for capital investment to expand an enterprise or for home improvement. At still another time there may be a need to save for planned investments in the future. Failure to meet these diverse needs is one reason for high dropout rates at some microfinance NGOs that do not offer diverse products. While there has been no comprehensive assessment of credit union dropout rates, few commercialized credit unions worry about it. More typical are the findings of a recent study in El Salvador showing that 81 percent of credit union members were still using credit union services after five years (Almeyda 2000).

Aside from meeting members' needs, there is an institutional benefit from product diversification—diversification of risk. As a credit union diversifies its loan portfolio, it is able to minimize the consequences of over-lending to one segment of the population. Diversification of risk is important to credit unions because any significant deterioration in the quality of a loan portfolio can wreak havoc with its public image, its ability to mobilize savings, and ultimately its financial sustainability.

### Aggressive Market Penetration and Expansion of New Market Niches

The key to aggressive market penetration is to have a variety of high-quality financial products and services available to different segments of the population. If a commercialized credit union is successful at improving its physical image while simultaneously improving the quality of its financial products and services, it will act like a magnet in attracting new members. Two of the best ways to verify the usefulness of a credit union's services are monitoring the number of new people who join to access those services and measuring the number of existing members utilizing the services.

Table 5.3 illustrates the accelerated growth that can occur when a credit union offers a broad range of products and services to meet the diverse needs of its membership. The credit unions included in the table have developed marketing strategies for a variety of products, to attract new members.

Table 5.3: Membership Growth, 1997–2000

| Country | Number of Credit Unions | 1997 | 2000 | Change | % Growth |
|---------|-------------------------|------|------|--------|----------|
| Philippines | 12 | 39,314 | 92,407 | 53,093 | 135.0 |
| Romania | 24 | 78,290 | 108,569 | 30,279 | 38.7 |
| Ecuador | 23 | 567,199 | 844,058 | 276,859 | 48.8 |
| Guatemala | 11 | 118,088 | 199,332 | 81,244 | 68.8 |
| Bolivia | 15 | 137,950 | 147,613 | 9,663 | 7.0 |
| Totals | 85 | 940,841 | 1,391,979 | 451,138 | 48.0 |

### PEARLS Monitoring System

During the late 1980s an attempt was made to use the CAMEL rating system to monitor the financial performance of credit unions in Latin America.[7] After several unsatisfactory attempts, the CAMEL was discarded because it did not measure financial structure and growth, two key areas for credit unions operating in the developing world. Subsequently, WOCCU created the new monitoring and evaluation system called PEARLS. Credit unions in most developing countries must deal with volatile macroeconomic conditions that can radically affect their financial performance. PEARLS serves as an invaluable guide to improve significantly the decision-making capacity of management through highly volatile conditions.

PEARLS includes forty-five financial ratios designed to provide a complete measurement of the financial performance of any credit union (and most NGOs). It is a quantitative monitoring system that can produce financial performance information as often as a balance sheet and income statement are produced. The process of commercialization is multidimensional; it is not only about finances, yields, and efficiency. There can also be a significant social impact. The PEARLS monitoring system has the unique ability to measure financial performance while simultaneously promoting social impact. This is possible because each of the areas measured by PEARLS has both business and social consequences. Table 5.4 illustrates this point by linking each of the areas measured and analyzed by PEARLS with the commercial and social impact it creates.

**Table 5.4: The Commercial and Social Impact of PEARLS**

| PEARLS Area | Commercial Impact | Social Impact |
|---|---|---|
| Protection | Measures the complete process of credit administration: Delinquency control Loan-loss reserves Loan charge-offs Loan recoveries | Provides members with a safe place to deposit their money. |
| Effective financials structure | Helps to optimize institutional solvency, profitability, and liquidity. | Encourages community loans to members, community savings from either rich or poor members, and capital accumulation through earnings instead of member shares. |
| Asset quality | Optimizes profitability by minimizing nonearning assets and seeking to finance those assets with funds that have no explicit interest cost. | Applies pressure on delinquent members to cancel their debts without obligating others to pay. It also restricts the acquisition of fixed assets that are not affordable. |
| Rates of return and costs | Optimizes the balance between portfolio yields, savings deposit yields, dividends on shares, operating efficiency, and the capitalization of net earnings. | Institutional profitability is limited to recovering all costs instead of maximizing profits. It provides savers and shareholders with real rates of return on their capital. Employees are paid competitive wages for their services. |
| Liquidity | Optimizes the level of liquidity needed to satisfy member withdrawal requests. Minimizes idle liquidity. | Provides members with instant liquidity whenever needed. Promotes the timely payment of all debt obligations. |
| Signs of growth | Enables balance-sheet account comparisons between structure and yield, while simultaneously trying to achieve real growth. | Promotes the affiliation of any person who follows the rules. Promotes thrift and savings among the membership. Promotes the acquisition of needed goods and services through loans to creditworthy members. |

### Stakeholder Equilibrium

In the competitive world of capitalism, the ultimate purpose of a for-profit company is to generate profits for shareholders. In recent years, the use of the word *stakeholders* has become a popular way to describe those with a "stake" in that process. In the credit union world the term is also applicable. Credit unions, as well as NGOs, must make a profit to build capital reserves, an essential element for meeting international standards for capital adequacy and solvency. Profits are also needed to develop and maintain high-quality financial products and services. However, while credit unions and NGOs must seek profitability, it is with the aim of fulfilling their social mission of helping the poor and underprivileged improve their socio-economic condition. It is from this ideology that the term *stakeholder equilibrium* becomes relevant and significant. The concept of stakeholder equilibrium means that each and every stakeholder should benefit to the fullest extent possible without causing undue harm to other stakeholders. The great challenge of any MFI is to find that delicate balance.

There are five main groups of stakeholders in a credit union:

- *Shareholders.* The member-owners who have contributed their own share capital with the expectation of receiving access to the financial products and services offered, while also expecting to receive a real dividend yield greater than inflation.
- *Depositors.* Some of the member-owners who have deposited their savings with the expectation of receiving a real return (greater than inflation) on those deposits.
- *Borrowers.* Some of the member-owners who have borrowed money for various purposes and who expect to pay as little interest as possible on their loans.
- *Employees.* Management and staff who receive financial remuneration for their time and efforts. They expect to receive a competitive salary for their services.
- *The institution.* The credit union itself, even though inanimate, is an interested party because it needs a continual source of net income to provide capital for quality goods and services, and to build sufficient capital reserves to protect the member-owners against operating losses.

How can all of these groups benefit at the same time without suffering undue harm? The answer lies in the ability of management to understand current market conditions and then align the institutional policies of the credit union appropriately, so that everyone receives a fair share. This means that borrowers pay a market rate of interest on their loans, savers receive a market rate of interest on their savings, employees receive a competitive salary for their wages, member-owners receive a competitive dividend on shares, and the credit union produces enough profit so that capital reserves meet established norms of safety and soundness while providing for the acquisition of quality goods and services.

As the interests of each stakeholder are carefully harnessed and delicately balanced with the others, a powerful synergy is created that produces impressive results. The best example of this principle is found in the case of Guatemala, where the eleven credit unions mentioned above have done an excellent job of balancing the interests of all stakeholders. In a country where the inflation rate is 5.1 percent, borrowers are paying a very attractive rate of 21.7 percent (which is the same rate commercial banks charge), and savers are receiving a real rate of return on their savings accounts (which is about 2.0 percent higher than the banks are paying). Additionally, shareholders receive a dividend of 7.5 percent (which is almost comparable to the current savings deposit interest rates in Guatemala), employees are paid very competitive salaries, and the overall operating-expense ratio of 7.1 percent is impressively low when compared with that of other MFIs.[8] Finally, the net return on assets after dividends, 2.4 percent, is an amount that was sufficient to build the institutional capital reserves to 13.3 percent of total assets at year-end 2000.

How does stakeholder equilibrium relate to commercialization? In its fullest sense, credit union commercialization means harmonizing external market conditions with internal credit union operating policies so that each stakeholder is fairly treated and the overall mission and ideology of the institution are accomplished and followed. Credit union commercialization is about not only adopting more market-based principles but also integrating those principles with the social mission.

## MFI COMMERCIALIZATION AND SOCIAL MISSION: ARE THEY COMPATIBLE?

A debate is raging between two camps within the microfinance industry: the business-minded institutionalists versus the social-minded welfarists. Apparently neither group believes that its objectives are totally compatible with those of the other. The biggest complaint from the welfarists is that in order to achieve institutional sustainability, you must suffer "mission drift," or abandonment of the very target niche of poor people you want to reach. The institutionalists, meanwhile, complain that by dealing only with the poorest segments of society, institutions never can be fully sustainable and must always depend on donor subsidy to survive. The credit union sector has not been exempt from this debate, as credit unions from different parts of the world have lined up on both sides of the issue. The answer to this conundrum can be found in the following paradox: "The more business-minded you are, the more social-minded you can become."

At first glance this statement appears to be contradictory, but it should become part of the operating mantra for any commercialized MFI. In order to understand how this statement is true, it is first necessary to define what is meant by the term *social minded*. Commercialized credit unions and NGOs have sought to define their social mission and how they fit into the larger context of poverty alleviation by taking a holistic approach to meeting people's daily physical or temporal needs. This holistic approach is rooted in one key point: true poverty alleviation can only occur as the poor and disenfranchised are assimilated into their local mainstream financial economies. This can only happen if a broader selection of financial products and services are offered to poor people, so that their daily needs are fully satisfied. In its fullest sense, to be social-minded means that an MFI is financially able to meet the daily needs of the poor people it serves. This daunting task requires a volume of financial resources far greater than the donor community alone can provide. Such a volume of resources can only be accessed in the commercial financial markets of the world. The degree to which an MFI is able to access adequate financial resources will determine whether or not it can fulfill its social mission.

The multiple financial products and services of a commercialized credit union are like rungs on a ladder that elevate or improve the income and wealth of the members/clients who use them. For example, the first rung of the ladder represents the most basic level of savings and loan services for the poorest segment of the membership, which has little wealth or income. As income increases and members/clients establish credit records, larger loans can be granted for both business and personal needs. Loans for such things as housing, education, and medicine are additional rungs that help elevate the membership to a higher standard of living. As wealth increases, a broader range of savings products is also needed (including term deposits, savings clubs, and retirement accounts) to fulfill expanding

Table 5.5: The Compatibility of Commercial and Social Objectives Using WOCCU Methodology

|  | Commercial Focus | Social Focus |
|---|---|---|
| **Accounting and reporting transparency** | Facilitates proper decision-making, eliminates bureaucracy, and improves operating efficiency. | Inspires member/client confidence and trust, and empowers people to make better-informed decisions. |
| **Financial discipline and prudential standards** | Promotes institutional transparency and facilitates the correct measurement of financial performance. | Creates a "level playing field" where members (investors, creditors, and clients alike) can conduct business among themselves without being unduly harmed because of unsafe or unscrupulous practices. |
| **Operating efficiency** | The cornerstone of competition. The more efficient an MFI is, the greater likelihood that it will be able to remain profitable and continue to be a permanent, long-term provider of financial services, notwithstanding the competition. | Translates into more favorable interest rates on loans and savings deposits, and directly benefits members and clients by helping them accumulate wealth more rapidly. |
| **Financial restructuring** | By optimizing distribution of the key balance-sheet accounts, a credit union can maximize profitability, solvency, and liquidity. For example, the single most profitable asset is the loan portfolio. Profitability can be maximized by investing up to 80 percent of total assets in loans. | By investing more money in the loan portfolio in local areas, the credit union can help more people than if it were to invest the money in short-term bank deposits. Profitability helps protect individual savers by increasing capital reserves. |

Table 5.5—*Continued*

| Physical-image enhancement | Stimulates the growth of total assets and hence improves operating efficiencies because of the larger volume of resources. | Provides members with more quality services, shorter lines, improved security, and greater privacy to conduct business. |
|---|---|---|
| Savings mobilization | It is more cost-effective to capture savings deposits from the public than to borrow money from a bank. The ensuing reduction in financial costs can improve profitability and facilitate more favorable lending rates. | Encourages thrift and saving among members, stimulates capital formation, and provides a safe place for poor people to deposit their precious resources. |
| Product diversification | Allows for greater risk diversification and flexibility in generating alternative sources of income. | Provides members with specific products to meet diverse financial needs. |
| Aggressive market penetration | Provides for greater volume and allows for lower transaction costs by allocating a higher percentage of fixed costs to areas where greater margins can be earned. | Attracts a broader cross-section of society and satisfies a more diverse set of financial needs through the principle of mutual self-help. |
| PEARLS monitoring system | Accurately measures and quantifies all key areas of credit union financial performance and pinpoints areas of weakness and risk. | Promotes social impact in each of the six areas it measures. |
| Stakeholder equilibrium | Facilitates the recovery of all institutional costs, both explicit and implicit, in the delivery of quality financial services. | Eliminates unfair and onerous internal subsidies by maximizing benefits to each stakeholder without causing undue harm to the other parties. |

financial needs. These types of products provide additional rungs on the ladder to elevate microentrepreneurs, as well as other poor members/ clients, out of poverty and toward complete assimilation into the mainstream financial economies of the world.

## A COMMERCIAL AND A SOCIAL MISSION: CAN THEY BE MERGED INTO ONE?

The debates between the institutionalists and the welfarists have failed to recognize a third, more powerful alternative. In reality, there is a high degree of compatibility between commercial and social objectives, as outlined in Table 5.5. It is important to emphasize that the ten-point methodology promoted by WOCCU may be replicated by any commercialized MFI; it is not unique to credit unions.

In summary, the process of commercialization brings numerous financial and social advantages if external market conditions and macroeconomic variables are harmonized with the internal institutional operating policies and ideologies. By harmonizing these variables and harnessing their advantages, commercialized credit unions and NGOs can provide significant competitive advantages to the people they serve.

### Commercialized Credit Unions and NGOs: Is There a Convergence of Operating Methodologies?

The recent interest in the commercialization of microfinance offers a unique opportunity to compare the early operating methodologies of the NGO industry with those of credit unions and to comment on the degree to which their differences are becoming less apparent as both seek to become more commercial.

For many years, credit unions viewed NGO best-practices methodologies and techniques with skepticism, because they seemed rigid and expensive to use. The cost of an average NGO loan was usually much higher than that of an average credit union loan, and the "special" way of reaching low-income microentrepreneurs did not seem to reach that many more low-income people.

On the other side of the argument, the NGO industry criticized credit unions for being stodgy, conservative, and unimaginative institutions. Credit unions did not target low-income entrepreneurs with specific loan products, and they appeared to be more interested in the middle class, who usually borrowed for consumption or housing. Credit unions, the

Table 5.6: NGO versus Credit Union Methodologies

| Early NGO Methodologies | Early Credit Union Methodologies | Commercialized Microfinance Credit Unions and NGOs |
|---|---|---|
| Solidarity-group guarantees serving as a collateral substitute. | Individual unsecured loans or two or three co-signers providing a fiduciary guarantee. | Individual lending with loans secured by cash flow, co-signers, and real collateral (for large loans). Continued group lending for very-low-income microentrepreneurs until credit records have been established. |
| Rigid loan cycles and "stepped" loan amounts with graduation to larger loans and longer terms after clients proved their creditworthiness. | "Cookie cutter" loan analysis and credit rationing (share/loan ratio) that ignored adequate loan sizes and capacity to repay. | No credit rationing or predetermined loan amounts or terms. All lending conditions tied exclusively to the client's repayment capacity. Multiple loan products offered, for commercial use, housing, transportation, health, education, and consumption, tied to client needs, repayment capacity, and individual or collateral guarantees. |
| Credit-only emphasis with financing provided by donors. | Credit-only emphasis with financing provided by member shares and donors. | Balanced emphasis on both savings deposit mobilization and credit, with financing provided by deposit savers, commercial bank credit, and capital investors. |
| Targeted clientele: low-income entrepreneurs (particularly women). | Small cliques, director-controlled favoritism, and preferential treatment. | Open membership with no special targeted groups or clientele quotas. No favoritism. |
| Disregard for market-driven operating efficiency. High-cost service delivery mechanisms. | High staff turnover because of low salaries and poor facilities. | Emphasis on market-driven operating efficiency and competitive pricing by simultaneously catering to different market niches. Renewed emphasis on increasing asset volume as means to lower operating-cost ratios and, hence lower lending rates. |
| Donor-subsidized lending methodologies | Cheap credit through member-subsidized lending rates. | Total operational and financial sustainability without external or internal subsidies. |

argument went, simply did not have the interests of the poor at heart, because they did not attempt to reach down to the poorer segments of society. The truth of the matter is that both sides were wrong.

Table 5.6 summarizes the early lending methodologies of NGOs and credit unions and shows how both sides now are gravitating toward a third, more commercialized approach. Both types of institutions have begun to provide a mix of loan products, including individual and group loans, as well as financing for activities beyond the original and exclusive emphasis on microenterprise lending, including agriculture, housing, and consumption. NGOs and credit unions have begun to focus more on savings mobilization as an effective way to lower financial costs while also improving client satisfaction. Finally, as asset volumes have increased and greater operating efficiencies have been attained, both groups have demonstrated the capacity to compete with commercial banks and others that have started to enter into this expanding market niche.

Today, a unique opportunity exists for credit unions and microfinance organizations to learn from each other. For example, credit unions could learn much about how to use group lending to reach the extreme poor in their communities. Equally important, NGOs could learn much from credit unions about deposit mobilization, loan product diversification, and techniques for improving operating efficiency and customer satisfaction.

The combined populations of low-income clients now being served by credit unions and microfinance organizations represent an extremely small percentage of the vast numbers of people who can only dream about access to fairly priced and much-needed financial services. The authors of this chapter are hopeful that both sides will now collaborate more closely so that by learning from each other, both types of organizations can march forward with renewed vigor to reach as many of these marginalized people as possible.

## NOTES

1. WOCCU is the largest of several international credit union apex organizations whose purpose is to provide advocacy, technology, and development services to its members. At year-end 2000, WOCCU represented more than 108 million members from thirty-six credit unions throughout ninety-one countries of the world, with total assets exceeding US$536 billion.

2. PEARLS stands for **P**rotection, **E**ffective financial structure, **A**sset quality, **R**ates of return and costs, **L**iquidity, and **S**igns of growth). The PEARLS Monitoring System Monograph may be downloaded free of charge from WOCCU website: www.woccu.org.

3. Institutional capital is defined as all permanent capital reserves, such as legal reserves, undivided surplus, and retained earnings. Institutional capital is a permanent, non-withdrawable source of capital that can be used to cover all types of operating risks and losses.

4. The gross financial margin is the difference between what is charged on loans and what is paid on savings and shares, before deducting operating expenses.

5. Data from only eleven credit unions are used because these institutions have computerized databases to sort their loan portfolios by different loan ranges, providing the corresponding number of accounts and volume of assets in each range. Total accounts include member, nonmember, youth, and infant accounts.

6. The poorest of the poor are defined as those with savings account balances below US$300. Lower-middle-class members are defined as those with savings accounts above US$1,000.

7. There are many different CAMEL systems in circulation around the world with varying key formulas and ratios. (CAMEL stands for **C**apital adequacy, **A**sset quality, **M**anagement, **E**arnings, and **L**iquidity.) It is noteworthy, however, that most CAMEL systems do not address the same areas as PEARLS. The CAMEL system used by WOCCU in 1988 came from the National Credit Union Administration in Washington, D.C.

8. Even though the dividend rate is greater than the inflation rate, it should be greater than the savings rate to reflect the greater risk associated with ownership capital. This is the one area that could still be improved upon in the equilibrium matrix. The operating-expense ratio used here is defined as total administrative expenses, less loan-loss provisions, divided by the total average assets. This differs from the formula promoted by CGAP.

## Part III

# Commercial Entrants
# into Microfinance

# 6

# Commercialization and Crisis in Bolivian Microfinance

**Elisabeth Rhyne**

In international development circles, Bolivia has been viewed as a model for commercial microfinance. Bolivia is known for its successful microfinance institutions (MFIs), which have transformed from their original status as NGOs into regulated commercial institutions, including BancoSol, the first and perhaps best-known transformed microlender. These MFIs constituted a thriving microfinance industry operating largely on commercial principles through the mid 1990s. Bolivia's experience of commercial microfinance took on a new dimension toward the end of the 1990s, caused by the growth of the transformed MFIs to a level that saturated the market for prime urban microfinance clients and by the entry (and subsequent retreat) of consumer lending. A third trend, commercial organizations taking up microenterprise lending, also affected Bolivia, but in a much smaller way. These events took place at the same time that Bolivia's economy, like other economies in South America, suffered a major shock and recession, felt especially hard by microentrepreneurs. These events led to a crisis in microfinance starting in late 1999 and still ongoing throughout 2001, in which borrowers became over-indebted and institutions suffered dangerously high delinquency and falling profits.

This chapter is adapted from Elisabeth Rhyne, *Mainstreaming Microfinance: How Lending to the Poor Began, Grew, and Came of Age in Bolivia* (West Hartford, Conn.: Kumarian Press, 2001), chap. 6.

This chapter discusses the state of the industry before the crisis, the changes that shook the industry, and the responses of microfinance institutions and regulators. It illustrates several issues at the core of microfinance commercialization: the dynamics of overlending, pressure on traditional microfinance methodologies, the interconnections of consumer lending and microfinance, and the impact of commercialization on clients. Such changes have thrust microfinance decisively into a new era.

After a brief scene-setting discussion, we will look at three sets of commercial players in Bolivian microfinance: the traditional microlenders who had transformed into these commercial institutions, a number of new purely commercial entrants, and the consumer lenders.

In 2000, approximately 400,000 microenterprise loans were outstanding in Bolivia. Total coverage of microcredit included a large share of the estimated national market of 600,000 to 1 million microenterprises, although there is no way to know how many separate clients this number represents, as borrowers often take loans from several institutions at once. The total active loan portfolio associated with these microenterprise loans was US$379 million at the end of 2000, representing just over 10 percent of the overall loan portfolio of the financial sector. In terms of numbers of clients, microcredit exceeds the rest of the financial sector. The majority of microloans are provided by formal financial institutions without significant external subsidies (cooperatives, BancoSol, and private finance funds), and the remainder (NGOs) have reduced their subsidy dependence drastically over the past five years.

## PRECONDITIONS:
## A MODERNIZING BOLIVIAN FINANCIAL SYSTEM

Bolivia's financial sector reforms in the late 1980s and early 1990s, together with inflation control, set favorable conditions for the creation of advanced MFIs as well as for commercial entry into the low end of the banking market. As in many developing countries, most Bolivian banks were traditionally controlled by a single individual, business group, or family. Most were inefficient and slow to innovate, until financial sector reforms turned the oligopoly upside down.

The reforms aimed to restore the confidence shattered during Bolivia's 1984–85 hyperinflation, which left the entire Bolivian banking sector with only US$60 million in loans outstanding.[1] Successive governments gradually rebuilt trust by liquidating the hopelessly ineffective state banks, which lost money, were corrupt, and lent exclusively to elites. They modernized the legal framework for the banking system and gave the Superintendency of Banks significant independence from political control. New legislation also prohibited insider lending, endemic in Bolivian banking. With these tools, authorities began weeding out weak, undercapitalized banks, restructuring or closing fifteen of the thirty-five banks. Finally, the government began allowing foreign banks to enter, alone or with local partners. Bolivia needed foreign banks to supply the equity capital local banks lacked. Moreover, banks with foreign partners could invest in modernization and innovation, guided by their partners' knowledge of the latest technologies.

These reforms brought depositors back into the financial system. From a few million dollars in 1985, the total amount of loans outstanding reached US$4.9 billion at the end of 1999, before falling back to US$4.2 billion in the recession of 2000.[2] Interest rates and spreads also fell throughout the reform period, suggesting improvements in efficiency and more competitive pricing.

The entry of foreign banks increased competition. The foreign-owned banks began luring prime corporate customers, using their access to cheaper funds to offer lower interest rates. Local banks started searching for niches down-market. Yet at this level, too, foreign banks are a formidable force, with advanced techniques for retail banking, particularly consumer lending.

Critics of financial sector reform often charge that without directives, banks will ignore the poor. Reform advocates answer that market forces will press financial institutions down-market. Bolivia's experience proves both views partly right. Competitive pressure in Bolivia has indeed driven banks down-market. However, Bolivia's experience also shows that banks need to see and understand how profits may be made in these markets. In Bolivia's case, although two models were available for reaching down, the formal banks felt much more comfortable with consumer lending than with microenterprise credit.

## THE PLAYERS IN BOLIVIA'S COMMERCIAL MICROFINANCE INDUSTRY

### The Transformed Microfinance Institutions

In Bolivian microfinance, private, formal financial institutions provide the majority of services. The dominance of formal financial institutions is a relatively recent development, however, as microfinance in Bolivia originated with donor support to NGOs that later transformed into formal financial institutions. These transformed institutions demonstrated to Bolivia—and to the international microfinance movement—that microfinance could operate commercially. The process of transformation has been one of the major contributions of Bolivian microfinance to international experience.[3]

## BancoSol

The first transformed institution, Banco Solidario (BancoSol), is now a licensed commercial bank.[4] On the strength of its core product, solidarity-group lending, BancoSol generated performance indicators that placed it at the top of the Bolivian banking industry during the mid 1990s. The Superintendency of Banks publishes data rankings annually on the banking system's performance. In 1999, as in each of the previous three years, the newspaper headlines stated that "BancoSol was the best local financial entity."[5]

Throughout the 1990s BancoSol consistently topped the list for return on assets (5.2 percent in 1998), asset quality (0 percent arrears), and capital adequacy (16.3 percent).[6] These are unusual and outstanding figures for a bank in any country. Although BancoSol was never the leader in return to shareholders' equity, not being as highly leveraged as other banks, its 29 percent return on equity in 1998 placed it among the top-performing banks. Only in administrative efficiency did BancoSol score below the norm, reflecting the high administrative cost inherent in microfinance relative to corporate banking. These indicators brought BancoSol to the attention of the financial mainstream in Bolivia and gave it international prominence.

BancoSol has been hard hit by the recent crisis in microfinance, as we will discuss below. Nevertheless, it retains a leading market position.

## Fondos Financieros Privados (FFPs)

The next tier of microfinance providers is the private financial funds (FFPs). FFPs are formal financial institutions licensed to engage in a wide range of lending and some savings activities. Their minimum capital requirements are lower than those for commercial banks, and they are not allowed to provide certain services banks provide. The government created this category in 1994 especially to accommodate the emerging microfinance industry. Much of the work to create the regulations for FFPs revolved around ProCrédito, an NGO that spawned the first FFP, Caja Los Andes. Several other microfinance NGOs have since become FFPs.

Each of these institutions has a unique personality. Caja Los Andes is a no-nonsense, focused financial institution, whose strong individual loan methodology makes it a formidable competitor. FIE, another La Paz-based individual lender, has a somewhat softer image and aims to support the broader development of the enterprises it serves. Prodem, the original NGO from which BancoSol was born, became an FFP in 2000. After it spawned BancoSol, Prodem turned to the still unserved rural population, developing the best nationwide outreach in rural areas, which gives it a strong market position as other institutions begin pushing out from the major cities.

None of the FFPs is primarily savings based, although most are licensed to offer savings accounts and time deposits. In general, this bias reflects their histories as NGOs not authorized to take savings and as consumer lenders. It also reflects prevailing attitudes that poor Bolivians don't save and/or that capturing deposits from them is too costly.

## NGOs

Bolivia's microfinance sector also includes strong NGOs that do not intend to become regulated institutions. The NGOs tend to have a more poverty-oriented and rural focus than their commercial counterparts. At the height of the growth phase of FFPs, it looked as though NGOs were becoming less relevant in Bolivian microfinance, particularly from the point of view of portfolio size, where they make up only 17 percent of the total microloan portfolio. However, several NGOs are growing rapidly, and together they account for 38 percent of active microfinance clients. Although they will likely remain NGOs, these organizations are deeply affected by the commercialization around them, in areas ranging from financial performance standards to competition for clients. This chapter does not examine all the NGOs but provides some examples from one urban village-banking NGO, Pro Mujer, to give some flavor of the experience of NGOs during the crisis.

## Commercial Entry into Microfinance

Several private sector institutions observed the microfinance lenders and decided they could compete profitably in the same marketplace.

Though relatively small, this kind of entry is potentially important because it represents movement into microfinance independent of donor
subsidies. We will look briefly at three entrants: a specialized lender,
FASSIL FFP; a bank with an interest in going down-market, Banco
Económico; and the credit cooperatives.

Alfredo Otero, the founder and former chief executive of FASSIL,
observed that Bolivian banks provided poor quality services to their retail customers and thought he could do better. He assembled eight local
investors, who met the initial US$1 million capital requirement for an
FFP, and opened FASSIL in 1996. FASSIL's strategy was to start with
consumer lending to build volume and profits quickly while its microcredit
portfolio grew to a profitable level. Gradually, it planned to increase the
share of business devoted to microcredit.

To launch consumer credit, FASSIL's founders studied Chilean consumer lenders and contracted a team of Chilean consultants. To launch
microcredit, they recruited experienced microenterprise lenders, largely
from BancoSol. Otero's team applied the BancoSol solidarity-group
methodology with a few alterations, and added products, including a jewelry pawn loan service. When FASSIL entered microenterprise credit,
competition was increasing quickly. Yet FASSIL lacked the start-up subsidies and access to preferred sources of loan capital that the donor-backed
MFIs enjoyed. Nor did its investors have the deep pockets of an international banking partner, and thus FASSIL faced a competitive disadvantage compared to some of the transformed MFIs. (For more information
on FASSIL, see Chapter 7.)

Another commercial entrant into microfinance was Banco Económico,
a commercial bank launched by eighteen private business people in 1991
to serve small and medium enterprises in Santa Cruz. During the mid
1990s Banco Económico showed returns on equity between 18 and 35
percent, higher than any other Bolivian bank, including BancoSol. Early
on, Banco Económico included microenterprises in its target market without distinguishing greatly between microenterprises and other businesses.
It began locating branches near large, informal markets, recognizing that
many informal operators move large sums of money. In 1997 Banco
Económico opened its Presto division specifically for micro and consumer credit. Two years later the crisis in the Bolivian microfinance and
consumer-credit sectors led Banco Económico to close Presto and re-
move itself completely from the microcredit market.

A third source of commercial entry into microfinance is represented
by several Santa Cruz–based savings and credit cooperatives that launched

specific microenterprise credit products. Although the cooperatives have historic connections to donor agencies, it is now appropriate to consider them commercial entrants because they operate commercially and their funding derives from private member savings. Although cooperatives have always included microenterprises in their overall target market, they only recently started using the methodologies of the self-identified microfinance institutions. By early 1999 at least five of the cooperatives in Santa Cruz offered solidarity-group loans as a regular part of their business, using techniques taken directly from the leading MFIs, often by hiring staff from BancoSol and others.

FASSIL, Banco Económico, and the large cooperatives illustrate the limited way the private sector approached microcredit. Only FASSIL staked its future on microcredit. The others experimented with microcredit at the margins of a wider array of markets and services.

## THE RISE OF CONSUMER CREDIT

Consumer credit has had momentous impact on microfinance in Bo- livia. This lending methodology was imported into Bolivia from the de- veloped world of salaried workers and consumer durables. It arrived in Bolivia via Chile, where it had burgeoned during the past decade.

Acceso FFP, the largest consumer lender in Bolivia, was owned by Empresas Conosur, a large Chilean holding company with subsidiaries in several countries operating home improvement centers, automobile dealerships, and other businesses that appeal to the growing Latin Ameri- can middle class. Acceso reached ninety thousand loans outstanding dur- ing its first three years, a scale that BancoSol had not achieved in its twelve-year history. This build-up was part of a strategy to reach scale quickly in order to gain market share and begin earning profits after a short time.

Acceso was not alone. Nearly all the Bolivian banks also started con- sumer credit. It was estimated that in mid 1998, the Bank of Santa Cruz's Solución program had another forty thousand clients, as did Union Bank's CrediAgil program.[7] One banker estimated that the system peaked at about US$150 million in consumer loans outstanding, approaching the aggregate size of commercial microcredit.

If consumer lending had been offered strictly to prime salaried em- ployees, it would have overlapped with microlenders to some degree because many families include both salaried and independent people—

sometimes even the same individual. But there was greater overlap than that, exacerbated by Bolivia's scarcity of prime employers. To achieve desired volumes, consumer lenders moved to smaller employers and to microenterprise lending. Acceso's managing director, André La Faye, estimated that about 30 percent of Acceso's clients were microenterprises. This percentage would represent more than twenty-five thousand clients, similar to several microfinance FFPs in number of microenterprise loans. Thus, consumer lenders competed directly with microlenders. By offering a product that on its face was similar to microfinance, often to the same clients, the consumer lenders challenged microfinance at its roots (see Table 6.1).

The fundamental basis for consumer lending is the ability to tap a borrower's salary for loan repayment. When Acceso first entered Bolivia, it sought customers among the employees of large, stable employers who provided trustworthy information about a loan applicant's employment and salary and arranged repayment through payroll deduction. For customers with less-than-prime employers, Acceso relied on its own sophisticated credit scoring model. Credit scoring models distill vast experience into a powerful though mechanical predictive process, where formerly that experience would have found expression in a set of policies applied through the judgment of a veteran credit officer (see Lewis 1993).

The consumer lenders also challenged microfinance's credit-administration philosophy. Microcredit places full responsibility for client performance on loan officers, while consumer lending is often described as a credit factory. Separate staff enter data, verify data accuracy, apply a credit score, verify client identity, notarize documents, disburse, and collect. In assembly line fashion, each person performs his or her task efficiently, but responsibility for outcomes is diffused. In contrast to microcredit, consumer-credit officers have no role in the important steps of verification, evaluation, or collection. They are essentially salespeople earning their money on commissions.

Consumer lending also challenged the microfinance culture of low delinquency. The consumer lenders built expectations of late payment into their pricing. According to staff, FASSIL's projections assumed delinquency around 17 percent, with write-offs of about 7 percent. Coming from more developed countries, consumer lenders use automated collection measures, mailing form letters to delinquent clients, a dramatic contrast to the immediate personal follow-up of microlenders. Consumer lenders charge fines for late payment that increase their revenues when

**Table 6.1: Comparison of Bolivian Microcredit and Consumer Lending**

| Parameter | Microenterprise Credit | Consumer Lending |
|---|---|---|
| Loan terms | Average near US$1,000, short term, fast turnaround, competitive interest rate | Average near US$1,000, short term, fast turnaround, competitive interest rate |
| Basis for loan approval | Enterprise and household cash flow, credit history, group guarantees | Salary, credit "score" |
| Basis for repayment | Motivation for continued access to credit, peer pressure | Steady salary and ability to garnish wages, employer cooperation |
| Tolerance for delinquency | "Zero tolerance"; expected delinquency: less than 3-5% | Not worried until after thirty days late; expected delinquency: 15-20% |
| Method of follow-up | Immediate, personal visit | Letter by mail |
| Staff organization | Loan officer responsibility for client | Assembly-line loan processing |
| Basic philosophy | Trust and responsibility | Information management |

clients are a little late, making a few days or a week of delinquency actually welcome from the consumer lender's perspective. Bolivian microlenders saw such practices with alarm.

Microlenders were even more upset about some of the new entrants' aggressive marketing. Instead of adopting lending techniques designed for microenterprises, consumer lenders piggybacked on the microlenders. The technique was simple: lure the good clients away from microlenders by offering them larger loans (also faster and at lower rates). The consumer lenders thought they would be safe if they targeted clients in good standing among microlenders, a low-risk strategy to invade the microcredit market. As it turned out, the consumer lenders should have given more heed to the market knowledge of the microlenders. After what in hindsight turned out to be reckless entry, default shot up among consumer lenders and microlenders alike during 1999 and 2000, creating the crisis of over-indebtedness.

## THE CRISIS OF 1999–2000

### *Causes of the Crisis*

By 1997 there were nearly 300,000 active microfinance loans in Bolivia, with the number of consumer loans also approaching that level. Market penetration by microfinance alone was near 50 percent, a rate probably unprecedented in the microfinance world.

Clients took advantage of the offer of quick and easy credit from so many institutions, maintaining two or more loans at a time. In an increasing number of cases, clients borrowed more than they could handle. Some let repayments slip or, in worst cases, began "bicycling" loans—using the proceeds of one loan to pay off another. Such behavior seriously damaged the carefully constructed culture of repayment in microcredit.

When delinquency began to rise at BancoSol, it was concentrated among clients with loans at other institutions. According to Juan Domingo Fabbri of BancoSol's marketing department, clients did not see multiple loans as risky: "The logic of clients is that they will earn more by investing more. Multiple loans have even become a status symbol." Moreover, clients felt that maintaining access to two or more institutions reduced their risk by widening their choices, when in reality, for most borrowers, too much credit is a quick route to financial disaster. Carmen Velasco, Pro Mujer's executive director, describes searching a poor section of Cochabamba where delinquency had surged and finding delinquent Pro Mujer borrowers in the offices of several other microlenders. In fact, a recent study showed that a major share of Pro Mujer clients also had loans at BancoSol. In mid 2000, analysis showed that among the microcredit FFPs, 28 percent of clients and 34 percent of the portfolio involved clients with loans in more than one institution. The equivalent numbers were even higher for consumer lenders.

Just as the microfinance market was approaching saturation in 1999, Bolivia suffered its first serious economic setback after fifteen years of progress. The economic crisis sprang from troubles throughout South America, starting with Brazil. The ensuing recession hit microfinance clients particularly hard, reducing demand for their wares both inside Bolivia and in export markets. At the same time, authorities cracked down on the "informal" importing and exporting so important to many Bolivian microenterprises.

When over-indebtedness coincided with economic shocks, a significant problem swelled to crisis proportions. After years of relative quiet, Bolivia experienced heightened social unrest, with mass protests about basics like water and electricity prices. Microfinance, too, felt the anger of the powerless. Interactions with clients started to sour, as loan officers spent more and more time wheedling collections from customers faced with too much debt and shrunken demand. These conditions set off a backlash against microcredit.

## The Debtors' Revolt

A handful of "professional" union organizers began gathering borrowers into debtors associations to protest against the consumer and microfinance lenders, attracting recruits with promises of debt forgiveness. The leaders, who claimed to speak for several thousand borrowers, staged protests, mainly at the offices of Acceso, CrediAgil, and other consumer lenders, but even at Caja Los Andes and BancoSol. A few association members engaged in hunger strikes, a tactic with a long history in Bolivia. Through such tactics, the associations attempted to take the moral high ground by painting the lenders as exploiters of the poor. In petitions to authorities, they accused the lenders of using humiliating practices against debtors—hiring mariachi bands to perform outside a debtor's house, painting the word *debtor* on the house, or broadcasting the names of debtors over the radio. They blamed the lenders for provoking every kind of social ill from suicide to prostitution. They demanded full debt forgiveness.

The affected institutions, working through their newly created association, ASOFIN, sought aid from the courts to stop the demonstrations. But although ASOFIN hired high-priced lawyers, the tearful testimony of a few market vendors carried the day. In fact, ASOFIN had scant legal basis for stopping the associations from mounting street protests. Eventually, the debtor associations forced a dialogue with the Superintendency of Banks and ASOFIN, in which the microfinance lenders agreed to consider debt relief to association members on a case-by-case basis. Only a handful of cases were resolved, however. Shortly thereafter, the microlenders rejoiced when the debtors associations threw their own leaders in jail. Apparently one association was a pyramid scheme in which leaders illegally collected debt service payments due to the microlenders and used them to make new loans. Leaders of another more legitimate association mishandled membership dues, a less spectacular crime, but enough to bring them down.

After a few months hiatus, the associations surfaced again with new leaders. They gradually moderated their aims: while acknowledging their obligations to repay debts, they asked for extended grace periods, longer loan terms, and annual interest rates of 2 percent. Tactics escalated again, however. In the most extreme example, demonstrators wearing sticks of dynamite took over the offices of the Superintendency of Banks, holding employees hostage and threatening to blow up the building. Although the debtors associations forced their way into negotiations with government and financial institutions through such tactics, the concessions granted them have so far been minor. The major importance of the debt protestors has been to politicize microfinance, changing attitudes about credit and damaging Bolivia's once-excellent repayment culture. The microfinance industry will have to live with the debtors associations, or at least the attitudes they represent, for the foreseeable future.

### The Fall of Consumer Credit

The members of the microfinance community were not the only ones concerned about the consequences of growing delinquency among the consumer lenders. The Superintendency of Banks issued regulations in early 1999 to place consumer credit on a sounder footing.[8] The most important provision limited the client's total debt service to 25 percent of salary. Clients who already had substantial car, home, or business loans would likely not qualify for a consumer loan. The response to this move varied. FASSIL sharply curtailed consumer lending, switching almost completely into microcredit. Banco Económico exited quickly from both. Acceso, it was widely rumored, went on much as before, simply paying the penalty the regulation carried.

The regulations came too late, however. By mid 1999 the consumer-lending movement crashed. When the level of bad debt grew large enough to erode the equity of the two largest consumer lenders, Acceso FFP and CrediAgil, the Superintendency intervened directly in those institutions. At the end of 1998, Acceso had had eighty-eight thousand clients, a portfolio of US$93 million, and delinquency of 19 percent. Two years later, Acceso had only eighty-four hundred active clients and a portfolio of

US$5.4 million.[9] Much of the difference was written off. Acceso's investors lost their money and will not make any new loans.

In retrospect, it is easy to see that the consumer lenders came into Bolivia without understanding the market. The models that worked in middle class Chile were not suited to less formal Bolivia. The lenders were also seduced by the success of the microlenders to think that their superior technologies could out-compete the charity-inspired institutions. They failed to recognize that their "credit factory" techniques lacked essential elements that made lending to microentrepreneurs work. Finally, they were unlucky to have run up huge portfolios just before an economic crisis.

## Microfinance in Crisis

After consumer credit vanished as quickly as it had come, it left behind a weakened microcredit industry. Liliana Bottega of Caja Los Andes stated, "Acceso and CrediAgil have closed, but the damage has been done to the system. Who knows if it can recover?" Four indicators help tell the story: the end of growth in numbers of clients, rising portfolios as microlenders go up-market, the highest delinquency in the history of Bolivian microfinance, and a dramatic fall in profits. To the extent that the difficulties of this crisis result from the economic downturn, similar problems prevail throughout the Bolivian banking sector.

During 1999 and 2000, none of the microlenders grew as they had in the past. BancoSol lost 25 percent of its clients and Prodem lost 45 percent during those two years. Much of this reduction presumably represents elimination of clients with loans from multiple institutions. Caja Los Andes continued adding clients, increasing active clients by 31 percent during the two-year period. To achieve this growth, however, Los Andes had to work much harder than previously, because a larger share of old clients left and a larger share of new applicants failed to qualify. The new FFP, Eco Futuro, also added clients, but most of its growth may result from transfers of existing clients from its founding NGOs.

Slower growth and higher delinquency showed up immediately on the bottom lines of all the microlenders. BancoSol's return on equity dropped from 29 percent in 1998 to 4 percent in 2000. FASSIL's profits dropped from 12 percent in 1998 into the negative range in 2000. Caja Los Andes, the least affected by the crisis, managed to keep its return on equity at a respectable 14 percent, making it the third most profitable financial institution (including banks) in Bolivia in 2000.

## Delinquency and Responses

Every microfinance lender experienced unprecedented delinquency in 1999 and 2000 as the lenders, in part to keep up with their consumer competitors, had also rushed to lend more money to the same clients. At the end of 1997, the regulated microlenders had only 2.4 percent of their portfolio overdue. This rate rose steadily, reaching 11.2 percent in 1999 and 12.6 percent in 2000, not including rescheduled loans.

Microlender responses to increased delinquency have included both internal strategies and cooperation with government. A first line of defense was the Superintendency's Central de Riesgo (credit bureau). Bolivia had a reasonably good system, designed for formal banks and reliant on Bolivia's national system of identification cards. Through the credit bureau, staff at banks, FFPs, and now microfinance NGOs can obtain an online report on the outstanding indebtedness of any prospective applicant. This information should reveal whether a client is over-indebted, but the information on the system was not complete or recent enough to prevent overlending (see Chapter 13).

Microlenders, spurred by tougher regulations from the Superintendency of Banks, increased emphasis on individual repayment capacity relative to past group performance. They also increased focus on tangible collateral, assisted by a new law to establish a registry of moveable goods that will allow clients to mortgage their equipment, an improvement over the current general purpose *prendaria* lien. The authorities also stepped up requirements for formal loan documentation, such as sales receipts. As such requirements creep higher, the difference between microfinance and conventional banking diminishes.

As a last resort, microlenders began to reschedule loans. Until 1999, the microfinance lenders rarely rescheduled or refinanced loans, considering such practices highly risky. But in the midst of the economic crisis, they saw few alternatives. The Superintendency granted a temporary amnesty on rescheduling. Normally, rescheduled loans carried a 20 percent provisioning requirement. Under the amnesty, however, a rescheduled loan returned to the low-risk category, as if it were never late. BancoSol reported rescheduling US$6 million and Caja Los Andes US$1 million during 1999. Further rescheduling was introduced in the government's economic revitalization program in early 2000. Although rescheduling is in some cases a realistic approach to clients with real debt-service problems, its widespread use can have a long-term negative effect on repayment discipline. And regulations allowing rescheduled

**Table 6.2: Indicators of Financial Performance for Leading Bolivian MFIs December 1997–December 2000**

|  | 1997 | 1998 | 1999 | 2000 |
|---|---|---|---|---|
| **BancoSol** |  |  |  |  |
| Loans outstanding (Number) | 76,216 | 81,555 | 73,073 | 60,976 |
| Loans outstanding (US$ million) | 63.1 | 74.1 | 82.3 | 77.8 |
| Portfolio at risk (>1 day, percent) | 2.1 | 2.5 | 7.0 | 12.3 |
| Return on equity (percent) | 24 | 29 | 9 | 4 |
| Average loan size (US$, rounded) | 830 | 910 | 1,130 | 1,280 |
| **Caja los Andes** |  |  |  |  |
| Loans outstanding (Number) | 27,876 | 32,482 | 36,815 | 42,643 |
| Loans outstanding (US$ million) | 20.4 | 28.6 | 35.9 | 46.8 |
| Portfolio at risk (percent) | n/a | 5.7 | 6.5 | 7.7 |
| Return on equity (percent) | 36 | 27 | 14 | 14 |
| Average loan size (US$) | 730 | 880 | 980 | 1,120 |
| **Prodem** |  |  |  |  |
| Loans outstanding (Number) | 38,248 | 47,130 | 39,909 | 26,096 |
| Loans outstanding (US$ million) | 18.2 | 24.2 | 21.8 | 23.6 |
| Portfolio at risk (percent) | 0.7 | 5.6 | 7.0 | 4.8 |
| Return on equity (percent) | 25 | 22 | 3 | 1 |
| Average loan size (US$) | 480 | 510 | 550 | 900 |
| **FIE** |  |  |  |  |
| Loans outstanding (Number) | 22,086 | 20,848 | 24,111 | 23,402 |
| Loans outstanding (US$ million) | 12.1 | 14.1 | 18.5 | 22.5 |
| Portfolio at risk (percent) | n/a | 1.5 | 6.2 | 7.9 |
| Return on equity (percent) | n/a | 32 | 8 | 10 |
| Average loan size (US$) | 550 | 680 | 770 | 960 |
| **FASSIL** (includes consumer loans) |  |  |  |  |
| Loans outstanding (Number) | 19,257 | 35,000 | 27,461 | 23,493 |
| Loans outstanding (US$ million) | 15.0 | 21.7 | 18.2 | 15.4 |
| Portfolio at risk (percent) | n/a | 12.4 | 13.8 | 17.2 |
| Return on equity (percent) | 11 | 12 | 1 | -10 |
| Average loan size (US$) | 780 | 620 | 660 | 660 |

ASOFIN, CIPAME, and FINRURAL, *Boletín Financiero: Microfinanzas* (various issues); Superintendencia de Banco y Entidades Financieras, *Boletín Informativo* 12/149 (December 2000).

loans to be treated as on time give an overly rosy picture of solvency in official statistics.

## COMPETITION'S ROLE IN BOLIVIAN MICROFINANCE

We now reflect broadly on Bolivian microfinance commercialization and its crisis by looking at four critical dimensions: the impact of lending competition on methodology, the dynamics of overlending, outreach to the poor, and the relationship between microfinance and consumer lending.

### Competition's Impact on Methodology and Service Quality

Up to this point this chapter has focused on how difficult increased competition and commercialization have been for microfinance *institutions*. However, for most microfinance *clients*, this same story is extremely positive (as long as they avoid over-indebtedness). Commercialization and competition have brought lower prices, quicker and easier service, and a variety of new products to customers. They have allowed access to credit to become virtually universal for Bolivia's urban micro-entrepreneurs, and increasingly for those in secondary cities and market towns. In this way competition is the culmination of the microfinance quest. This major victory should not be forgotten as the microfinance field struggles with the challenges commercialization poses.

Increased competition in microfinance alters the balance of power between lender and borrower. As a FASSIL loan officer stated, "Before, the institution selected the clients. Now the client selects the institution." When clients have a choice, they choose the lenders that offer the best service and the best deal. This freedom of movement plays havoc with the methods of microcredit in use throughout most of the 1990s, which sacrificed client convenience to minimize lender risk. Group guarantees, immediate follow-up of delinquency, frequent meetings, and small initial loan amounts all pose inconveniences that clients accept only if they have no alternative.

Competition forced Bolivian microlenders to scrutinize their methodologies, looking for ways to make themselves more attractive to clients. Interest rates dropped, and lenders strove to turn loans around in hours rather than days or weeks. BancoSol increased its product range from two lending and two savings products at the end of 1997 to eight lending, four payment, and two savings products in 2001.

Solidarity-group loans, pioneered in Bolivia by Prodem and BancoSol, require clients to put their own assets at risk for their colleagues. If groups go wrong, as they often do, clients can lose a great deal of time, money, and peace of mind in repairing the situation. Village-banking methods, like those of NGOs Pro Mujer and Crecer, are even less flexible. They tie the timing of a client's access to credit together with thirty others and require weekly attendance at meetings. Many observers and practitioners believe that individual lending gives Caja Los Andes and FIE a tremendous market advantage over group lenders, for reasons long articulated by IPC and shared by Claudio González Vega and others at Ohio State University. As validation of their views, IPC and Ohio State point out the stronger performance of Caja Los Andes relative to BancoSol and Prodem during the crisis (see Table 6.3).

**Table 6.3: Institutions with Largest Portfolios in Loans Below US$500**

| Institution | Portfolio (US$ millions) |
|---|---|
| **Commercial MFIs** | |
| Caja los Andes | 5.0 |
| FIE | 3.0 |
| BancoSol | 2.4 |
| Eco Futuro | 2.1 |
| Prodem | 1.6 |
| **NGOs** | |
| Crecer | 3.3 |
| Pro Mujer | 2.8 |
| FADES | 2.7 |
| ANED | 2.5 |

ASOFIN, CIPAME, and FINRURAL, *Boletín Financiero: Microfinanzas* (December 2000), 36–37.

BancoSol's former managing director Hermann Krützfeldt notes that in a recession the group mechanism may even augment risk; in difficult times, all members are weakened, and the need to help one member can be too much for the others. In fact, the majority of BancoSol's delinquency since the crisis was concentrated in its solidarity portfolio. In essence, group lending addresses idiosyncratic but not systematic risk.

BancoSol's market research showed that a significant portion of clients prefers group loans. Clients cannot or do not want to provide the tangible guarantees that individual lenders require. Market researcher Domingo Fabbri says that these clients use the credit history of their group in the role of equity for leveraging larger loans. Nevertheless, by mid 1999 BancoSol greatly expanded individual lending. By the end of 2000, BancoSol's solidarity-group loan portfolio had decreased to 34 percent of the total portfolio, although it still represented 62 percent of active clients. In Bolivia, the ratio of individual to group loans has grown. In December 1997 individual loans made up 41 percent of the nation's microloan portfolio, while in December 2000 they accounted for 78 percent.[10]

Even village-banking NGOs feel this pressure. One Pro Mujer response was to enhance flexibility by increasing the use of client internal (group-managed) accounts from which clients can readily borrow. However, Pro Mujer's main bulwark against competition has been its attempt to segment the market, targeting clients who are too poor or inexperienced to qualify for loans at the commercial MFIs. In the competitive setting it is becoming more difficult to find a stratum of clients excluded from other microfinance programs and yet still able to service debt. Moreover, after a couple of Pro Mujer loans, clients qualify with other lenders—witnessed by so many of its clients having loans from BancoSol and others. If Pro Mujer narrows its market to clients who cannot borrow from other lenders, however, it becomes harder to achieve financial viability.

### Unhealthy Competition: Overlending

Unquestionably, most microfinance clients benefit from the advent of competition. More people have access to financial services, they can choose their supplier, and they can demand favorable terms. These benefits for the majority of clients are, or should be, the main story about the arrival of competition. However, the good news is tempered by questions on two fronts: over-indebtedness and mission drift.

Poaching clients from other institutions by offering larger loans has proven to be an extremely successful marketing technique in Bolivia, as elsewhere. Problems arise because clients are not good judges of their own debt capacity. Apparently, credit is like good food: when seated in front of a feast, many of us eat too much and regret it later. Perhaps more experienced borrowers than Bolivian microentrepreneurs can learn to exercise restraint, but the fact that overborrowing occurs in many societies (and is, for example, a chronic problem in the United States) suggests a common trait of human nature. The truly unfortunate dynamic is that if clients patronize lenders that offer too-large loans (or multiple loans that exceed debt capacity), responsible lenders are virtually forced to follow suit. Worse, if clients begin using one loan to pay off another, the game becomes, as Elizabeth Naba of FIE says, "Who collects first?"

The market dynamics associated with overlending require a collective response, supported by regulatory standards. In such a situation, only a central body, like the Superintendency of Banks, can stop the spiral, with regulations such as those put in place for consumer loans in 1999. The problem of multiple loans requires top-quality credit bureaus, while the problem of excessive loan sizes requires industry-wide lending norms. In every country where microfinance is growing, credit bureau development should be high on the agenda.

### The New Microfinance Industry and the Poor

Perhaps the greatest anxiety about the commercialization of microfinance is the fear that the profit motive will cause microfinance institutions to move up-market, away from the poor. As BancoSol regional manager German Sanchéz noted, loan officers are naturally tempted to pursue larger clients, especially when trying to meet portfolio and income targets. Pancho Otero, BancoSol's first managing director, recalls, "There's no problem making larger loans to more successful clients, even individual loans. The difficulty is to stay excited about the smaller clients."

The starting point for considering this issue in Bolivia is the recognition that the commercially oriented MFIs in Bolivia never served the extremely poor. Data from 1995 show that 78 percent of BancoSol clients clustered just below or just above the poverty line, with most of the rest clearly non-poor. At FIE and Caja Los Andes, most clients were above the line (80 percent and 74 percent, respectively). Only 2 or 3 percent of the clients at these institutions were in the categories of indigent or poorest (González-Vega et al. n.d., 26). Only the rural lenders Prodem and Sartawi served primarily people below the poverty line.

Since the early 1990s, average loan sizes have been increasing at all the leading commercial MFIs. In 1992 BancoSol's average loan balance was US$250. By 1995 this figure had doubled, and by the end of 2000 it was US$1,276.[11] To some degree, growing average loan sizes are inherent in the microcredit methodology of increasing loan amounts to growing customers. In addition, BancoSol added new loan products aimed specifically at larger microbusinesses. But mission drift would only occur if the organization stopped lending to new clients at the low end or failed to retain existing low-end clients.

In the mid 1990s BancoSol and ACCION analyzed the portfolio and concluded that most of the growth was coming from repeat clients and not mission drift. An Ohio State study concurred. "There is no evidence of drift from the organizations' mission of lending to the poor, even though the average size of loan has grown as their portfolios have matured." In fact, OSU found that Caja Los Andes was actually moving down-market during this period as it opened its doors increasingly to market vendors (González-Vega et al. n.d., 22).

In 2000, available numbers indicate that the commercial microlenders remain active at the bottom end of the spectrum (see Table 6.3). In fact, the institution with the largest portfolio of loans below US$500, including NGOs and commercial MFIs, was Caja Los Andes. The small-loan portfolios of other commercial microlenders were similar in size to those of the largest NGOs. It is possible that the NGOs reach farther down within the under US$500 category, but the distribution of loans under US$500 across institutions offers important reassurance about the continued activity of commercialized institutions at the lower market level.

Staff members at microfinance institutions have long believed that small loans lose money and must be cross-subsidized by larger loans. For clients whose loan sizes stay small—or who leave the bank after a first or second loan—the overall relationship is not profitable. During the pre-competitive years, this observation underscored the importance of turning every customer into a repeat customer.

If commercially driven lenders take over a major share of the top end of the microfinance market, they leave the mission-driven organizations, whether commercialized or not, with some unpleasant choices. To remain competitive, mission-driven organizations may have to reduce cross-subsidization in order to offer the upper end clients better terms. Alternatively, they may be left with a client group whose loans are too small to be a basis for profitable operation. Perhaps much of this dilemma could be solved simply, through differential pricing to boost the smallest loans above the break-even threshold. Differential pricing is already in place in FIE and some other organizations.

BancoSol has decided to enter a more upscale market, but senior managers argue that this is in addition to its original focus. Poverty-focused lenders like Pro Mujer face a starker choice. If Pro Mujer continues to be exclusively focused on the lowest end, its ability to keep larger clients and become financially viable may be threatened. Pro Mujer's choice to remain a poverty-focused NGO may help it retain access to the donor funding that is increasingly aimed at the very poor. Such access could become essential if competition continues to bite into the upper portion of Pro Mujer's target group.

In Bolivia generally, intense competition is giving institutions a great incentive to seek new, less-saturated market niches. Some observers believe that this force will lead to innovations that will make smaller loans profitable. This long-term push toward new markets could mean that competition will ultimately result in deeper outreach toward the poor. But for the near future, gains for the very poor are likely to come from the move of microfinance into rural areas and from the development of specially tailored savings services.

### Consumer Lenders and the Public Identity of Microfinance

MFIs everywhere must come to grips with the consumer-lending challenge. Despite the debacle it suffered in Bolivia, consumer lending is a rapidly growing phenomenon. Microfinance lenders operating with consumer lenders must face an awkward fact: to a client, their products look very similar in size, duration, interest rate, turnaround (a few days), and rhetoric about client benefits (growth and prosperity). The borrowers' revolt demonstrated how thin the line is between microfinance, with altruistic motives, and consumer lending, a purely profit-seeking activity often considered unscrupulous. The debt protesters did not greatly distinguish between the two. The borrower revolt and the overlap with consumer lending should provoke microfinance practitioners and donors to serious rethinking.

One line of rethinking concerns the public image and values of microfinance. What actually distinguishes lending that is good for the client from destructive lending? If the private sector contains unscrupulous elements, how should the microfinance industry position itself? The Bolivian experience suggests that the principal public-image issues for microfinance are high interest rates and the consequences of default—age-old concerns about moneylending. It is ironic that the Bolivian debtors associations played the interest-rate card, even though rates had never before been at issue between microlenders and their clients and even though rates were declining under competition.

Microlenders must also worry about public condemnation of practices leading to debt addiction. Microfinance has been zealous in ensuring that its borrowers can handle their debt, while consumer lenders routinely

expect 7 to 10 percent of clients ultimately to default. Bolivia's consumer lenders tolerated a level of default that the microlenders considered unconscionable because of its toll in broken families and because
other borrowers had to pay for those failures. The burden is on
microfinance to define and promote ethical lending practices, recognizing that the human weakness for fast cash may make a purely market-
based solution less than ideal.

Another line of rethinking concerns the competitive pressure on
microfinance to expand its scope to include the low-income salaried sector. Many salaried employees in poor countries receive incomes as low
or lower than microentrepreneurs. The microfinance profession has seen
a burgeoning interest in new product development, including savings,
housing finance, and insurance. In the process of exploring such new
products, should microfinance focus exclusively on the non-salaried segment of the population, on the grounds that the market will not provide
for this segment, or should it be all-inclusive, on the grounds that the
same product can serve both segments? In part, this is an empirical question: as financial innovation progresses, the salaried/non-salaried distinction may or may not remain relevant for selecting clients.

Those in the microfinance field for whom poverty alleviation and
empowerment are central profoundly distrust the private sector. They
fear that the private sector will take up the vehicle but not the values.
Once commercialization begins, however, the truth appears that utopian
microfinance institutions cannot operate in isolation. The prudent course
is to work with the private entrants to ensure that they adopt the values
and practices the promoters of microfinance endorse. Like it or not, as
Bolivia shows, the future of microfinance requires engagement with the
mainstream.

## REFLECTIONS

In reflecting on the Bolivian experience of commercial microfinance,
it is important to separate commercialization from the crisis. Regarding
commercialization itself, two points stand out. First, the commercialization of microfinance in Bolivia has largely followed one particular path—
the transformation of NGOs into financial institutions. Other models,
such as downscaling of banks and financial institutions and creation of
new commercial entities are also relevant. Pure private entry into
microenterprise lending, while present, has not been dominant, and the

crisis has ensured that it is unlikely to be a major factor for some time to come. So we look to Bolivia as one important variation in the overall commercialization story, but not the whole story.

Second, it is important to reiterate the effects of commercialization on service quality, methodology, and new product development and to emphasize that these emerged independent of the crisis. These far-reaching and mainly positive results will not necessarily be accompanied by the kind of crisis Bolivian microfinance has faced. Indeed, studying the Bolivian example may help policymakers and lenders achieve the positive results without falling victim to the negative ones.

But neither can one simply set aside the crisis as an unfortunate confluence of events unique to Bolivia. Perhaps the arrival of economic and political problems in Bolivia at just the time when the lenders had overextended themselves was bad luck. But this kind of bad luck is characteristic of collective financial behavior: economic downturn reveals the risk a system has taken on. Perhaps the behavior of the Bolivian consumer lenders and to a lesser degree the response of its microlenders was just poor judgment. But those judgments sprang from motivations and conceptual paradigms that are widely prevalent among consumer and microenterprise lenders in many countries. Although we may not see as dramatic a series of events in other places as in Bolivia, it is almost certain that some of the underlying patterns will be part of the future of commercialized microfinance.

## NOTES

1. Mario Riquena, Ministry of Finance, interview with author. In this chapter, quotations or paraphrases of individuals are from interviews with the author during March 1999 and March 2000.

2. Superintendencia de Bancos y Entidades Financieras, *Boletin Informativo* 12/149 (December 2000), 10.

3. For a detailed account of the Bolivian model of microfinance transformation, see Elisabeth Rhyne, *Mainstreaming Microfinance: How Lending to the Poor Began, Grew, and Came of Age in Bolivia* (West Hartford, Conn.: Kumarian Press, 2001), chap. 5.

4. BancoSol's transformation is detailed in Deborah Drake and Maria Otero, *Alchemists for the Poor: NGOs as Financial Institutions,* Monograph Series No. 6 (Washington, D.C.: ACCION International, 1992); Amy Glosser, "The Creation of BancoSol in Bolivia," in Maria Otero and Elisabeth Rhyne, eds., *The New World of Microenterprise Finance: Building Healthy Financial Institutions for the Poor* (West Hartford, Conn.: Kumarian Press, 1994); and Cheryl Frankiewicz, *Building Institutional Capacity: The Story of PRODEM, 1987–1999* (Toronto: Calmeadow Foundation, 2001).

5. *La Razon, Economia y Negocios* [La Paz] (February 21, 1999), 1.

6. Ibid., 5. The delinquency indicator used in the newspaper is more lenient than the indicator used elsewhere in this chapter.

7. Müller and Associates, "Evaluación del Sistema Financiero Nacional," *Informe Confidencial* 115 (March-April 1998), 13.

8. Government of Bolivia, Superintendency of Banks, Circular 282 (La Paz, January 4, 1999).

9. ASOFIN, CIPAME, and FINRURAL, *Boletín Financiero: Microfinanzas* (December 2000).

10. Author's calculation based on ibid., 31.

11. Claudio González-Vega et al., "A Primer on Bolivian Experiences in Microfinance: An Ohio State Perspective" (Columbus, Ohio: Rural Finance Program, Ohio State University, n.d.), 23; Banco Solidario, "Memoria 1998" (La Paz, 1999), 112; and ASOFIN, CIPAME, and FINRURAL, *Boletín Finaciero: Microfinanazas* (December 2000).

# 7

# The FFP Experience
## *FASSIL Case Study*

### Lynne Curran

Fondo Financiero Privado FA$$IL (FASSIL) represents an illustrative case of the commercialization of microfinance and the impacts of a difficult economy and competitive environment on commercial microfinance institutions. Here, an overview of FASSIL's experience as a regulated financial entity to date is provided, including the ways in which the microfinance institution was affected by the crisis that hit the Bolivian microfinance sector in recent years, which occurred subsequent to the original study. The case study of FASSIL clearly illustrates a number of internal and external factors that encouraged the financial institution to penetrate the microenterprise market, slowly at first and then more rapidly.

## BACKGROUND

The Bolivian Fondos Financieros Privados (private financial funds), or FFPs, are considered non-bank financial entities because they cannot directly offer current accounts or foreign exchange services and therefore do

This chapter is an update of a case study included in Jeffrey Poyo and Robin Young, "Commercialization of Microfinance: The Cases of Banco Económico and Fondo Financiero Privado FA$$IL, Bolivia" (Bethesda, Md.: Development Alternatives, Microenterprise Best Practices Project, 1999).

not participate in the process of expansion and contraction of the money supply. FFPs, like other non-bank financial entities, lie between fully regulated banks and microfinance NGOs on the spectrum of financial institutions providing microfinance services. The minimum capital requirement for FFPs is 630,000 Special Drawing Rights (SDRs) or approximately US$1 million, compared to the minimum capital required for a full service bank in Bolivia of two million SDRs or approximately US$3 million. The FFP structure, created by the Bolivian Superintendency in 1995, was designed specifically to provide an adequate legal structure for institutions offering financial services to micro and small enterprises (MSEs).

Shortly after the FFP structure was created in Bolivia in 1995, a group of private investors from the construction, commercial, and telecommunications sectors of Santa Cruz de la Sierra, Bolivia, decided to form an FFP to offer financial services to a critical segment of the population: low-income salaried workers and microentrepreneurs with limited access to the banking system. The eight initial shareholders who formed FASSIL were moved to create an FFP by the evidence of the large number of Bolivians without access to credit. FASSIL's founders, as well as the first general manager, who had extensive experience in the commercial-banking sector in Bolivia, recognized that there was a strong profit potential in the microfinance sector.

Within a year of the decision to form an FFP, FASSIL had received its operating license from the Bolivian Superintendency of Banks and Financial Institutions, and the institution began operations in August 1996. Its main products since that time have been consumer credit, microcredit, and a gold-backed pawn-loan product, as well as limited deposit and payment services.

## EVOLUTION OF THE FFP

FASSIL's institutional mission is to "provide financial intermediation and creative services to our clients in an easy, fast and opportune manner, maintaining a profitability that allows us to direct our efforts to promote emergent economic sectors, supporting the growth and development of the country." The founders of FASSIL have always viewed the institution as a microfinance institution whose primary focus is to serve microenterprise clients. However, the institution's initial drive focused more heavily on growing a consumer-credit portfolio, believing that this approach could be more profitable in the short term. By year-end 1998, FASSIL's consumer-credit portfolio represented 58 percent of its entire portfolio of US$21.7 million. Within the microenterprise credit portfolio, which represented the remaining 42 percent of the total portfolio, solidarity credit represented 68 percent, association/group credits encompassed 18 percent, and individual credits comprised only 14 percent.[1]

Today, FASSIL could be considered a completely different institution from that which was originally researched for the 1998 case study. A number of factors that affected consumer credit, including the Bolivian economic crisis, changes in legislation regarding consumer credit, and laws imposed on contraband trading at the borders with Brazil, have combined to cause the management and board of directors to change many aspects of the institution's operations. By year-end 2000, the institution had turned completely away from consumer credit and was focusing all efforts on growing its microenterprise portfolio. At that time FASSIL's consumer-credit portfolio had declined to represent only 22 percent of the entire portfolio of US$15.4 million. Within the microenterprise credit portfolio, which represented the remaining 78 percent of the total portfolio, solidarity credit represented 44 percent, individual credits 43 percent, and association/group credits 13 percent.

FASSIL's total outstanding portfolio declined almost 30 percent, from US$21.7 million to US$15.4 million between December 31, 1998, and December 31, 2000. The majority of Bolivian microfinance institutions (MFIs) experienced decreasing portfolio size during the same period, as both financial institutions and their clients felt the impact of the economic recession that began in 1999. Moreover, the declining portfolio size is a reflection of FASSIL's move to increase its focus on microenterprise credit over consumer credit. The credit analysis required to disburse microenterprise loans is much more detailed and time consuming than that required for consumer loans, and as such the process to grow a healthy microloan portfolio is longer.[2] Within the microloan portfolio, total growth over the two-year period between December 31, 1998, and December 31, 2000, was a strong 31.84 percent, from US$9.2 million to US$12.1 million. Most of this growth occurred in 1999, when the portfolio increased 29 percent, from US$9.2 million to US$11.8 million. During 2000, although the portfolio did increase slightly, the institution was more focused on collecting the past-due portfolio and determining future strategies than achieving large expansion within the microloan portfolio.

FASSIL was created to provide financing via two main approaches: consumer credit and microcredit. As stated previously, however, FASSIL initially focused on growing its consumer-credit portfolio, assuming that a profitable microcredit portfolio would take longer to develop and that the rapid expansion of consumer credit would provide the funding necessary to allow the microenterprise portfolio to grow at a healthy pace. FASSIL was operationally sustainable after only eight months of operations due to this approach. However, by 1999 FASSIL began to suffer a downturn in its loan portfolio quality, which had a direct negative impact on the income and sustainability of the institution.

Bolivia's entire microfinance sector began to see an increase in delinquency at that time, as the overall banking system was faltering as well. As Elisabeth Rhyne explains in Chapter 6, the declining portfolio quality could be attributed to a combination of factors, including increased competition and the regional financial slowdown. By that time microfinance in Bolivia had experienced explosive growth, with NGOs, FFPs, and BancoSol, the one commercial bank devoted to microfinance, fighting for clients among themselves as well as with commercial banks providing consumer credit. This increased access to microcredit quickly led to a saturation of the market, over-indebted clients, and declining portfolio qualities.

Just a few years into operations, FASSIL's board and management decided to grow the microcredit portfolio more quickly than originally planned, while reducing consumer-credit activities. In addition to the increased competition in the Bolivian microfinance market, there were a number of factors that led to this mid-1999 decision, including the economic recession that was beginning in Bolivia and was already strongly felt in Santa Cruz, as well as changes in legislation put in place by the Superintendency of Banks in early 1999, which tightened the reins on institutions operating in consumer credit. Legislative changes included increased provisioning requirements that sharply and negatively affected the profitability of consumer-credit operators. There were numerous institutions offering consumer credit in Bolivia by early 1999, and many of these institutions were offering consumer loans to the same clients, which led to increased over-indebtedness among those clients. This directly marred the consumer-credit portfolio of FASSIL and the other consumer lenders, because many clients were unable to repay all the loans they had taken from a variety of consumer lenders. The Superintendency saw this as a dangerous situation for the financial institutions that might not recover their loans, and thus increased provisioning requirements for consumer-loan portfolios.

The increased competition and increased provisioning requirements made it much less attractive for FASSIL to offer consumer credit as its main product, and the strategic decision was made to reduce the focus on the consumer-credit portfolio while increasing the microenterprise credit activities.

Shortly after the Superintendency of Banks imposed increased provisioning requirements on institutions offering consumer-credit products, tax requirements were changed to reduce significantly the amount of contraband goods arriving into Bolivia at the borders, especially the borders with Brazil. As the sale of such goods was the primary business of many microentrepreneurs in Santa Cruz, their repayment capacity was greatly damaged by the increased taxes. This hurt the portfolio quality and profitability levels of all MFIs operating in Santa Cruz, including FASSIL. FASSIL has survived the crisis thus far and has succeeded in growing its microloan portfolio. However, today FASSIL's management is facing the important challenge of identifying its niche in what continues to be a very competitive market in a difficult macroeconomic environment; it must do so if the institution is to return to previous levels of profitability and to recapture a healthy microfinance portfolio.

### Products and Services

When FASSIL's founders chose the FFP structure over that of a full-fledged commercial bank, they recognized that the cost of creating a commercial bank was too high to be able to provide the additional services banks are allowed to offer, such as checking accounts and foreign-exchange services. By forming FASSIL as an FFP rather than an NGO, however, there has been the advantage of being able to provide a somewhat more diversified range of products and services to its clientele than NGOs can provide. At the same time, as a regulated institution, FASSIL has been required to adhere to the strict provisioning requirements established by the Superintendency of Banks.

FASSIL continues to classify its loan products within two main subcategories: microcredit and consumer credit. The division is based more on loan size than credit methodology, however, as commercial and mortgage loans are included within the consumer portfolio and gold-backed pawn-loans are classified within the microcredit portfolio. FASSIL's increased focus on microcredit has included an increased focus on the gold-backed pawn-loan product. FASSIL management discovered that many microentrepreneurs and other low-income clients like the product, as they are practically guaranteed immediate disbursement of the loan. There are constantly clients waiting in the branches to be attended to by staff dedicated to the pawn loan, and up to twenty loans may be disbursed on any given day.

FASSIL has experimented with a number of additional products since its inception, although not all of the lines have been successful, as in the case of association/group loan product. This product, which places loans through merchant associations, never met expectations, and FASSIL no longer offers association/group loans. Also, in early 2000, a rural credit product was introduced, but it was quickly determined that FASSIL was not prepared to offer and support such a product. By year-end 2000, there were only twenty-one rural loans outstanding. Today, the institution offers the following nine credit products:

| **Consumer Credit** | **Microcredit** |
|---|---|
| Loans to salaried persons | Solidarity group loans |
| Loans to self-employed persons | Individual loans |
| Commercial loans (to businesses) | Group/association loans |
| Personal commercial loans | Pawn loans |
| Mortgage loans | |

### Consumer Credit

FASSIL's consumer-credit model was similar to the model used by Chilean consumer-credit companies, a model that was imported to a number of financial institutions in Bolivia at the same time.

This model has been referred to as a "credit factory," with a high degree of specialization and the incentive for the sales team depending entirely on the amount of credit disbursed. At the height of the activity in FASSIL's consumer-credit portfolio, there were ninety sales officers who were responsible only for promoting the product and obtaining required information from the customer and guarantors. Responsibility for information verification, analysis, approval, portfolio management, and loan collection was distributed among several other staff members.

The Chilean model of consumer credit is designed to be used with a statistical-analysis model or credit scoring. However, neither FASSIL nor the other Bolivian institutions that entered the Bolivian consumer-credit field at the same time had any credit-scoring model, and thus the push to disburse many credits resulted in the disbursement of many poorly analyzed loans. The resulting high portfolio at risk led FASSIL quickly to recognize the need to examine and reform certain elements of its credit technology in an effort to control delinquency and increase the profitability of its consumer-loan product.

During 1999 and 2000, FASSIL management focused efforts on reducing the consumer-credit portfolio. By year-end 2000, there were twenty-five staff members dedicated solely to collecting the consumer portfolio. It is expected that the portfolio will disappear completely by 2002, and those staff members will transfer to microcredit activities. However, the management team recognizes that the change in focus to microcredit will not be easy. The reputation of institutions that participated in the Bolivian consumer-lending frenzy has been tarnished, and FASSIL needs to take steps to improve its institutional image in the eyes of both clients and potential funders.

## Microcredit

Although there was an early drive to grow the consumer-credit portfolio, it was understood that the reason for this drive was to provide the internal financing necessary to grow the microcredit portfolio at a slower, healthier pace. Currently, the microloan portfolio has the largest representation within FASSIL's overall loan portfolio. Originally, FASSIL's main microcredit product was the traditional solidarity-group product, although slight modifications were made to the traditional methodology, such as larger loan sizes and flexibility regarding the number of members per solidarity group.

Today, there is an interesting phenomenon in Bolivia; almost all microfinance institutions, both regulated and non-regulated, are moving away from solidarity-group loans as their primary product. As clients have become more knowledgeable about credit and group members face increased difficulties in repaying their own loans, such clients are less willing to take on the risk of providing solidarity guarantees for other group members. FASSIL began offering individual loans slightly before the competition, which helped the institution to establish a strong customer base. FASSIL quickly identified the need to offer individual credits for clients who graduated from solidarity lending and for other potential customers with more established businesses who were applying for consumer loans.[3]

**Figure 7.1**

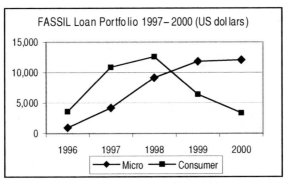

**Figure 7.2**

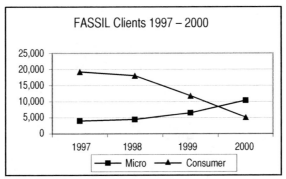

## Other Products and Services

In addition to its loan products, FASSIL has taken advantage of its structure as a regulated entity to offer a number of other financial services, including savings accounts and time deposits. FASSIL also has a contract with a local utility company to accept payments in FASSIL branches; and there is a FASSIL cashier located in six of the utility company's locations throughout Santa Cruz. Although this has not proved an important source of revenue for FASSIL (basically providing just enough income to cover the cost of providing the service), it has brought in many potential clients. FASSIL also offers other services, including salary payments for local businesses and the receipt of tax payments.

## FASSIL'S FINANCIAL RESULTS

FASSIL reported positive net income within its first year of operations, generating an average return on equity (ROE) of 10.56 percent in
1997 and 12.44 percent in 1998. However, the Bolivian crisis affected
FASSIL's operations by 1999, and net income declined from US$292,000
in 1998 to US$41,000 in 1999, only a 1.34% ROE. The institution's net
loss of US$297,000 for 2000 resulted in an ROE of negative 10.15%.

**Figure 7.3**

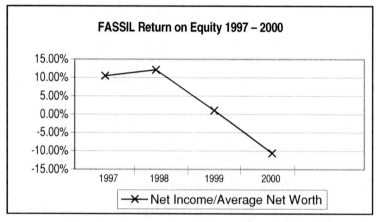

The main reason for the institution's declining profitability levels is
the provision expense related to the portfolio quality. By December 1998
the portfolio at risk of the consumer-credit portfolio was 20.16 percent,
while the portfolio at risk of microenterprise credits was only 1.74 percent.[4] Even with the switch to focus on the microcredit portfolio, the
institution has continued to be hit by the need for high provisions, as the
Bolivian economic recession has led to worsening portfolio qualities
throughout the system. ASOFIN reported that the combined portfolio at
risk for all regulated microfinance institutions in Bolivia was 12.6 percent on December 31, 2000. By December 2000, FASSIL's total portfolio at risk was 13.00 percent over thirty days; the microcredit loan portfolio was showing delinquency levels of 9.82 percent, and the
consumer-credit portfolio was 24.47 percent past due.

Along with growing the gold-backed pawn-loan portfolio, FASSIL
management has also developed better ways to ensure repayment of the

pawn loans. Since these loans are fully guaranteed by gold jewelry, which is not that difficult to sell should the client be unable to repay, they have dramatically improved the portfolio quality of the product from 1998 to 2000.

## FASSIL'S FUNDING SOURCES

One of the main arguments for microfinance NGOs to transform to regulated institutions is the increased access to diversified funding sources. Since its inception, FASSIL's primary external funding source has been large certificates of deposits held by local investors, maintaining a debt/equity (leverage) ratio between 5:1 and 9:1. In 1999 the institution began a campaign to increase client savings. One promotion included lowering interest rates for clients who chose to deposit at least 10 percent of their loan into a FASSIL savings account. Again, however, the difficult economic environment impeded any significant increase in client savings. Although client savings did increase 42.24 percent between 1998 and 1999, there was a 51.31 percent decrease from December 1999 to December 2000.

Given the worsening economic environment and impending crisis facing Bolivian microfinance institutions, by late 1999 FASSIL's management and board decided to look for international funding. In early 2000 the institution obtained a soft loan from the multilateral institution Corporación Andina de Fomento (CAF) for approximately US$500,000. Table 7.1 illustrates FASSIL's main funding sources as of December 1998, 1999, and 2000.

**Table 7.1: FASSIL's Portfolio Funding Sources (US$)**

|  | December 1998 | December 1999 | December 2000 |
|---|---|---|---|
| Savings Accounts | 757,398 | 1,077,332 | 524,577 |
| Certificates of Deposit | 20,898,459 | 17,148,295 | 13,845,728 |
| National Bank Loans | 823,348 | – | 333,381 |
| Subsidized Debt | – | – | 514,778 |
| TOTAL | 22,479,205 | 18,225,627 | 15,218,464 |

## LESSONS LEARNED

When discussing the commercialization of microfinance, it is important to keep in mind that there is no magic formula in terms of legal form for any institution working in microfinance; it all depends on the strategy, needs, and economic environment of the institution. Additionally, it is important for an institution to have a clearly defined market strategy, which, in FASSIL's case, analyzing experience to date, appears to have been somewhat weak. It was supposedly always an institution whose primary focus was microfinance, but management may have gotten carried away by a rush to profit through consumer credit. Commercial microfinance institutions will obviously want to obtain profits, but as in any line of business the board and management should be aware of the institutional market strategy, have a clearly defined market niche, and not lose sight of the vision of the institution and what its real objective is in providing microenterprise credit.

As clearly illustrated in Chapter 6, the economic recession and the crisis that have hit microfinance in Bolivia have affected institutions of all shapes, sizes, and legal structures. Instead of looking back and analyzing what should have been done, FASSIL's board of directors and management team now face the challenging task of determining where to go from here. To continue operating and to overcome the crisis, they need to determine where FASSIL's appropriate niche market lies. The board and management of the institution have not ruled out a merger with a more stable institution. Decisions to make will include whether there will even be a place for FASSIL in what will most likely emerge in Bolivia as a much more consolidated microfinance market.

## CONCLUSIONS

It is still too early to reach any definitive conclusions regarding the commercialization of microfinance based on FASSIL's experience to date. With so many factors contributing to the problems at FASSIL in its first few years of existence, it is difficult to determine whether its incorporation as a regulated commercial institution helped or hindered its performance. Tentatively, it is possible to conclude that crises such as that which the Bolivian microfinance sector has suffered in the past few years affect the microfinance sector at large, regardless of the legal structure of institutions operating in the field. In December 2000 ASOFIN reported that Bolivian FFPs as a whole reported portfolio at risk over thirty days of 9.70 percent, while BancoSol, the only commercial bank dedicated to microfinance, reported portfolio at risk of 12.33 percent, and NGOs had a combined portfolio at risk of 16.70 percent. This doesn't necessarily mean that FFPs weather crises better than other forms of MFIs, or that commercial institutions handle crises better than NGOs, as profitability indicators tell a different story. In fact, FFPs showed the largest loss in the system in 2000, and NGOs as a whole reported much greater profitability for the year.

There are some undeniable costs as well as benefits of being a regulated financial entity, which FASSIL has encountered. Some of these costs and benefits are outlined below.

### FFP vs. NGO

The main cost of being a regulated institution rather than an NGO during the Bolivian crisis has been the requirement to adhere to the Superintendency's strict provisioning requirements. FASSIL provisioned 9.66 percent and 12.60 percent of its portfolio in 1999 and 2000, respectively. As a non-regulated institution, FASSIL may have been able to create lower loan loss reserves safely and been able to use that savings to build a bigger capital base and further grow its loan portfolio. Another cost that FASSIL management has identified during the crisis was its lack of access to donor funding and difficulties accessing low-cost funding from international agencies.[5] However, one of the main arguments for the commercialization of microfinance is to end dependence on donor funds and subsidized credit. Not only will such funding run out eventually, but also it has been proven that even in times of crisis there are significant delays in the disbursement of donor funds. FASSIL's incorporation as a regulated entity allowed the institution to capture deposits, mainly in the form of large CDs, which were arguably received much more rapidly than any donation would have been received. Also, FASSIL's ability to offer products other than microcredit loans has been positive for the institution, as it has built up the pawn loan product and other services, which, although less profitable, have brought clients into the institution.

### *FFP* vs. *Commercial Bank*

The primary benefit of forming an FFP over a commercial bank is clearly the significantly smaller minimum capital required to establish an FFP. However, as FASSIL matures as an FFP, the restrictions placed on the services an FFP is allowed to provide may impede further growth in active clients. FASSIL management has observed that as clients are maturing and becoming more knowledgeable about financial services, they are interested in gaining access to additional services, such as checking accounts and credit cards. Since FASSIL cannot provide these services, management is concerned that the heavy investment made in capturing clients will be lost as these clients move to the wider range of services available through commercial banks.

Another challenge faced not only by FASSIL in Bolivia, but by non-bank financial entities in many countries is that of establishing a good reputation. In Bolivia, although FFPs are a separate legal structure created specifically for microfinance institutions, they are considered to be *financieras* by the general public, like any other non-bank financial entities. For various reasons the *financieras* have a poor reputation in many regions. In some areas it is because the consumer-credit companies who flooded the market were *financieras*, and their quick disbursement of credit led to the over-indebtedness of many poor Bolivians. Other *financieras* provide credit for the purchase of goods such as cars or household appliances and are known for charging exorbitant interest rates. FASSIL has begun to invest in publicity campaigns to gain client trust; it recognizes that further investment is necessary to create a well-known and respected image among target clientele.

## RECOMMENDATIONS FOR FURTHER STUDY

As Bolivian MFIs emerge from the current crisis, it will be important to study the impact of the crisis on the various types of institutions operating in microfinance, as well as the reactions of management. Such analysis will allow players in the microfinance field to determine whether there are similar effects of crises on non-bank regulated entities, for instance. This will help microfinance institutions who encounter similar economic and/or portfolio quality crises in the future determine proper actions to take in response to the crisis. Such preparedness may prevent extreme losses suffered by institutions, including FASSIL, during the Bolivian crisis.

## NOTES

1. With group/association lending, part of the work for analysis, payment, and selection is shifted to a third party, namely, a merchant association. The goal of this type of lending is to transfer the cost and risks to the association, while increasing the benefits offered to members of merchant associations.

2. Consumer-credit loans are disbursed much more rapidly (often the same day that an application is received), as the credit analysis is traditionally based on credit-scoring models and collateral. The credit analysis for microenterprise loans usually involves interviews and visits to the microenterprise involved, which makes the process much longer.

3. In microfinance, the term *graduation* is used when a client "outgrows" the solidarity-group methodology. Traditionally, solidarity-group loans are small in size, and as clients need to access larger loans and are able to provide different forms of guarantee, they are more interested in obtaining individual loans.

4. Portfolio quality ratios for all consumer-credit portfolios in Bolivia were around the same level during this period. For further detail, see Chapter 6 herein.

5. Although some MFIs do still have access to donor and subsidized funds, especially in times of crisis, FASSIL found that having bypassed the NGO stage completely, board members and management did not have the necessary relationships with donors to be able to access such funding rapidly.

# 8

# Corposol and Finansol
## Institutional Crisis and Survival

Patricia Lee

## BACKGROUND

On August 22, 1988, a group of Colombian business leaders led by Alvaro Arango and Oscar Giraldo founded the NGO Actuar Bogotá, which at a later stage of its evolution would be called Corposol.[1] The mission of the organization was to provide business credit and training to Bogotá's microentrepreneurs—poor business owners running small, often unlicensed businesses such as fruit stands, shoe repair shops, and small restaurants. At the time of Corposol's formation, this informal sector accounted for 40 percent of employment in Colombia, with approximately 1.2 million microenterprises employing 3.3 million people.[2]

Both Giraldo, Corposol's president, and Arango, the president of Corposol's board of directors, had business backgrounds and were personally committed to helping communities in need. Charismatic and ambitious, their personalities had an enormous influence on the growth of the organization in its early days. However, their personal and professional desire for success led them to pursue a strategy that was overly focused on growth, without sufficient emphasis placed on portfolio quality.

Part of that growth plan was to acquire a commercial finance company, Finansol, in 1993. Through its acquisition of Finansol, Corposol

---

This chapter is based on *The Rise and Fall of Corposol: Lessons Learned from the Challenges of Managing Growth* by Jean Steege, written in October 1998 for USAID's Microfinance Best Practices project.

became the second microfinance institution (MFI) in Latin America to enter the commercial arena.[3] For several years Corposol and Finansol appeared to work well together; Finansol issued microloans, while Corposol provided client training. Although Finansol was a separate company with its own management, staff, and board of directors, Corposol's majority ownership enabled it to control nearly every aspect of Finansol's operations and strategic direction.

In their heyday, the institutions were internationally celebrated for their rapid growth and success in serving a vast number of Colombian microentrepreneurs in need of credit. But by 1995 the loan portfolio and operations were beginning to exhibit significant weakness, with delinquency rates surging from 9 percent in 1994 to 17 percent in 1995 to a peak of 33.5 percent at year-end 1996. By September 1996 these weaknesses devolved into a full-blown crisis, revealing the mounting financial and operational troubles of both organizations. In 1996 Finansol was forced to establish a new management team and recapitalize its portfolio, enabling it to continue lending to this day. Corposol's fate was not as bright. In September 1996 the Colombian Superintendency of Companies (Superintendencia de Sociedades) ordered the official liquidation of Corposol. Since 1996 Finansol (renamed FINAMERICA in 1997) has rebuilt its business slowly and carefully. See Figure 8.1 for a history of the institution's active clients and outstanding portfolio.

This chapter details the accomplishments of Corposol's first several years, the events leading to its fall, and Finansol's ensuing recovery. Moreover, this chapter analyzes the strengths and shortcomings of both organizations and suggests lessons for other NGOs that have transformed or are planning to transform into commercial institutions.

**Fig. 8.1: Active Clients and Outstanding Portfolio, Corposol/Finansol/FINAMERICA, 1988–2001**

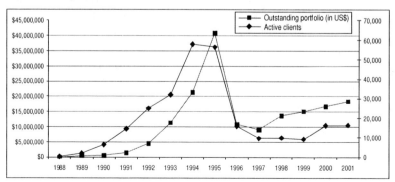

The history of Corposol/Finansol can be categorized in six distinct periods:

1. Controlled growth (1988–91)
2. Signs of trouble (1991–92)
3. Product over-diversification (1992–94)
4. The unraveling (1995–96)
5. The turnaround (1996–97)
6. Rebuilding (1997–2002)

## CONTROLLED GROWTH

From 1988 until 1991 Corposol experienced rapid yet controlled growth, with a focused and consistent lending methodology. During that time the institution was flourishing, boasting an outstanding portfolio of US$1.4 million and over fourteen thousand active clients after only two years of operations.

### *Operational Consistency*

Corposol's original lending methodology was to provide loans to solidarity groups—networks of four microentrepreneurs who were mutually responsible for the loan repayment of each member of the group. To induce growth and maintain controlled lending practices, loan officers were assigned specific geographic zones. They were not permitted to lend in a new zone until their existing territory was sufficiently served. Additionally, expansion into different zones would be considered only if a minimum of twenty solidarity groups were already established. Until 1990, this zone system seemed to work well. Loan officers were able to reach their performance objectives, which were based on the number of new clients and the number of renewed loans each loan officer made. Unfortunately, even at this early stage the system gave insufficient weight to loan repayment, often prioritizing lending volume at the cost of portfolio quality.

### *Funding Sources*

Corposol's founders planned to create an initial financial base through donations, but the portfolio grew faster than donations could support. To maintain its growth trajectory, they then pursued a larger, more reliable funding source—commercial bank loans personally guaranteed by Corposol's board members. But these guarantees were still not sufficient to support the organization's rapid growth, temporarily halting expansion.

In 1990, to overcome this financing constraint, Corposol turned to FUNDES, a Swiss business family foundation operating in Colombia, and ACCION International, a U.S.-based private nonprofit specializing in microfinance. ACCION and FUNDES co-guaranteed letters of credit to Colombian banks, greatly increasing the amount of funding available to the institution. As banks grew more familiar with Corposol and the successful repayment rates of their microentrepreneur clients, they became comfortable lending directly to Corposol. Eventually, banks even began accepting promissory notes signed by microentrepreneurs as collateral. By all accounts, Corposol's growth trajectory was sustainable, supported by ample funding, high client-demand, and the momentum of a motivated staff and management team.

## SIGNS OF TROUBLE

In 1991, however, Corposol's lending methodology and performance objectives were becoming increasingly unrealistic. In response to donor wishes and management's desire for expansion, there was a notable shift away from simple "growth" to "growth at all costs."[4]

### Operational Inconsistencies

Although the zone system worked well at the beginning, it began to falter after 1991. Management began demanding higher productivity from loan officers, despite feedback that zones were becoming saturated or consumer demand was waning. When loan officers requested to expand into new territories, management often refused, leading loan officers to deviate from the original, effective lending methodology. They began to lend arbitrarily in unapproved geographical areas, and worse, they issued loans for the sake of meeting requirements, without confidence that the client needed additional funds or had the ability to repay.

By 1992 it was nearly impossible for loan officers to reach their objectives and still practice standard lending procedures. With a strict incentive system based on lending volume rather than delinquency rates, increasingly risky loans were being disbursed. Loan officers who didn't meet the portfolio growth objectives incurred harsh penalties, from public reprimands to outright dismissal. At the same time, the rate of hiring new loan officers was increasing, while less emphasis was put on training. This contributed further to a departure from the earlier, more proven lending methodology.

### Funding Problems

In 1992 Corposol hit a major funding wall. With a capital to loan ratio of 1:16, the organization was over-leveraged and could not obtain additional credit from banks. ACCION International and FUNDES had reached the limits of their approved risk exposure, and neither institution could provide additional letters of credit to Corposol.

## PRODUCT OVER-DIVERSIFICATION

From October 1992 to December 1994 Corposol's organizational structure significantly changed. Its management introduced two new subsidiaries, Finansol and Mercasol. Finansol, the commercial finance company, offered four distinct credit products: construction loans (under the brand name Construsol), agricultural loans (under the brand name Agrosol), individual loans, and solidarity-group loans (see Table 8.1). Although the establishment of these subsidiary programs, collectively called Gruposol, was consistent with the overall mission of Corposol—to provide the poor with tools to increase their income-generating capacity and quality of life—they were initiated with insufficient market research and unrealistic implementation plans.

By the end of 1994 Gruposol reported that it was collectively serving fifty-eight thousand clients, a 190 percent increase since it had begun to diversify its services, just two years earlier.[5] This produced a 1994 outstanding loan portfolio of US$21.3 million, nearly double its value from the previous year. This growth was made possible by Corposol's 1993 acquisition of Finansol.

### The Acquisition of Finansol

Corposol's management and board realized that to reach a substantial number of Colombia's microentrepreneurs, they would need to become a regulated commercial finance institution. After years of feasibility studies and assessments of alternative options, Finansol was launched on November 2, 1993, as Corposol's for-profit commercial finance company (CFC). Finansol was charged with managing all credit operations for Gruposol.

### Exploring the Bank Option

Before the opportunity to transform into a CFC presented itself, however, the management and board of Corposol had planned to create a fully regulated bank. At the beginning of 1993 a feasibility study concluded that the creation of a bank would solve the recurring capital shortage problem, ensuring fund availability in the long term. As a bank, Corposol would have been able to:

- Capture funds directly from the public (including savings deposits)
- Maintain a capital to loan ratio of 1:10
- Eliminate commercial banks as intermediaries, thereby reducing the cost of its loans to borrowers

Despite the advantages, becoming a bank required a minimum capitalization of US$13.7 million, which neither Corposol nor its international supporters could afford.

### Pursuing the CFC Option

Later in 1993 a change in Colombia's banking law made an alternative option available to Corposol. Previously, companies held one license for both leasing and financial services, even if they only offered one of the two services. The new law separated the license into two distinct parts, rendering the license to make loans unnecessary for Financiera Fenix, a local leasing company. Corposol, along with several external partners, purchased Financiera Fenix's financial services license on September 30, 1993, for US$250,000. The acquisition involved only the license to operate, with no transfer of the portfolio, employees, or even the company's name. By purchasing an existing license, operations could begin in two months; it would have taken over a year to apply for government authorization to create a new commercial finance company. Capitalized at US$3 million, the new CFC was named Finansol.

**Table 8.1: Gruposol in 1994**

| Name | Year Established | Non/For-Profit | Mission |
|------|-----------------|----------------|---------|
| Corposol | 1988 | Nonprofit | Corposol provided strategic leadership, administrative support, public relations, and general coordination for the entire group. Corposol was the majority shareholder in Mercasol and Finansol, and served as a fundraiser for the nonprofit arms. Corposol also provided training to microcredit clients. All Gruposol clients were automatically charged a training fee that was tied to the disbursement of their loans. Although clients were not obligated to attend training courses (or could send family members or employees), they were still charged the fee, which generated significant income for Corposol. |
| Finansol | 1993 | For-profit | Finansol was a private commercial finance company (CFC) supervised by the Superintendency of Banks; it served as the financial intermediary of the group. Finansol issued loans for each part of Gruposol that had credit operations. Its operations were primarily funded by issuing certificates of deposit (CDs) to the Colombian government and local commercial banks. As the only regulated entity in Gruposol, Finansol was accountable for the quality of the aggregate portfolio. |
| Mercasol | 1991 | For-profit | Mercasol was a commercial retailer, selling inventory to microentrepreneurs through lines of credit. Mercasol purchased in bulk from suppliers and passed the savings on to clients, while allowing them to purchase in small quantities. |

**Table 8.1—*Continued***

| Agrosol | 1992 | Line of Credit through Finansol | Agrosol was a line of credit issued through Finansol. Agrosol provided loans, training and technical assistance to rural clients. |
|---|---|---|---|
| Construsol | 1994 | Line of Credit through Finansol | Construsol was a credit product offered through Finansol, providing loans to clients making physical improvements to their homes or businesses. Construsol also provided, for a fee, the technical assistance of architects, engineers and lawyers to help clients plan and execute construction projects. Corposol created Construsol with the intention that it would eventually become financially self-sustainable and be spun off as its own private institution. |

Corposol was the majority shareholder of Finansol with 71 percent of the shares. Minority shareholders included private individuals, ACCION International, Calmeadow, and FUNDES.[6]

The Finansol acquisition was viewed favorably by Colombia's Superintendency of Banks. Corposol had a strong board of directors, including prominent members of the Colombian banking, business, and law communities and the financial and governance support of several international shareholders. Furthermore, its leaders, Arango and Giraldo, were well known to have with strong backgrounds in both business and social development.

Finansol handled all of Gruposol's lending activities, and inherited thirty-two thousand clients, a high-quality portfolio, and a successful track record from Corposol and Agrosol. As a CFC, Finansol could obtain funds through certificates of deposit or bond issuance but was prohibited by law from offering savings and checking accounts. Corposol remained an NGO, offering training to clients and administrative support to Finansol. Notably, the loan officers remained the employees of Corposol. This put Finansol in the awkward position of being legally responsible for portfolio quality but having no management authority over the loan officers who actually disbursed the loans.

Finansol established its own board of directors and management team. However, it was never a completely autonomous institution as Giraldo, the president of Corposol, closely monitored the day-to-day activities of Finansol's management. More than half of the board of directors of Finansol were also members of Corposol's board, and Alvaro Arango was the president of both boards of directors.

Although formally Finansol and Corposol were separate entities, Corposol used its majority ownership of Finansol to support projects that contributed to growth (Corposol's goal), with less focus on the financial integrity of the organizations (Finansol's responsibility). These divergent goals and mismatched responsibilities eventually impaired the successful marriage of the two organizations.

## THE UNRAVELING

Through early 1995 Gruposol continued to grow, and the institutions seemed to be running smoothly, reporting over fifty-six thousand active clients, whose loans generated an outstanding portfolio in 1995 of US$41 million. Finansol's success was widely considered proof that the commercial approach to microfinance worked. However, although its performance appeared robust, the structure behind it proved to be shaky.

In May 1995, after eight months of delays by Corposol's management, ACCION International performed a diagnostic assessment (CAMEL) that pinpointed a deterioration of operations that had begun as early as 1992.[7] The assessment brought to light several problems, including:

- Deterioration in asset quality, efficiency and profitability, with a 24 percent decrease in net income from 1992 to 1993[8]
- Ambiguity caused by dividing management of the credit function between Corposol and Finansol
- Ineffective information flow within the organization, negatively influencing the efficacy of management and decision-making
- A high rate of employee turnover, a costly symptom of broader organizational problems
- Inconsistent statistics, which set off alarms concerning the accuracy of Corposol's reporting practices

By mid-1995 it became clear that Finansol and Corposol had undertaken some unscrupulous business practices. Finansol had performed extensive loan refinancing and had even sold part of its poor-quality portfolio to Corposol in order to defer the required provisions and write-offs of its many bad loans.

Adding to the crisis, Arango and Giraldo purchased Urban Solutions, a low-income housing developer, in May 1995. The purchase was poorly timed, given Gruposol's already-troubled portfolio, and led to further distrust by the board in management's ability to make wise business decisions in the face of a financial emergency.

To oversee the institution during the crisis, Luis Fernando Tobón, a respected banking professional, became Finansol's third president in October 1995. As Finansol's first president independent of political ties to Corposol, Tobón's arrival marked a key improvement in the administration of Finansol. He implemented a series of corrective measures, including the termination of the development of new credit products as well as a reinstatement of the ACCION lending model, from which the institution had deviated during its drive for growth.[9] He completely separated the operations of Finansol from Corposol and formulated a plan to streamline financial management. He put in place plans to improve management information systems, day-to-day operations, and human resources. Additionally, Tobón made the collection of doubtful loans a priority for Finansol. Despite these corrective measures, Corposol's situation was becoming increasingly desperate.

By May 1996 Finansol's continued losses had eroded its equity to less than half of what it had been at the start of the fiscal year, rendering the organization insolvent. By then, Corposol was unable to meet payroll, much less repay its creditors. Together with Finansol's board, the Colombian Superintendency of Banks agreed to a restructuring plan accompanied by a recapitalization. Aware of the gravity of the institutions' financial situations, the Superintendency declared a moratorium on the issuance of new loans.

The moratorium was logical from a regulatory standpoint but had two unintended negative effects. First, certain "good clients" began to go into arrears when they learned that their loans might not be renewed because of the Superintendency's ruling. Second, Finansol's losses were aggravated as the overall loan portfolio was shrinking and its fixed costs were now covered only by the interest on existing loans versus interest received on new loans.

## THE TURNAROUND

Tobón resigned in March 1996 to take another position within the Colombian banking sector. His replacement, María Eugenia Iglesias, was a twenty-year Citibank veteran and former consultant to Corposol. Iglesias was an ideal candidate to lead Finansol's turnaround. As a friend and former colleague of Tobón, she was well aware that the institution teetered on the brink of disaster. She performed the difficult and crucial task of removing all 260 loan officers from the Corposol payroll and incorporating them into the structure of Finansol.

ACCION then attempted to spearhead a commercial private-equity placement to solve the capital adequacy needs of the institution. This entailed engineering the involvement of a major global financial player, Citibank Colombia. However, the issuance of equity failed, due mainly to the deterioration of the Colombian financial markets and the damaged reputation of Finansol. In July 1996 another Finansol recapitalization effort began.

ACCION and Citibank put together an investor group that included ProFund and a government development bank, the Instituto de Fomento Industrial (IFI), as major partners. As Finansol's creditor, IFI accepted the role of principal shareholder to avoid the need to provision Finansol's debt. As a second-level funder, IFI could convert Finansol's debt into equity and have the chance to recoup its losses. Calmeadow, Citibank-Colombia, ACCION International, Fondo Nacional de Garantías (Colombia's National Guarantee Fund) and Fundación Social (one of Colombia's leading nonprofit foundations) participated as well. Support also came from the microfinance sector itself, with participation from ACCION's Latin American Network and other Colombian microcredit institutions. Together the group raised US$9.1 million in 1996 to absorb the losses of the old portfolio and lay the foundation for future growth.

In September 1996 the Colombian Superintendency of Companies ordered the complete separation of Corposol and Finansol. Corposol ceded its shares in Finansol to creditor banks including Banco de Colombia, Banco de Estado, Corfiunión, and Coopcentral, whose loans to Corposol had been collateralized by those shares. Buckling under outstanding loans from seventeen financial institutions and debts equaling US$15 million, Corposol was unable to restructure the rest of its debt with its remaining creditors. Corposol—along with Agrosol, Construsol, and Mercasol—was completely dissolved in September 1996. Finansol remained, the only surviving entity within Gruposol.

From July 1996 to July 1997, with higher expenses due to increased provisioning for loan losses coupled with the reduction of the loan portfolio, Finansol's net income fell rapidly. A second tranche to the initial recapitalization equaling US$1.9 million was launched in July 1997, bringing the total recapitalization effort to US$11 million.

To break its association with its tumultuous past, Finansol was renamed FINAMERICA in 1997. A new president, José Manuel Montaño, was hired to take FINAMERICA into its post-crisis phase.

**Table 8.2: Ownership Structure in FINAMERICA**

| Shareholder | 1997 | 2001 |
|---|---|---|
| IFI | 44.95% | 45.78% |
| ProFund | 26.58% | 25.77% |
| Acciones y Aportes Ltda. | 4.34% | 3.25% |
| Incame (Instit. de Cap. Microemp.) | 4.29% | N/A |
| Citibank (Repfin Ltda.) | 4.28% | 3.20% |
| Fundación Social | 4.18% | 3.13% |
| Fondo Nacional de Garantías | 2.94% | 2.20% |
| Stichting Triodos Doen | 2.28% | 2.27% |
| ACCION International | 1.74% | 1.97% |
| FUNDES | 1.73% | 5.80% |
| Inversiones Ramoresa | N/A | 0.32% |
| Calmeadow | N/A | 0.32% |
| ACCION Gateway Fund L.L.C. | N/A | 4.69% |
| Other | 2.69% | 1.30% |

## REBUILDING

From June 1997 until August 2001 Jose Manuel Montaño served as president of FINAMERICA. Under Montaño's leadership FINAMERICA's portfolio improved steadily and the institution regained stability, although it has not yet returned to the level of success characteristic of its early days. In 2001 Germán Contreras, a former IFI executive, succeeded Montaño as FINAMERICA's president. Because the institution had focused on larger microbusinesses in the years immediately following the crisis in an effort to regain financial stability, one of Contreras's priorities is to ensure that all segments of the microenterprise market are being served.

With net losses in 1999, 2000, and 2001 totaling US$491,000, US$198,000 and US$267,960 respectively, FINAMERICA's short-term goal is to achieve profitability by year-end 2002.

# WHY DID IT FAIL?

Transforming from an NGO to a regulated finance company allowed Corposol to increase its access to funding sources, an effective way to realize its goal of reaching more poor Colombian microentrepreneurs. So what caused the failure of this seemingly successful example of a commercialized microfinance institution? Its failure can be attributed to problems within the institutional relationship between Corposol and Finansol as well as a flawed governance structure.

## *Institutional Relationship Between Corposol and Finansol*

Much of the institutional dysfunction between Corposol and Finansol was due to ambiguity of authority and of responsibility within the credit process, fundamental cultural differences between Corposol and Finansol, and an institutional structure that allowed financial problems to be hidden.

### *Mismatched Responsibilities*

Within Corposol and Finansol, staff responsibilities were inconsistent with ultimate accountability. Loan officers, as the primary liaisons between the clients and Gruposol's many services, remained Corposol staff until 1996. Their responsibilities went beyond evaluation of clients' creditworthiness and repayment capacity. They also reviewed the possibilities for additional credit lines offered by Construsol or Mercasol and advised clients on training options. Because all of Corposol's income was generated through mandatory training fees, there was an inherent conflict of interest. Priority was placed on the one-time training fee that clients brought in, not the long-term relationship, or, most important, the probability that clients would repay their loans.

Finansol, as the regulated institution within Gruposol, was responsible for the quality of the portfolio yet had no managerial control over the loan officers who were in the position of making the loans and following up with clients in arrears. Finansol's role was limited to loan disbursements, financing Gruposol—including tapping the financial markets—and reporting to the Superintendency. Essentially, Finansol acted as a checkbook for Corposol, with no control over who received the checks. When loan officers were finally incorporated into Finansol's organizational structure in 1996, it was too late to ameliorate the portfolio problems.

## Cultural Differences

The nonprofit culture of Corposol and the banking culture of Finansol were often at odds throughout the history of the institutions. Finansol's survival was dependent on solid financial performance and a high-quality portfolio. These concerns were not as important to Corposol as an NGO, causing tension between the employees of the two organizations.

### *Informal* vs. *Formal Cultures*
In an industry that traditionally represents a hybrid of financial and social mentalities, Corposol staff felt that Finansol bankers did not understand the lending methodology or the idiosyncrasies of their microentrepreneur clients. They also felt that Finansol staff members were excessively bureaucratic and that their higher budget and salary expectations were not in keeping with the overall mission of helping the poor.

Additionally, the attitude of informality that had driven Corposol's operations throughout its history conflicted with Finansol's need to be accountable to its shareholders and the Superintendency. By the time Finansol was established, the "growth at all costs" mentality and consequent methodological shortcuts were firmly entrenched in the lending operation, as was the practice of refinancing to sweep bad loans under the rug.

An unwritten code of flexibility also permeated clients' repayment culture, which damaged the portfolio quality. Clients were accustomed to Corposol overlooking late payments, as long as they eventually repaid their loans. By August 1995 there was a significant deterioration in Finansol's credit portfolio, because Corposol consistently failed to collect in a timely manner. The stricter collection culture of Finansol confused clients and fostered a negative perception when they began incurring penalties and interest on payments in arrears. As a result, some clients resisted repaying their loans at all.

For Corposol, the price of these sloppy lending procedures had been inconsequential. However, once Finansol was required to make provisions for portfolio at risk in accordance with the Superintendency regulations, the goal of breaking even was overwhelming for the struggling new financial institution.

*Differences in Lending Methodology*

As Corposol and Finansol continued to grow, a distortion of the lending methodology emerged. Under pressure from Corposol's management to bolster the number of clients (in order to collect the mandatory training fee), loan officers allowed larger loans for longer terms, without following traditional, more stringent lending criteria.

Due to rapid growth and product diversification goals, by 1995 Gruposol programs often made parallel loans to the same client without proper lending analysis. Furthermore, Corposol's management allowed loans to be refinanced to circumvent provisioning requirements, creating the conditions for the future crisis.

As it turned out, there were other serious problems that would contribute to the Corposol and Finansol crisis. Finansol was in the practice of financing long-term assets with short-term capital, paid little attention to the systemization of financial data, and was vulnerable to fraud due to a lack of checks and balances. For example, as early as 1992, a group of loan officers was fired for making loans to "ghost groups"—groups that did not actually exist. At that time such indiscretions were still the exception, but by 1995 fraud was increasingly prevalent. In a diagnostic undertaken by Tobón in 1995, he discovered ghost groups and self-lending (funds disbursed to loan officers themselves) totaling US$200,000 in several branches.

### Ability to Hide Problems

By working through a non-regulated entity, Finansol was able to avoid government regulations when they were inconsistent with the institution's strategy or needs. For example, when the Superintendency imposed blanket limitations on the lending growth of financial institutions in 1994, Finansol simply issued loans through Corposol, thus avoiding an interruption to its loan disbursements and skirting the intent of the Superintendency. When Finansol's portfolio began to deteriorate, the worst loans were restructured and sold to Corposol, whose portfolio was not subject to provisioning requirements or review by the Superintendency. Such tactics allowed Finansol to hide the quality of the overall portfolio and to avoid developing operational standards with the required rigor of a regulated entity. This opportunistic swapping of loan portfolios was one of the most detrimental practices undertaken by the two institutions. At the same time, Finansol did not have to bear its own full operational cost (as loan officers were supported by Corposol until 1996), further camouflaging its true financial condition.

### Flawed Governance Structure

Strained dynamics between the boards and managements of Finansol and Corposol, as well as within the Finansol board itself, were born largely out of Corposol's mandated majority ownership of Finansol. The resulting dysfunction in Finansol's management and board of directors contributed directly to the crisis.

### Management Constraints

For the first several years of its existence, Finansol's management lacked autonomy because Corposol maintained ultimate control through Arango's position as board president. Additionally, the lack of continuity due to turnover in the position of Finansol's president further enabled Giraldo and Arango to guide the strategic decisions of the CFC.

Finansol's first two presidents lacked autonomy for different reasons. The first president, Mario Rodriguez Escallón, came from a banking background and had trouble adjusting his banking practices to Corposol's more informal practices. In May 1994, after less than six months as president, he was fired. He was replaced by José Antonio Jaime Escobar, who lacked autonomy because of his close relationship with Giraldo and Arango. He had been a senior manager at Corposol since its inception in 1988. When he became president of Finansol, he continued to view his job with Corposol's interests in mind. He resigned in September 1995, leaving behind a troubled portfolio, which had been refinanced before his departure, giving the impression that it was in better shape than it actually was.

Finally, in late 1995 Corposol's management was finally challenged with the arrival of Luis Fernando Tobón Cambas, an independent thinker and former Citibank executive. Tobón had been on the team that conducted the original feasibility studies to acquire Finansol. He played a key role in the restructuring of the institutions at the beginning stages of the crisis. Six months later, in March 1996, Tobón resigned to take the position of president at Banco Superior, a leading Colombian bank.

María Eugenia Iglesias became the fourth president of Finansol in March 1996. She accepted the position because she knew Tobón well and was interested in the social impact of the institution. She had also participated in the feasibility study to acquire the CFC and understood the precarious state of Finansol's portfolio when she took over. After overseeing the successful recapitalization of the organization, Iglesias resigned in August 1997 to make way for the organization's next phase.

José Manuel Montaño became the fifth president of Finansol in July 1997. He had held distinguished positions in the most important financial institutions in Colombia for twenty years, followed by nearly two years at FUNDES, before accepting the position at the institution now called FINAMERICA. Montaño turned around the institution's field operations and implemented a strict system of checks and balances between the board and management, enabling FINAMERICA to recover from the crisis.

Germán Contreras succeeded Montaño as president of FINAMERICA in August 2001. Contreras had been on the FINAMERICA board of directors since 1996 and was an executive at IFI for a decade before becoming the sixth president of FINAMERICA. With over thirty years of experience in Colombia's financial sector and a sound understanding of the institution itself, Contreras's focus is to bring the institution to profitability while broadening the client base to include the very poor microentrepreneurs that comprised Corposol's original target market.

## The Board of Directors

The inability of Finansol's board of directors to prevent the institutional crisis was due to the weak structural relationship between the Corposol and Finansol boards. Finansol's statutes mandated that majority control of its board must always remain with Corposol, the primary shareholder. This governance structure was fundamentally flawed because it placed the decision-making power of a for-profit institution in the hands of an NGO. Their differing missions and responsibilities were inherently at odds.

With five Finansol board seats occupied by Corposol representatives, the Finansol board played only a nominal role in governance of its own institution. Furthermore, with no rotation of the presidency of Finansol's board—Alvaro Arango always held the position—there was a lack of new opinions to challenge the status quo. Given his daily meetings with Giraldo and his dual position as president of Corposol's board, Arango was unable to consider Finansol's best interests at all times. Especially in key events leading to the Corposol crisis, Finansol board members did not exercise their power to override the decisions of management as they should have. When the Finansol board finally took action and demanded that the recovery of doubtful loans become a priority, in October 1995, it was too late to save Corposol.

## WAS THE BAILOUT WORTH IT?

The Finansol board realized that the failure of the CFC would hurt its clients in particular and the microfinance sector in general. But was spending US$11 million and countless person-hours worth the salvation of the apparently capsizing institution?

After five years of the "new" FINAMERICA, the organization has only been profitable one year (1998). Its poor profitability has been due largely to the losses the institution absorbed from the crisis and a small margin due to interest rate caps in an environment of deep recession. Still, FINAMERICA's year-end 2001 loan portfolio was only equivalent to Finansol's 1994 levels. Critics maintain that the cost of salvaging the institution was substantially higher than starting a new institution from scratch. Additionally, Finansol's public image underwent irreparable damage, as evidenced by a donor community still hesitant to support FINAMERICA to this day.

It must also be noted, however, that the crisis came at a critical time in the burgeoning microfinance industry. A failure of Finansol—the second regulated MFI in Latin America—might have convinced others that the commercial approach to microfinance was ineffective. ACCION International and other shareholders were committed to rebuilding Finansol because they believed that the implicit cost of its failure would be much greater than the rescue costs. Furthermore, despite the declining portfolio quality, forty thousand small-business owners depended on Finansol's financial services to maintain their businesses. Taking away their source of funding would have been detrimental to the individual businesses, as there were few alternative microlenders that could have replaced Finansol. Furthermore, the termination of Finansol might have precluded clients from trusting the integrity of subsequent microfinance institutions, further damaging the future of microfinance in Colombia.

## LESSONS FOR OTHER
## COMMERCIAL MICROFINANCE INSTITUTIONS

In hindsight, a clear set of factors contributed to Corposol's downfall. Yet during the critical years when steps might have been taken to identify and halt the institutional and operational weaknesses, necessary improvements were not made. The following summary suggests lessons that can be learned from Corposol's experience so that other commercial MFIs can avoid the same mistakes.

### Lesson One:
### Increase the Autonomy of the Regulated Institution

The relationship between Corposol and Finansol was structurally flawed. Corposol, the NGO, retained the credit officers and maintained control over disbursement decisions, while Finansol, the financial institution, served only as a booking and financing agent. Additionally, Corposol management controlled the board of Finansol. These factors prevented Finansol from controlling loan placement and from making independent organizational decisions.

The Corposol experience suggests that the NGO should be responsible for training and administration only. Regulated institutions should have control over the lending and collection processes, as they are ultimately responsible to the Superintendency and their shareholders for the quality of the portfolio.

### Lesson Two:
### Consistent Performance Objectives Should be Applied

Corposol's management imposed performance objectives upon loan officers and other staff without consistent grounding in past performance as a measure of feasibility. Loan officers became resentful as performance objectives became increasingly unrealistic.

To avoid uncertainty and ambiguity among staff, MFIs should define and apply consistent, attainable, and transparent performance evaluation criteria. By clearly linking positive performance to rewards and employing analysis of poor performance as input for feedback and subsequent follow-up, employees will take ownership of their own performance. Furthermore, managers should pursue a system of hiring, firing, and promoting based on clearly defined, predictable, and objective parameters to ensure staff motivation and accountability.

### Lesson Three:
### Manage Portfolio Growth

Corposol's mandate for growth was effective when the organization was small. Yet as the institution grew, structures were not put in place to accommodate growth. This caused gaps in information flow, inhibiting good decision-making and limiting the effectiveness of middle management. For example, training new loan officers had been a priority in the first several years of Corposol's existence, but the practice became increasingly rare as the rate of hiring new staff increased.

Pursuing a growth rate consistent with demand and institutional capabilities will allow MFIs to mitigate risks related to institutional growth (Churchill 1997). MFIs should not only be vigilant of the number of loan officers required to serve the client base, but also the number of new loan officers the existing supervisory capacity can handle.

## Lesson Four:
### Design Channels for Board Intervention

Finansol's board did not act quickly when it had misgivings about Corposol's risky lending activities and management decisions. Furthermore, the high representation of Corposol's board on the Finansol board created a governing body that did not always consider the best interests of the regulated institution.

To ensure the proper functioning of governance, the board of directors of the regulated institution must be able to question managerial decisions. All representatives should have equal authority and feel empowered to voice their concerns and to make suggestions. As part of their governance duties, board members are obliged to exercise independent judgment and participate actively in strategic decisions (see Chapter 11).

## Lesson Five:
### Effectively Manage Product Diversification

Without soliciting the opinions of their clients or loan officers, Corposol began offering new financial products with little evidence of sufficient demand. Furthermore, Corposol expanded products and services without the appropriate supply channels or business plans to deliver the services. Product diversification appeared to offer new avenues for growth while meeting a broad range of client needs. Yet the structure and policies that governed the new products encouraged loan officers to give multiple loans to the same clients, augmenting the risk of over-indebtedness and contributing to portfolio instability.

Before developing new initiatives to meet institutional objectives, organizations should analyze markets to ensure that sufficient client demand exists, while keeping the clients' best interests—repayment and debt capacity—in mind. Time should be dedicated to develop, pilot, monitor and adjust new initiatives. Management should provide support to each functional area preparing for new responsibilities associated with new products.

### Lesson Six:
### Resolve Corporate Culture Differences
### Between the Regulated Institution and the NGO

Employees of the nonprofit Corposol had different ideas about microlending than did the staff of the for-profit Finansol. Corposol viewed the organization's purpose as primarily social, while Finansol had a greater focus on the financial aspect of microfinance. These divergent mentalities often generated resentment between the two institutions.

Some element of conflict is inevitable when an organization is created or reshaped from two different organizational cultures. However, communication and training can minimize the negative perceptions and encourage employees to learn from each other's strengths and diverse backgrounds. MFIs should identify sources of variation in institutional culture; recognize that any shift in strategy, operations, or personnel can affect institutional culture; and develop a strategy to adapt to those changes. Above all, organizations should communicate frequently with all levels of staff.

### Lesson Seven:
### Commit to Transparency

Corposol and Finansol unethically swapped the loan portfolio to avoid detection of poorly performing Finansol loans by the Superintendency of Banks. At its most extreme, Finansol sold its bad loans to Corposol the day before the end of the month (when reporting was done) and bought them back a few days later.

By committing to transparent financial management, MFIs can ensure ongoing quality control and long-term sustainability, reducing the temptation to engage in fraudulent and unethical practices.

### Lesson Eight:
### Avoid Centralized Control

Strong charismatic leadership set the tone for Corposol in its early days. As it grew, however, upper management exercised its power without soliciting advice from other management or staff.

Because a weak or subservient staff will undermine the goals of the institution in the long term, organizations should develop strong middle managers and empower them to make real decisions. Although parameters should be established to guide operations, some degree of staff autonomy should be encouraged.

### Lesson Nine:
### Focus on the Mission, Not Public Expectations

Corposol's positive public image initially inspired employees and attracted new clients while building the credibility necessary to access funding. But as Corposol's image grew rosier than its actual performance, protection of that image led to misrepresentation of statistics and refinancing to hide portfolio deterioration. This pattern was destructive in that it valued image above substance, which subsequently affected lending behavior.

Exerting excessive pressure on field operations to succeed without adjusting performance objectives and lending methodologies to changes in the market may result in compromised lending standards. Organizations should celebrate success while continually redefining success in relation to the realities of the economic and competitive environments.

## SUMMARY

Entry into the commercial arena is a wise decision for many microfinance institutions that want to expand their reach, provide better services to their clients, and access commercial financing. However, as institutions pursue these lofty goals, lessons from Corposol and Finansol can provide guidance, helping them avoid the pitfalls of commercialization, such as an ineffective institutional structure and a flawed system of governance.

## NOTES

1. For the purposes of this chapter, we will refer to the nonprofit organization as Corposol with the understanding that, from its inception until 1993, the name of the organization was Actuar Bogotá.

2. Compañia de Financiamiento Comercial (CFC-Actuar), "Estudio de Factibilidad" (May 1993).

3. BancoSol in Bolivia was the first MFI in Latin America to be commercialized when it became a bank in 1992.

4. Growth was an operating premise that existed from Corposol's inception. At different moments in the institution's tenure, that mandate could be attributed to Corposol's desire to achieve significant social outreach, its need to demonstrate its ability to attract donors or establish credibility with the financial sector, its attempt to achieve sustainable scale, and its aspiration for public recognition of its success. As time went on, Corposol's management pushed for "growth at all costs," leading to poor lending procedures and burned-out loan officers. This mentality was entrenched in the organization by the time Finansol was acquired.

5. When the 1994 loan portfolio was examined in later years, it was discovered that many of the same clients were receiving loans from several product lines within Gruposol. In fact, some of the performance indicators reported at the time were inflated by as much as 30 percent.

6. Calmeadow is a Canadian nonprofit charity with over fifteen years of experience in microfinance. Based in Toronto, Calmeadow focuses its efforts on mobilizing and managing capital for direct investment in developing microfinance institutions.

7. ACCION International conducts CAMEL evaluations (based on a similarly named assessment tool developed by U.S. bank regulators) to assess the financial and managerial soundness of its microfinance affiliates in Latin America.

8. Asset quality was measured by delinquent portfolio as a percentage of outstanding portfolio and as a percentage of equity. Efficiency was measured in terms of both operational costs and physical productivity of loan officers.

9. The ACCION lending methodology aims to meet the needs of the poor while paying for itself. Loans are provided on a commercial basis and are for short periods, as few as two months. Loans start small—as low as US$100—to build confidence and a repayment record. Clients become eligible for larger loans as earlier loans are repaid (step lending). Clients with no collateral borrow in solidarity groups of three to five people, in which each member cross-guarantees the others' loans.

**9.**

# Creating a Microfinance Bank in Peru

## Acción Comunitaria del Perú's Transformation to Mibanco

### Anita Campion, Elizabeth Dunn, and J. Gordon Arbuckle Jr.

## FROM NGO TO COMMERCIAL BANK

Political and economic challenges and changing regulatory options characterized the transformation of the Peruvian NGO Acción Communitaria del Perú (ACP) into the commercial bank Mibanco in May 1998. As Peru's first commercial bank dedicated to microfinance, Mibanco offers a variety of savings products as well as housing, consumer, and microbusiness loans. Its yellow, pink, and green signs stand out in poor neighborhoods throughout Lima and beyond, with twenty-six branches and an outstanding portfolio of $59.6 million and nearly seventy-eight thousand active clients at year-end 2001.

ACP began operations as a nonprofit NGO on January 13, 1969, launched by a group of businesspeople with the objective of creating development opportunities for low-income Peruvians. Until the 1980s

Much of the first part of this chapter is extracted from the findings of the case study presented in Anita Campion and Victoria White, *Institutional Metamorphosis: Transformation of Microfinance NGOs into Regulated Financial Institutions*, MicroFinance Network Occasional Paper No. 4 (2000). Much of the second part of this chapter is based upon Elizabeth Dunn and J. Gordon Arbuckle Jr., "The Impacts of Microcredit: A Case Study from Peru," AIMS Project Report (Washington, D.C.: USAID/G/EG/MD, Management Systems International, 2001).

ACP operated like many NGOs at that time, working on several aspects of community development, with projects such as community savings, housing construction, and education.

In the early 1980s ACP developed its first long-term strategic plan focused on microenterprise development in response to a survey showing that access to credit and business training were the greatest needs of poor entrepreneurs. From 1982 through 1998 ACP provided these services to microentrepreneurs through a credit program called Programa Progreso. ACP targeted microenterprises in the capital city of Lima, which was experiencing astounding population growth due to migration from rural areas of Peru.[1] Over its sixteen-year history, Progreso consistently experienced rapid growth, temporarily stunted only by economic and financial crises in the mid 1980s.

## Interrupted Growth (1983–1989)

ACP grew to become the largest microfinanace institution (MFI) in Latin America in 1986. By the end of 1987 ACP's Progreso project had reached a level of annual disbursements in excess of US$5.8 million to nine thousand microentrepreneurs. Economic crisis and hyperinflation in 1988, however, nearly erased all the advances Progreso had made. Economic policy and the resulting hyperinflation were not conducive to providing microcredit. From 1985 to 1990 regulations prohibited the issuance of loans in foreign currencies. The usury rate was lowered to 32 percent in 1987, while inflation skyrocketed to more than 7,000 percent. By the end of 1988 two of ACP's four existing branches were closed, and its loan portfolio had withered to US$99,000.

## Expansion of ACP (1990–1998)

With the installation of Alberto Fujimori's government in 1990, a series of structural changes was implemented to liberalize the financial sector. Usury laws were abolished, and the government targeted the microenterprise sector in its plans to promote economic growth. A separate microenterprise division was created within the Superintendency of Banks (SBS), further demonstrating the government's commitment to microenterprise.

Along with an improved regulatory environment, economic stability and lower inflation returned to Peru, allowing ACP to begin a second growth phase. This period was marked by ACP's strong drive to increase its loan portfolio and accumulate equity to protect itself against future instability. By the end of 1995 ACP had an outstanding loan portfolio of US$6.8 million and 19,100 clients, charging an effective annual interest rate of 125 percent. Inflation came down from 7,650 percent in 1990 to just 10 percent in 1995, allowing ACP to quickly recapitalize and accumulate net equity of more than US$5.5 million by the end of the year. At the time of its transformation to Mibanco on May 4, 1998, ACP had 32,000 clients and an outstanding loan portfolio exceeding US$14 million. At that time ACP's director, Manuel Montoya, estimated that the institution reached only 2 percent of Peru's microenterprise market, which totaled approximately 600,000 microenterprises in Lima alone.[2]

### Transformation Plans

ACP's transformation plans evolved with Peru's changing regulatory and political environment. Institutional transformation was considered the only way to expand services to Peru's largely unserved microenterprise market. An estimated 60 percent of Peru's work force is employed in the microenterprise sector. In the 1990s donor funds, which had been readily available for the startup of microenterprise programs in the past, began drying up. Institutional transformation would allow the MFI access to new sources of capital, including US$16 million of Inter-American Development Bank (IDB) funds being channeled through the Corporación Financiera de Desarrollo (COFIDE), a second-tier financial institution that onlends exclusively to regulated financial institutions.

ACP's board believed that being regulated would force the MFI to improve its financial transparency and accountability. They hoped that becoming part of the formal financial system would help uncover inefficiencies and identify cost-cutting measures. ACP also viewed transformation as a way to institutionalize its commitment to self-sufficiency.

### The Financiera Option

In 1994 ACP explored the possibility of becoming a financiera, a type of formal financial institution that would allow the institution to collect term deposits. The minimum capital requirements of a *financiera* were US$3 million, substantially less than the amount required to create a full-service bank. In terms of ACP's desired future product offerings, the inability to offer passbook savings was the only long-term limitation to the *financiera* structure. Despite commissioning a pre-feasibility study and an extensive client survey, ACP never formally presented its *financiera* proposal to the SBS because changes in banking laws presented a new transformation possibility: the EDPYME.

## Entidades de Desarrollo para la Pequeña y Microempresa (EDPYME)

In December 1994 the SBS created new laws to encourage the transformation of NGOs into regulated financial entities called Entidades de Desarrollo para la Pequeña y Microempresa (EDPYMEs or small business or microenterprise development institutions). Minimum capital requirement is only US$256,000. EDPYMEs are not allowed to collect savings deposits in any form. The government designed the EDPYME laws as an interim step for NGOs to grow eventually into fully regulated financial intermediaries, while familiarizing regulators with microfinance.

This cautious and gradual approach to transformation appealed to ACP because it did not plan to mobilize savings deposits in the short term. The EDPYME option would allow ACP access to additional bank funding and special rediscount credit facilities from the IDB that were unavailable to *financieras*. ACP conducted a legal review, a feasibility study, and an operational plan, and identified potential investors over the course of eighteen months. In October 1996 ACP's proposal to establish an EDPYME was approved by the SBS, but operations had not yet begun when a third possibility arose.

## The Peruvian Government's Microfinance Challenge

In a public address in July 1996, President Fujimori challenged the Peruvian formal financial sector to create a bank for microentrepreneurs. Although the traditional banks were interested in microfinance, they preferred to reach the microenterprise sector through their existing institutions rather than to create new specialized institutions. The president, unsatisfied with this response, named a commission to oversee the development of a microfinance bank. The government's objective was to create a competitive environment for microfinance institutions that would effectively serve microentrepreneurs on a large scale and at reasonable interest rates. Fujimori recognized microfinance as both economically and socially profitable, and therefore politically attractive.

Fujimori's administration acknowledged its lack of familiarity with microfinance and formed a technical committee of microfinance experts in the autumn of 1996 to carry out an IDB-funded study of what he referred to as a private-sector initiative. In February 1997 Fujimori attended the Microcredit Summit in Washington, D.C. There, in an effort to gain public recognition and support, he announced his commitment to create a microfinance bank in Peru.

As the largest microfinance NGO in Peru contemplating transformation, ACP was the obvious choice to become the country's first microfinance bank. ACP's decision to follow the government's plan of transformation was a calculated risk. While the government could offer support through the regulatory approval process and increased public awareness, there was legitimate concern that Mibanco would be confused with a public-sector effort. Neither banks nor government institutions have positive reputations with Peru's microentrepreneurs. In negotiating the agreement, ACCION International and ACP attempted to minimize the potential for future government intervention.

In April 1997 an agreement was reached between ACP, ACCION and ProFund to transform ACP into a microfinance bank.[3] The government agreed to facilitate the process but to hold no direct equity in the new institution. By July 1997 private-sector investors had been identified, which included two Peruvian banks, Banco Wiese and Banco de Crédito, and the partnership was announced publicly.

### The Creation of Mibanco

In July 1997 a new feasibility study was conducted on the possibility of transforming ACP into a multipurpose bank named Mibanco. With this, ACP was agreeing to become the most regulated type of financial institution, with the highest level of minimum capital requirement (US$5.6 million). This structure, however, would allow the institution to offer passbook savings accounts, a financial service that the institution had hoped to provide its clients in the long run.

The feasibility study took approximately five months to develop. The proposed concept of transformation was to transfer the majority of the employees and lending operations of ACP into the new bank, while leaving a few employees with the NGO to continue providing business-development services to microentrepreneurs. The objective was to find ways in which ACP and Mibanco could complement each other in serving the microenterprise sector.

Regulatory approval by the Peruvian SBS consisted then, as now, of a two-step process: (1) approval of the proposed institution's financial plan and board of directors, and (2) approval of the institution's operational plan. The financial plan includes a detailed financial history and projections, along with information on investors and their ability to satisfy the minimum capital requirements. The operational plan explains how the business will operate and presents an organizational chart and details of the various levels of responsibility. For approval of the second step, the institution must have proof of its paid-in capital and be registered publicly. The Peruvian government's involvement was decisive in expediting Mibanco's regulatory approval.[4] The feasibility study presented to the SBS was approved in November 1997, thereby concluding the first step of the process.

## Transformation Process

The transformation process took one year, with most of the time spent discussing the organizational and financial aspects of the shareholders' agreements necessary to create a bank. The majority of the operational transformation, however, occurred in just six months, from initial regulatory approval in November 1997 to Mibanco's official opening in May 1998.

### Organizational Transformation

As part of the transformation process, ACP contracted a banking technical advisor to work with management to develop and implement a strategic plan, including an organizational framework and budget. In preparing for the transformation, ACP identified investors and determined the governance structure for the new bank.

#### Investor Identification

ACP's board of directors identified and negotiated with potential investors in Mibanco. Representing both the private and nonprofit sectors, Mibanco's investors included ACP (60 percent), ProFund S.A. (19 percent) ACCION International's Gateway Fund[5] (7 percent), Banco de Crédito and Banco Wiese (each at 6.6 percent).

Together, the five investors subscribed US$14 million of capital, of which US$5.6 million represented the required paid-in capital. Additionally, a government-promoted plan was written into the bylaws to offer Mibanco shares to interested clients. The plan is to sell preferred stock of US$1 million to client shareholders at some time in the future. However, given Mibanco's high level of capitalization, this is not currently a priority.

In 1999 the Corporación Andina de Fomento (CAF) became an additional Mibanco shareholder, owning 3.8 percent of Mibanco's total equity, which exceeded US$13 million at the end of 1999.[6] As of June 2000, Mibanco still had a low debt-to-equity ratio of 1.25:1, an extremely conservative gearing ratio that will permit additional leverage in the future.[7]

### Governance Structure

Mibanco's shares are designed so that each initial owner has at least one seat on the board.[8] The ACP board members selected owners with the desirable mix of business, banking, legal, investment, and microfinance expertise. The nine-member board is comprised of five representatives from ACP and one representative each from ProFund, ACCION, Banco de Crédito and Banco Wiese.[9] In recognition of the government's support in creating a microfinance bank, President Fujimori was invited to send one non-voting representative to participate in board meetings for Mibanco's first two years of operation.

There are several potential conflicts of interest inherent in Mibanco's board. The primary conflict lies in the fact that the NGO, ACP, maintains majority control with its 60 percent ownership of Mibanco. Additionally, five of the ACP's eight board members are also Mibanco board members. Manuel Montoya, director and CEO of Mibanco, considers that any possible conflict is eliminated by defining ACP as a nonfinancial-services institution and Mibanco as a financial institution. The board members representing ACP on the Mibanco board hold no personal equity in either institution. This potentially reduces the intended benefits of private ownership, such as increased accountability, profitability, and access to additional sources of capital.

Mibanco's private-sector investors, Banco de Crédito and Banco Wiese, are the two largest commercial banks in Peru and, as competitors, represent a possible conflict of interest. At this point there is little conflict because the shareholder participation of each is small and the microfinance market is far from saturated. Currently, the two banks' board representatives provide unique insights into the formal financial sector in Peru. In the future, however, competition will likely increase, and the banks' investments in Mibanco, which represent a very small portion of their overall holdings, could hinder the two board members from providing adequate oversight and fulfilling their duty of loyalty to Mibanco (see Chapter 11).

## Financial Transformation

In conjunction with ACP's organizational transformation, the investors considered the financial aspects of transformation, including the transfer of assets and liabilities from ACP to Mibanco, regulatory implications, and access to new funding sources.

### Transfer of Assets and Liabilities

Mibanco assumed ownership of ACP's loan portfolio as loans renewed, circumventing the need for an official transfer of the loan portfolio. Mibanco agreed to administer ACP's existing loan portfolio at no cost for the first year. The loan portfolio to be renewed by Mibanco was estimated at US$10 million. The agreement stated that ACP would continue to receive the interest payments on all preexisting loans until they came due. Because most ACP loans had three- to four-month terms, 80 to 90 percent of the portfolio was fully transferred to Mibanco by September 1998. The remaining loans transferred by April 30, 1999, the end of Mibanco's first year in operation.

Mibanco paid ACP a premium of US$1 million in cash for access to ACP's client base and US$3.6 million on credit for fixed assets. Through a promissory note, Mibanco agreed to pay ACP for the fixed assets at an annual interest rate of 19.5 percent. Donor limitations on the transfer of assets did not present a problem, as ACP retained control of US$6 million in assets, far exceeding the US$1.8 million in grants the NGO had received since its inception. Grant limitations on the use of the initial funds required that they remain in a like institution, but most such limitations had expired by 1990. No liabilities were transferred in the transformation process except one loan fund of US$500,000 that had previously been lent to ACP by CAF for its microlending operations; it was redirected to Mibanco.

### Regulatory Implications

As a regulated financial institution, Mibanco is subject to many legal requirements that were not applicable to ACP. For example, Mibanco must pay a 30 percent tax on net income, whereas ACP was tax exempt.[10] As a bank, Mibanco is subject to loan-provisioning requirements, which are stricter than they were under ACP and more conservative than those required by the SBS.

Mibanco is required to keep 7 percent of its domestic-denominated deposits on reserve at the central bank and 20 percent of its international-denominated deposits on reserve (of which 13 percent must be kept on reserve at the central bank and the remaining 6 percent can be kept as cash in the vault).

As a microfinance NGO, ACP was required by the SBS to report weekly on donations received, number of clients, and account balances. As a regulated bank, Mibanco must complete all of the following of the SBS's bank-reporting requirements (Rock 1997, 73):

- Daily report on interest charged
- Semimonthly report on reserve position
- Monthly financial statement
- Monthly report on effective equity level and risk-weighted assets
- Monthly report on principal debtors
- Quarterly report classifying debt quality to establish credit rating
- Annual report

In response to regulatory requirements, Mibanco upgraded its security systems to include guards, protective doors and walls, and new safes in all its branches. The SBS requires an annual external audit conducted at the bank's expense. This is not a requirement of microfinance NGOs in Peru, although ACP did conduct annual external audits. The SBS also requires banks to have an internal audit department. ACP formerly had one person who performed this function but who was not a professional auditor. Mibanco's new internal audit department has three internal auditors and reports directly to the board.

### Access to New Sources of Funds

As a formal financial institution, Mibanco has access to a range of sources of loan capital. Through the second-tier financial institution COFIDE, Mibanco has various credit facilities available in the local currency (with effective annual interest rates ranging from 13.27 percent to 21.50 percent), from which it was accessing US$14.3 million at year-end 2001. In addition, the International Bank of Luxembourg (IBL) in conjunction with a French bank, AXA, launched a pilot project (the DMCF—BlueOrchard Debt USD), from which Mibanco received US$1 million at six-month LIBOR (London InterBank Offering Rate) plus 4 percent in January 2001. CAF has a bridge fund, from which it has lent US$1.5 million to Mibanco since the transformation at an effective rate averaging 4.9 percent per year.

Mibanco's funding sources have also included a four-year US$2.9 million credit line from the Agencia para la Cooperación Internaciónal de España. In October 2001, Banco de Crédito extended a US$3.2 million, three-year loan with a 50 percent guarantee from ACCION's Latin America Bridge Fund to Mibanco. The International Finance Corporation (IFC), the private-sector arm of the World Bank Group, provided a five-year US$5 million loan at six-month LIBOR plus 5.75 percent to Mibanco in 2002 to support its portfolio and expansion plans. Other sources of funding include a US$800,000 loan from Stichting Triodos Doen, a US$300,000 loan from Stichting Hivos-Triodos Fonds, and a loan from Fondo Mivivienda for US$800,000.

Transformation to a commercial bank grants Mibanco the right to mobilize savings deposits. To draw on this stable source of capital, Mibanco began offering passbook savings in July 2000. At year-end 2001, over seventy thousand microentrepreneurs were accessing passbook savings through Mibanco. Other savings products include time deposits, compulsory savings, and current accounts.

## Operational Transformation

Mibanco's staff implemented the majority of the organization's operational transformation in the six months prior to the opening of Mibanco. This time frame was extremely short, considering the numerous changes required in staffing, systems, and processes. Mibanco would have preferred more time to develop new products or services before opening its doors, so that existing clients would see immediate benefits.

### Staff Changes

Mibanco's strategic plan proposed that the bank designate a mix of NGO and bank managers that could provide the security of a formal bank while catering to the microenterprise market. In the past, community-development professionals had managed ACP, with three senior management positions under the managing director. Mibanco broadened its organizational chart to include five senior management positions under the managing director: finance, human resources, operations, business management, and development. In January 1998, in preparation for the transition, management let go fifty employees deemed poor performers. Many of those released found employment at higher salaries in traditional banks that were adding microfinance departments, which led to the voluntary departure of additional staff.

Despite these employee reductions, the total number of staff increased from 235 employees to 260 from December 1997 to September 1998. The new hires included several traditional bankers, especially within upper management. Due to some unanticipated staff departures, upper management became heavily represented by the traditional banking sector.

From the beginning ACP had an informal management style in which information flowed freely and managers met with all staff to discuss changes before implementing them. The bankers, however, formalized the communication style, causing employees to feel that they were less involved in the transformation decisions. This lowered employee morale and increased the polarization between former bankers and former NGO staff.

Mibanco's managing director and the board quickly recognized and rectified the situation. By November 1998 Mibanco had restructured its key management positions, resulting in the same balance of traditional bankers and NGO staff as the bank's original structure. Now, former ACP employees hold the key positions that require an intimate understanding of microfinance and that have the most contact with branch staff.

Like many MFIs, Mibanco is now facing the challenge of developing strong branch managers. Although loan officers tend to have strong interpersonal and analytical skills, few have the ability to manage employees or operate a profit center effectively. Mibanco is working with ACCION International to develop a leadership program to groom potential loan officers for eventual promotion to management.

### Systems

Prior to its official opening, Mibanco identified and began implementing a new computer system. To avoid duplicating previous efforts, Mibanco bought software used by other banks and adapted it to fit its needs. Management selected two systems, SIAF, which manages general banking operations at headquarters, and FINESSE, platform software that tracks loan approvals, disbursements, loan management, monitoring, and collections at the branch level. To accommodate multiple currencies and regulatory reporting requirements, Mibanco revised ACP's accounting system and purchased new accounting software compatible with SIAF. The total systems implementation cost to Mibanco was approximately US$1.5 million, which includes about US$50,000 to adapt the accounting system.

### Processes

One of the lessons Mibanco learned in its transformation is the unique nature of the relationship between the bank and its clients. Mibanco experienced some difficulties as a result of hiring a traditional banker for the role of microenterprise director. Lacking microfinance expertise, Mibanco's initial microenterprise director began to implement procedural changes that were inconsistent with microfinance methodology. Clients temporarily perceived these changes as diminishing customer service. Most of the changes have since been reversed.

Under ACP's Progreso credit program, each loan required a new loan application and review. With the help of ACCION, Mibanco implemented a new loan-review process with two loan evaluation methods and more quantitative information than the ACP process. All first loans undergo a thorough evaluation, known as the Type A evaluation. For subsequent loans, clients with an excellent repayment history receive the simpler, less restrictive Type B evaluation, which allows for faster loan processing. Clients whose repayment practices become less than excellent must again submit to a Type A review. This system provides better tracking of poor performers and rescheduled loans, and ensures better customer service for excellent clients.

For a short time after the transformation, the turnaround time for first loans increased from three to five days. This was because all clients had to undergo the Type A loan evaluation. Now that Mibanco has gone through its consolidation period, first loans are processed more quickly.

### Training

Mibanco has maintained ACP's interactive approach to training, spending more than US$180,000 in one year preparing employees for the transformation. All employees were trained in how to use the new computer system, and loan officers were trained in the new loan-review process, loan sales, and collections. Special emphasis was placed on training loan officers in loan sales, helping them overcome a fear of or distaste for selling. The new sales training instructs loan officers to pursue an active sales strategy in which they help clients understand how a loan could potentially benefit their businesses and increase their income. Additionally, loan officers learned to conduct the technical and financial analyses required by the new, more quantitative loan-evaluation method.

In preparation for the transformation, ACP implemented a new loan-officer orientation system that combines both classroom time and fieldwork. This process, now in use, ensures that the bank hires only candidates who enjoy working with the informal sector. Self-selection is encouraged; the orientation usually begins with sixteen candidates and ends with only seven or eight qualified trainees.

### Products

Mibanco began with only one type of product, working capital loans. Until October 1998 the loan product was exactly the same as the one ACP had offered, at a 125 percent annual compounded effective interest rate. In October 1998 the bank diversified interest rates according to loan size and credit history. The loan product has a maximum loan term of twelve months, with weekly, bimonthly, or monthly repayment intervals, and is available as an individual or solidarity-group loan.

Since its creation, Mibanco has introduced three new loan types: consumer loans, a fixed-asset loan to purchase industrial machines, and another to construct or repair buildings, such as modernization of a small factory or workshop. Mibanco also collects time deposits, current accounts, and offers foreign exchange services.

### Client Transitioning

In transitioning the existing loan portfolio from ACP, Mibanco renewed only 80 percent of it. Mibanco considered the remaining 20 percent non-creditworthy because of bad credit histories or over-indebtedness as identified by the new, more-restrictive loan evaluation process.

Mibanco communicated the transformation to clients through letters mailed to each customer, verbal communications from employees, and posters that described Mibanco's commitment to serving microentrepreneurs. Radio and newspaper advertisements aimed to attract new clients announced the transformation publicly. The government attracted free media attention, which was both positive and negative, given people's attitudes toward government involvement.

To ensure quality customer service throughout the transformation, Mibanco held client focus groups, offered incentive programs for client referrals, extended branch hours, and added cashiers.

Although there is some understanding about the organizational changes associated with commercialization, there is still very little information about what happens to clients during the commercialization process. The following section considers how ACP's clients may have been affected during the institution's process of transformation in becoming Mibanco. In particular, this section investigates whether any shifts occurred in the client target during the transitional period immediately following com-mercialization.

## CLIENTS AND COMMERCIALIZATION

Based on an analysis of data collected before and immediately after ACP's transformation to Mibanco, there is some surprising evidence of a shift in the client profile during the transition period toward poorer cli-ents. This could be interpreted as evidence that commercialization may not necessarily lead to mission drift, as many skeptics fear. These client-level findings could, however, simply reveal more about the transitional period associated with commercialization than they do about the long-term effects of commercialization on clients. In addition, there is anec-dotal evidence of increased transaction costs for clients and strains in customer relations associated with the transformation. These findings should be interpreted with caution, however, as they are based on data collected for USAID's Assessing the Impact of Microenterprise Services (AIMS) project, and not specifically for the purposes of this book.[11]

### *Data and Analysis*

### *The Original Impact Study*

The AIMS baseline survey was conducted in September 1997 and included a random sample of 400 ACP clients and a control group of 301 similar entrepreneurs who were not clients of ACP.[12] The second round of the survey was conducted in September 1999. Although the data were collected for the specific purpose of evaluating the impact of microcredit services, there were two coincidental events that increased the relevance of the data to understanding the effects of commercialization on clients:

- The clients of ACP became the clients of Mibanco in May 1998, an event that occurred between the two rounds of the survey; and
- Of the 301 entrepreneurs in the original control group for the im-pact study, twenty-three became new clients of Mibanco after the transformation and before the second round of the survey.

In addition to the survey data, the AIMS impact assessment included case-study data from in-depth interviews with clients in 1998 and 1999.

This qualitative information provides insights into clients' experiences during the transformation process and provides several examples that help to explain the survey findings.

### Adapting the Data to This Study

In studying the transformation of ACP to Mibanco, two types of new clients emerged: those who became new clients prior to the transformation and those who became new clients immediately after the transformation:

- The ACP *new entrants* are 220 individuals who became first-time clients of ACP in the fifteen months leading up to the baseline survey (June 1996 to September 1997).
- The *Mibanco new entrants* are twenty-three individuals who became first-time clients of Mibanco in the fifteen months immediately after the transformation of ACP to Mibanco and prior to the second round of the survey (June 1998 to September 1999).[13]

### Evidence of Client Shift

The Mibanco new-entrant group and the ACP new-entrant group were compared on several household-level and enterprise-level variables, including gender, income, poverty level, housing, income diversification, salary, location of microenterprise, business sector, age of business, type of business (formal, informal, home-based), license, assets, and revenue. The characteristics of the two groups are reported in Table 9.1 in terms of mean values and percentages for the thirteen variables. As can be seen in the table, the Mibanco new entrants differed significantly from the ACP new entrants in three variables: poverty, zone, and sector. In addition, the groups had marginally significant differences in three other variables: income, diversification, and assets. The two groups were similar for the remaining variables.

### Shift in Poverty Levels

The most interesting finding was that the Mibanco new entrants had a significantly higher average poverty rate than the ACP new entrants.[14] Fifty-seven percent of the Mibanco new entrants were poor, while only

**Table 9.1: Characteristics of ACP and Mibanco New Entrants**

| Variable | ACP New Entrants (n=220) | Mibanco New Entrants (n=23) | Significant (p value) |
|---|---|---|---|
| Gender (% male) | 35% | 30% | .694 |
| Income (in soles) | 6,075 | 4,383 | .111* |
| Poverty (% poor) | 26% | 57% | .011** |
| Housing (% own) | 86% | 87% | .937 |
| Diversification (% with more than one income) | 81% | 91% | .140* |
| Salary (% with) | 54% | 61% | .514 |
| Zone (% modern) | 23% | 9% | .043** |
| Sector (% comm.'l) | 76% | 95% | .002** |
| Age of micro-enterprise (yrs.) | 6.09 | 5.67 | .616 |
| Premises (% formal) | 32% | 43% | .318 |
| License (% with) | 55% | 57% | .853 |
| Assets (in soles) | 5,952 | 2,770 | .121* |
| Monthly gross revenue (in soles) | 5,178 | 6,702 | .519 |

*Difference is marginally significant at the .10<p<.15 level.
**Difference is statistically significant at the p<.10 level.

26 percent of the ACP new clients had household expenditures that fell below the national poverty line.

The higher poverty rate among Mibanco new entrants is consistent with the findings related to per-capita income, diversification, and enterprise fixed assets. The mean per-capita income of Mibanco new entrants was about 28 percent lower than the mean for ACP new entrants. In addition, Mibanco new entrants had somewhat higher levels of income diversification, with 91 percent having more than one source of income, compared with 81 percent of ACP new entrants. Finally, the mean value of enterprise fixed assets for Mibanco new entrants was less than half that for ACP new entrants. Although all three of these differences can be theoretically associated with the higher poverty levels among the Mibanco new entrants, these three findings are only marginally significant and should be interpreted with caution.[15]

## Shifts in Credit Terms

Although both groups of clients—ACP new entrants and Mibanco new entrants—received the same type of working-capital loans, there were some shifts in the terms of the loans received by the two groups. Six credit-related variables were measured, and differences between the two groups were tested using independent sample t-tests. As Table 9.2 indicates, there were statistically significant shifts toward longer loans and less frequent payments. The average loan length for the Mibanco new entrants was almost a month longer than for the ACP new entrants.

**Table 9.2: Credit Characteristics for Loans to ACP and Mibanco New Entrants**

| Variable | ACP New Entrants (n=220) | Mibanco New Entrants (n=23) | Significant (p value) |
|---|---|---|---|
| Amount of principal (in soles) | 1,316 | 1,182 | .475 |
| Loan length (in months) | 3.26 | 4.17 | .001* |
| Weekly payments | 26% | 9% | .015* |
| Biweekly payments | 54% | 36% | .089* |
| Monthly payments | 20% | 55% | .006* |
| Multiple loans | 19% | 17% | .884 |

*Difference is statistically significant at the p<.10 level.

### Clients' Perspectives on the Transition

In this section we draw from written transcripts of case-study interviews to explore clients' subjective perspectives on their relationships with the MFI before and after the transformation. The interviews were conducted in 1998 and 1999 with eleven ACP/Mibanco microfinance clients. The informants volunteered the examples provided here, as the interview protocol did not include any questions about the transformation specifically.

## Increased Transaction Costs

From the clients' perspectives, commercialization led to an increased emphasis on documenting repayment capacity and collateral, with clients reporting that they were adversely affected as they tried to comply with new requirements. One client specifically attributed this change to the transformation of ACP to Mibanco. She had always repaid her loans on time but, when she applied for a new loan, she was asked to provide documents that she did not have: "They just surprised us: now they have new personnel and one has to be documented. We thought it was strange, because we have worked [with ACP], and they're treating us as if we were new. . . . It's not just me; they're asking the same of everybody."

Another client, who had been borrowing from ACP for twenty years, had a loan disbursement delayed because of a late payment. Due to a combination of factors, including illness and substantial investments in the construction of a new market stall, the client overextended herself and missed one biweekly payment. Although she repaid the loan in full and on time, Mibanco lowered her loan ceiling from US$2,000 to US$1,200 and postponed disbursement of her next loan for twenty-two days. The client's husband, who is also her business partner, explained: "[We missed] a biweekly payment, but in two weeks we made both payments [at once] . . . so that they would give us [the next loan] more quickly, and in the end . . . they didn't give us [a loan right away]. It was hard to make two payments [at once]. . . . Instead of buying [inventory], I hurt myself." That their efforts to remain in good standing with Mibanco were not rewarded was frustrating for the couple, particularly because they had foregone profitable investment opportunities in order to pay their loan on time.

### Strained Client Relationships

As Mibanco adopted more stringent policies than those that existed under ACP, relationships with some clients became strained. The client described above was disappointed that Mibanco was not more understanding when she missed a payment. "I guess it's a punishment," she said. "But a client shouldn't be treated that way." Her husband added: "And despite having worked with Mibanco [ACP] for many years . . . since it began!" As a result of the delayed loan and lowered loan ceiling, she and her husband were considering other credit alternatives.

In another case Mibanco's efforts to document collateral drove a client away. Shortly after the transformation, the client, who had been borrowing from ACP for several years, was late on one or more payments. Although she repaid her entire loan on time, a credit agent visited her business to secure collateral for the next loan. The agent wanted the client to sign a notarized document giving Mibanco the right to several cases of goods in case of default. The client was offended: "My husband and I didn't like that, because it wasn't as if it was the first time I had worked with the bank. . . . The woman even knew me. . . . You know, if a person is a few days late, I don't believe it's worth doing all that. . . . There are ways to solve a problem. . . . There's no reason for them to treat us that way . . . so we told her no." Rather than comply with the new requirements, the client simply stopped borrowing from Mibanco.

### Increased Alternatives

At the time of ACP's transformation to Mibanco, many commercial banks were entering the microcredit market. Increasing competition for clients translated into more credit alternatives for entrepreneurs. Indeed, the client who stopped borrowing from Mibanco rather than comply with the bank's request for collateral was also borrowing from another bank at the time. Instead of tolerating a situation that was uncomfortable for her, she simply borrowed more from the other bank, which she viewed as having more flexible late-payment policies: "With the other bank . . . a few days would pass, or maybe we would forget [to pay], or maybe in that moment there wasn't [enough cash] . . . they gave me more [than Mibanco], up to 24,000 soles . . . and they never came and said, 'Señora, why this, that, and the other?'" Thus, Mibanco lost a valuable high-end client because its rigid late-payment policy compared unfavorably with that of another bank.

Anecdotal evidence suggests that clients noticed Mibanco tightening its policies and procedures immediately following the transformation. Clients' loans were delayed as they worked out new arrangements, leading some clients to feel slighted. As a result, certain clients' relationships with Mibanco deteriorated, even to the point of driving away creditworthy borrowers.

### Interpretations

The apparent shift toward poorer clients after ACP's commercialization is a surprising finding that can be explained by three possible interpretations: the "skimming" of wealthier borrowers, higher transaction costs, and loan terms better suited for the poor.[16]

## *"Skimming" of Wealthier Borrowers*

One possible explanation for the shift toward poorer borrowers could be that the wealthier borrowers had been "skimmed off the top." This could have occurred in two ways. At the time of the transformation, banks were entering the microcredit market. According to anecdotal evidence, loan officers from these banks flooded the more-established markets in Lima, offering larger loans and attracting the wealthier borrowers, leaving less wealthy borrowers to conduct their business with Mibanco.

Alternatively, the skimming may have occurred across time and be related to the way the sample was constructed for this study. Because the Mibanco new entrants were drawn only from areas where ACP had been operating for some time, it is possible that ACP had already attracted the wealthier borrowers within these areas, leaving only less-wealthy borrowers for the newly formed Mibanco. This interpretation is based on the fact that the sample of Mibanco new entrants was not representative of all new Mibanco borrowers. Rather, the sample consisted only of new borrowers in areas where ACP had already served large numbers of clients.

## *Transaction Costs*

Another possible explanation for the shift toward poorer clients is that increases in borrowers' transaction costs made Mibanco loans less attractive to wealthy borrowers with higher opportunity costs than poorer borrowers.

There are several indications that borrowers' transaction costs increased during the period immediately following ACP's transformation to Mibanco. The clients in the case studies reported that they were required to submit new documentation, and the average time needed to process a loan temporarily increased as both old and new borrowers were required to undergo the more thorough Type A evaluation. Wealthy borrowers may have been driven away by the increased red tape and wait time immediately following the transformation, whereas less wealthy borrowers did not react as adversely because of their lower opportunity costs.

## *Loan Terms Better Suited to the Poor*

A third possible explanation for the shift in the client profile toward poorer borrowers is the longer loan terms offered through Mibanco for the same size loans. The resulting lower payment amounts made the loans more attractive to poor households. In addition, allowing less frequent payments gave borrowers more time to accumulate the money needed for a payment.

If the above interpretation is correct, the shift toward poorer clients would not be a temporary change associated only with the transition period. Instead, it would suggest that longer loans and less frequent payments are a more appropriate lending technology for reaching the poor with working-capital loans. It is unclear, however, whether the shift in loan terms attracted poorer borrowers or the poorer borrowers influenced Mibanco to modify its loan terms.

## SUMMARY

As in most cases, Mibanco's institutional transformation was a costly endeavor in the short term. However, Mibanco is already realizing many benefits as a result of the change. It achieved its main objective for the transformation—to have access to additional sources of capital to fuel future growth.

Mibanco originally anticipated a net loss for its first year, but, because of higher than expected returns on investments, the bank yielded a net gain of US$120,000.[17] This was followed by a net income of US$731,000 in 1999, increasing to US$4.36 million in 2000, and US$3.2 million at year-end 2001. In the future Mibanco expects to yield a return on equity of 35 percent, with a minimum of 12 percent in difficult years.

In the past, because of a lack of competition and the ability to charge high interest rates, ACP was able to delay addressing its operational inefficiencies, such as its high level of administrative costs and low client-to-loan officer ratio. It was hoped that the transformation would automatically rectify some of the problems. However, given the rushed time frame, cost-effective decisions were not always made. A large challenge remains for Mibanco to implement cost controls and improve its operational efficiency.

To improve efficiency, Mibanco is looking at ways to diversify its portfolio to reach more businesses, speed up the loan-approval process, and reduce costs. Mibanco plans to increase the average number of clients per loan officer from 365 to 400, and its average portfolio from US$100,000 to US$160,000 in the next few years. However, the primary remaining concern is not branch costs but headquarters costs, which currently represent a significant portion of Mibanco's total operating costs.

While the microenterprise market is still widely underserved in Peru, traditional banks, EDPYMEs, microfinance NGOs, and the Cajas Municipales are all increasing their outreach. Mibanco needs to prepare for the increased competition, especially as clients become more educated due to an increase in publicity aimed at the microenterprise sector. Clients are becoming increasingly aware of alternative options and are comparing differences in interest rates, fees, and services. Mibanco will need to continue to improve its efficiency to remain competitive and retain its market share in the future.

According to the results of this study, commercialization may not lead to mission drift. These findings are tentative, at best, and need to be strengthened with additional empirical work on the client-level impact of commercialization. If commercialization enhances outreach to poor clients, this is a story that needs to be told. Future studies should seek larger representative samples of the transformed institution's new clients. To capture the long-term effects of commercialization on clients, any future studies would need to include information on what happens to clients once the transformed institution has had sufficient time to develop its new portfolio of products and services.

## NOTES

1. Hernando De Soto estimates that Lima's population increased by 1,200 percent over the four decades prior to 1989.

2. "Organo Informativo del Congreso de la Republica," *El Congreso* (September 15, 1998), 6.

3. ProFund is the world's first private equity fund solely dedicated to microfinance investment. Based in San Jose, Costa Rica, ProFund's strategy is to achieve superior financial returns through the purchase of debt and equity in regulated financial institutions dedicated to serving small businesses and microenterprises in Latin America and the Caribbean.

4. Discussion with José Zapata, microenterprise intendant, SBS, September 17, 1998.

5. ACCION Gateway Fund, LLC, was created in 1997 to support microfinance institutions in Latin America through equity or debt investments in new regulated MFIs; nonprofits in the process of transformation to a regulated financial status; and already-established regulated MFIs. In addition to providing long-term capital, the Gateway Fund participates in the governance of these microfinance institutions, helping to ensure that they remain financially sound and committed to a social mission. The Gateway Fund is capitalized with grants from the U.S. Agency for International Development (USAID) and the Consultative Group to Assist the Poorest (CGAP).

6. Corporación Andina de Fomento (CAF) is a multilateral financial institution based in Venezuela. Its mission is to promote the sustainable development of its shareholder countries and regional integration. It serves the public and private sectors, providing multiple financial services to a broad customer base composed of the governments of shareholder countries, public and private companies, and financial institutions.

7. According to ACCION International, a debt-to-equity ratio no higher than 6:1 is optimal for MFIs. According to the Basle Convention, the international capital adequacy standard for commercial banks is 12:1.

8. Mibanco created four different classes of shares to enshrine the right of the original shareholders to be represented on the board and to ensure that the original mission is maintained. Some of the shares do not transfer this right to a new owner if sold.

9. CAF was not an original owner and therefore does not have a seat on the board.

10. The tax rate would have been the same had ACP transformed into a financiera. As an EDPYME, ACP would have been subject to an 18–percent tax on total revenues.

11. The client-level data were collected as part of USAID's AIMS project. The purpose of the impact assessment was to evaluate the client-level impact of microcredit program participation on individual borrowers, their households, and their microenterprises. The results of the impact evaluation are reported in Elizabeth Dunn and J. Gordon Arbuckle Jr., "The Impacts of Microcredit: A Case Study from Peru," AIMS Project Report (Washington, D.C.: USAID/G/EG/MD, Management Systems International, 2001). By coincidence, the survey data for this longitudinal impact study were collected both before and after the transformation of ACP into Mibanco. Because the data were collected for a different purpose, they are not ideally suited for the current study. The Mibanco new entrants are not a random sample drawn from all new Mibanco clients. Instead, they are members of the control group for the original impact study who happened to take first loans from Mibanco between June 1998 and September 1999. This resulted in a sample of only twenty-three borrowers, and a sample that is not representative of all new Mibanco borrowers. The usefulness of the case study data is also limited because the protocol for the case-study interviews did not include specific questions about the clients' perspectives on the transformation. It should also be noted that Mibanco did not introduce any new products in the fifteen months after the transformation. Therefore, the findings of this study do not reflect any of the client-level effects that might be associated with the new products and services eventually offered by Mibanco. This could be considered both a strength and a weakness of the study. It is a weakness in the sense that the ability to introduce new products and services is often a motivating force behind commercialization, but the study findings do not reflect any client-level changes associated with this process. On the other hand, one strength of the study is that it is based on a comparison of clients who received essentially the same product: a short-term loan for microenterprise working capital. Thus

any observed changes in the client profile cannot be attributed to changes in the types of products offered.

12. For a complete discussion of the sampling design for the impact study and descriptions of the client and control groups, see Elizabeth Dunn, "Microfinance Clients in Lima, Peru: Baseline Report for AIMS Core Impact Assessment," AIMS Project Report (Washington, D.C.: USAID/G/EG/MD, Management Systems International, 1999).

13. To investigate possible shifts in the client profile associated with commercialization, the characteristics of the ACP new entrants were compared with those of the Mibanco new entrants using independent sample t-tests. The data for the ACP new entrants came from the 1997 survey, and the data for the Mibanco new entrants came from the 1999 survey. Credit data refer to the loans that were current at the time of each survey (the loans current in September 1997 for the ACP new entrants and the loans current in September 1999 for the Mibanco new entrants). All monetary values are reported in 1999 real values.

14. Household poverty level was measured using the same expenditures-based approach as the Living Standards Measurement Survey, which establishes Peru's national poverty line.

15. The standard criterion for statistical significance is $p=.10$ or lower. The results for these three variables do not meet this criterion but are relatively close, at $.10<p<.14$.

16. Given the limitations of the data, however, and the lack of previous empirical work from which to draw, these interpretations should be considered suggestive rather than definitive.

17. The first year was a short year, May 4 to December 31, 1998.

## Part IV

# Challenges
# to Commercial Microfinance

# 10

# Microfinance Institutions in Competitive Conditions

**Elisabeth Rhyne**

Until the late 1990s most microfinance institutions (MFIs) did not have to worry about competition. They enjoyed near monopolies, as a few, mostly small, service providers sought to reach a huge untapped market. The idea of competing for clients was so far from the mindset of early MFIs that when two of them operated in the same city, they often reached a gentlemen's agreement to divide the market geographically. This period of low competition was essential. It allowed MFIs the freedom to focus single-mindedly on making the breakthroughs in methodology and management necessary to reach scale and sustainability. These break-throughs have now brought microfinance to the threshold of competition.

In some countries, such as Bangladesh, Bolivia, and Nicaragua, the entire microfinance market is approaching saturation. However, even in localized regions, such as the area around Kampala, Uganda, MFIs are finding competitors vying for their clients. This competition is emerging from three sources: the expansion of the self-identified MFIs, the entry of new commercial players into microfinance, and the emergence of related businesses, primarily consumer lending, that serve many of the same clients as traditional microfinance (Rhyne and Christen 1999; Christen 2000).

Competition is having a profound effect on microfinance, seen most readily in the flowering of interest in market research and new-product development. These changes are bringing significant benefits to clients as MFIs become more customer-oriented. But for MFIs, competition makes life much more challenging. Most MFIs have not yet fully adjusted their business orientation to the demands of competition. This chapter attempts to analyze the effects of competition on MFIs and to encourage those institutions to analyze the consequences of competition for their business.

## OLD THINK AND NEW THINK

In the pre-competitive period the overall objectives of most MFIs were embodied in the mantra of outreach and sustainability. To achieve outreach and sustainability, MFIs had to focus internally. With the assumption that client demand was nearly limitless and with few other players on the scene, institutions could take external factors largely for granted. In this setting the future was always projected as an upward sloping trend line, and the questions surrounding the achievement of projections mainly concerned building the institution itself. Aside from general economic shocks or natural disasters, external events were unlikely to derail the projections.

Managers concentrated on streamlining operating systems to improve productivity and increasing client volumes to reach economies of scale. They sought efficiency to create profitable operations, which in turn brought access to the more plentiful and more commercial sources of funds available to successful MFIs. One of the great dynamic forces in microfinance throughout the 1990s was a drive to qualify for more plentiful sources of funds. This drive sparked the movement toward institutional transformation that began with BancoSol in Bolivia and has become widespread. It also sparked advances in the microenterprise field in the areas of financial management and operational efficiency.

With the arrival of competition, institutions are finding themselves subtly but fundamentally shifting their core objectives. They must replace the expectation of growth by a struggle to retain market share. Profitability (or sustainability) shifts from center stage, although it remains a requirement for survival. The core preoccupation of management becomes attracting and retaining clients. In this situation, institutions must pay more attention to the external environment, both clients and competitors. This requires the addition of capabilities not well-developed earlier—and in many MFIs lacking altogether—such as market research and product development. These functions must now be installed and integrated into decision-making. Even in traditional areas of focus, new driving forces appear. For example, the institution seeks efficiency not just to lower costs but to offer the customer faster service at better prices.

In this new environment the factors determining whether the organization's business objectives will be achieved are increasingly beyond its control. As in any game, the success of one player's strategy depends on the other players' moves. Thus, the future is far less predictable. What is certain is that the environment will not be static and that institutions must be prepared to change.

**Table 10.1: Concerns of Microfinance Institutions Before and During Competition**

| Pre-Competitive Stage | Competitive Stage |
|---|---|
| *Objectives:* to reach *more people* and to become *financially viable* | *Objectives:* to retain or increase *market share* while remaining *profitable* |
| *Driving motivation:* access to *funding* | *Driving motivation:* attracting the *customer* |
| *Management focus:* developing the institution's *internal* capabilities | *Management focus:* though internal issues remain, *external* focus is added: understanding the external environment and adjusting business strategy to it |
| *Growth: high* growth projections possible | *Growth: low* growth likely |
| Little need to take the behavior of other players into account | Must study the behavior of clients, prospective clients, and competitors |
| Client demand taken as given | Client demand can evaporate quickly if competitor provides better service |
| *Low risk,* predictable future; *high degree of control* over outcomes | *Rapid change,* high uncertainty; *lower control* over outcomes |

## DETERMINING COMPETITIVE STRATEGIES

For institutions in competitive settings, the process of choosing and refining strategies must change in two ways: increased external focus and readiness for frequent change. We can recognize a continuous cycle of four strategy steps: (1) analyze the market and client preferences; (2) analyze comparative advantages in light of competitors; (3) select and implement strategy; and (4) monitor outcome and competitor response. The external focus is reflected in the steps themselves, while the readiness for change is reflected in treating this process as a cycle.

Currently, the business-planning processes of MFIs are overwhelmingly devoted to internal considerations, primarily financial modeling. MFIs frequently include only a cursory look at competition and markets in their business planning (for example, a brainstorming session on strengths and weaknesses and some demographic information).

In the next section we look at how competition changes the relationship of MFIs to their markets and the tools that are emerging to assist MFIs in becoming more market responsive. The remainder of the chapter is devoted to the competitive analysis process.

## ANALYSIS OF THE MARKET
## AND CLIENT PREFERENCES

The central fact of competition in microfinance is that it changes the relationship between service provider and client. When there is competition, the customer has a choice of institutions, and experience in countries as diverse as Bolivia, Uganda, and Bangladesh shows that customers will exercise that choice. In fact, clients seem to revel in trying out multiple providers. Recent experience shows that strong client loyalty is not intrinsic to microfinance.

A microfinance institution can examine its relationship to existing and prospective clients at three levels: market preferences concerning the basic microfinance products it already provides (product enhancement), unfilled financial needs of existing clients (new products), and unserved market segments (new markets).

### *Product Enhancement*

The microfinance field has long recognized the client preferences associated with basic microenterprise loans, but until recently most practitioners have given greater weight to their own risk-control requirements. Early writings on microfinance recognized that clients seek good service quality: fast disbursement; convenient locations; simple processes; a welcoming, non-intimidating experience; and terms that fit their business rhythms (Otero 1986, 30–33). Although the standard microfinance methodologies incorporated some of these elements of service quality, there was little push to innovate, and methodological limits were often taken as a given. With competition, the following dimensions are moving to the forefront:

- Speed of loan turnaround has become a crucial point of competition in Bolivia.
- Clients of Mibanco in Peru talked of personal treatment: several long-time clients expressed a desire to change providers when sanctions were applied to them for minor lapses during difficult periods.[1] This experience demonstrates how quickly client loyalty, built over time, can diminish.
- Price sensitivity in competitive markets may be driving down the price of microloans in some countries, but the evidence is mixed (see Chapter 1). In Uganda, clients have become more aware of price, leading institutions to craft formulas that appear more attractive to clients, which in turn prompts regulatory concern about truth in lending.
- With access assured, clients are showing preferences for improved terms—longer maturities, larger loans, less frequent repayments, easier applications, and so on. And again, in Bolivia, loan size has emerged as a major competitive battleground, with lenders luring clients with promises of larger loans than their competitors.

One of the most salient dimensions of competition affecting microfinance products is the client preference for individual loans over group loans. Researchers on microfinance have long recognized that most clients prefer individual loans if given a choice (Churchill 1999, for example). While some clients do enjoy the security of a support group, most will trade that security for the flexibility and freedom individual loans offer. In Uganda, time lost in weekly group meetings was by far the most frequent complaint clients raised about their village-banking programs, even though many clients cited the social aspects of the group as important to them (Barnes, Gaile, and Kibombo 2001, 98). In Bolivia, the success of individual lenders, competing directly with solidarity-group and village-bank lenders has resulted in the rapidly increasing proportion of Bolivia's total microfinance portfolio in individual loans, from 41 percent in 1997 to 78 percent in 2000.[2] Group lenders such as Prodem and BancoSol have moved rapidly into individual loans (Navajas, Conning, and Gonzalez-Vega 1999). In Peru, Mibanco has also shifted dramatically away from group lending, to the delight of numerous clients in the AIMS study. In addition to the obvious difficulties of paying for troubled group members, the Mibanco clients pointed out how inconvenient it is to cede control of the timing of borrowing and repayment to the schedules of the group as a whole. Group lending, once viewed as the heart of microfinance, could become a niche product for clients of certain types.

### New Products for Existing Customers

The threat of competition coincides with results of AIMS and MicroSave-Africa research that emphasize the diversity of financial-management needs among microfinance clients.[3] Both the competitive force and new understanding pull MFIs toward new products for existing customers. Among the most important of these are lines of credit, housing finance, savings, money transfers, and insurance. This chapter will not discuss these new products, but a few general comments are in order.

The traditional microfinance product is a short-term working-capital loan with a repayment period between three and twelve months. There were a number of advantages to the one-product approach. Lenders found one product easy to deliver, monitor, and multiply. Clients could manage an all-purpose loan for a variety of purposes—working capital, fixed assets, home improvement, and school fees. Successful lending was based on the client's existing ability (and willingness) to repay, not on loan use. Bank Rakyat Indonesia's stunning success has been based on one loan product and three savings products, each flexibly structured for multiple uses.

If we accept that a few all-purpose financial products, when flexibly configured and effectively delivered, can meet a wide range of client needs, the burden is on specialized products to prove their added value. Before launching a new product, it is necessary to understand the extent to which it allows clients to accomplish more than they can with standard products. If clients can already do most of what a new product allows, then a new product may detract substantially from the existing one while adding internal management challenges. For example, a line of credit may offer customers better cash flow, but a lender would probably draw many line-of-credit customers from its existing microloan customer base. And lines of credit may be more difficult to administer. For existing clients, MFIs must also consider a client's total indebtedness, so as not to stretch beyond repayment capacity.

New products, if well-designed, have the potential to improve the value of financial services for clients. However, in the rush to compete for customers, MFIs must ensure that their new product introductions are more than marketing ploys, that they are genuine innovations offering added value.

## New Markets for Microfinance Institutions

Considerations are somewhat different in the case of new target groups. Competitive financial markets seem to have a tendency to saturate certain markets while ignoring others. Prime microfinance clients are hotly contested, while other market segments go largely untouched (for example, men in Bangladesh). Innovators who open new markets face the high costs and risks of learning while worrying that followers will make their market advantage short lived. Nevertheless, as competition becomes stronger, so does the pressure to try out new markets. Three new market segments are under exploration.

- *Frontier markets.* These include poorer and harder to reach clients, especially in rural areas. In several countries, donors are increasingly supporting programs attempting to penetrate poorer client groups, particularly in rural areas. Sustainable methodologies are likely to emerge, and the probability is high that the frontier will continue to move out.
- *Small business.* Most MFIs grow with their clients, but some are also adding distinct small business products aimed at formal enterprises. They may face a daunting challenge from mainstream banks that already serve this market.
- *Salaried employees.* In many countries a large number of salaried workers have incomes comparable to microfinance clients. These workers are a potential market for a range of products from enterprise and housing loans to savings accounts. Again, other lenders, especially consumer lenders, already reach a major portion of this market, and MFIs must determine whether they can add value or reach deeper.

## Tools for Understanding Markets

Although market research is a well-developed profession, the application of market-research techniques to microfinance is in its infancy. MicroSave-Africa and the AIMS Project have developed some market-research tools for microfinance that have swept quickly through the microfinance profession. Thanks to their efforts, among others, focus-group analysis and other tools are used more often and more effectively by MFIs. These tools are a good start for the industry, but more work is needed. Consider some of the questions associated with opening a new microfinance operation, each requiring a different form of investigation:

- Is demand sufficient in the area? (demand study)
- Where should the branch or office be located? (traffic-pattern study)
- What services do clients want? (client-behavior and preferences)
- What services do clients currently have access to and use? (client-behavior and competition assessment)
- How large should loans be and for what term? (assessment of income levels and business patterns)
- How should the service or institution be "pitched" to clients? (perceptions and branding)

At the moment, MFIs are on their own to sort out the methodology and scope of such research. When they have turned to professional market-analysis firms, they have often found organizations aimed at corporations and unfamiliar with ways to solicit information from the informal sector.

Because market research is a new aspect of microfinance, it is not routine in most MFIs. If done at all, it may not be well connected into the key decision-making processes at the MFI, preventing the MFI from getting the benefit of the knowledge gained. MFIs are unsure how much of their resources to put into such efforts, when to hire outside expertise, how often to conduct market research, and even where to situate market research within the organization. Organizations that develop the ability to use market research are likely to be better equipped to compete.

## DIMENSIONS OF COMPETITION AMONG MICROFINANCE INSTITUTIONS

### *Analysis of Competitive Advantage*

We now turn to the second aspect of competitive strategy development: analysis of competitive advantage. In the microfinance field, institutions have rarely used tools to analyze their competitive advantages. The only widely known tool is the SWOT (Strengths, Weaknesses, Opportunities, and Threats) analysis, which has rarely been applied rigorously. Frequently, the SWOT analysis has been treated as an occasion to engage the staff of an MFI in a soul-searching discussion about the institution, which then provides useful feedback to senior management and is summarized in a few pages in a business plan. However, this kind of session is far from the demands of hard-headed competitive analysis.

Although the SWOT does point toward the elements necessary for an effective competitive analysis, the need is for a more rigorous tool that can analyze the competitive advantage and disadvantage of an MFI and its competitors. Statements about each of these advantages and disadvantages would not come primarily from opinion but would be backed by investigation and data. The analysis would focus on the future evolution of the market, backed by the documentation of trends. A full analysis would involve detailed comparisons of the MFI and its main competitors in areas such as:

- Cost of and access to funds; equity cushion
- Staff productivity; human-resource capabilities
- Infrastructure and location
- Customer base
- Product range and service quality
- Pricing
- Corporate culture
- Brand and institutional image

The attributes examined might repeat those treated in a standard institutional assessment. However, the focus would be comparative and judgmental rather than descriptive, with comparisons between competing MFIs rather than against industry norms. No matter how systematic such analyses become, however, most writers on business strategy concede that the best and most inspired strategies combine information and analysis with the "gut intuition" only experience provides. In the end, competitive strategy remains an art.

### Strategies for Competition

This section discusses some of the strategies firms in general adopt to deal with competition, with applications to microfinance. We know from the economist's theoretical concept that perfect competition sharpens the focus on efficiency that drove MFIs during the low-competition stage of the microfinance industry.[4] The unrelenting pressure for efficiency should be borne in mind when thinking about competition, even though discussion often focuses on product differentiation. In the real world, firms struggle to make their own situations as unlike perfect competition as possible in order to insulate themselves from competition's demand for efficiency. A variety of strategies can place an organization in a less hotly contested position.

### First- and Second-Mover Advantages

The first firm (first mover) to spot and exploit a market opportunity or technological innovation can receive high returns after recouping its initial investment. However, if the new opportunity is attractive, other firms will follow, so this advantage is usually temporary. The early innovators in microfinance launched credit technologies that enabled them to reach a market segment previously considered unbankable, earning relatively high returns. For example, BancoSol, the first entrant in commercial microfinance in Bolivia, made high returns on equity during the mid 1990s (leading the entire Bolivian banking sector on several measures), but by the late 1990s competition was eroding its first-mover advantage and returns fell. By business standards the five years of low competition BancoSol enjoyed represent a relatively long period of insulation from competition. Because of the risks and costs associated with being first, MFIs have usually sought subsidies to enter new areas. This may be changing, as more MFIs have become established enough to finance some of their own innovation.

The first mover paves the way for others, who apply proven technology at lower cost and risk. ASA, in Bangladesh, captured what might be called second-mover advantage by building upon and innovating around the Grameen Bank methodology. Second movers have lower entry costs, but they also have lower expectations of profit, both because the market is partially taken and because of competition's effect on reducing profit margins. As Mommartz and Schor point out in Chapter 4, private banks considering microfinance in countries with strong, profitable MFIs may choose not to enter because they see a crowded market with falling returns. Such a calculation is undoubtedly one factor keeping private bankers away from microfinance in Bolivia.

### Protection

Firms of all sorts seek legal and regulatory means to reduce competition—tariff barriers, patents, copyrights, and licensing. For financial institutions, licensing is the main means of securing such advantages. Such advantages may be good for the public (for example, assurance of solvency), but the political process often includes pressure toward advantages that may serve the public less well (restricted entry). MFIs in competitive settings are already exerting pressure to enter the licensed arena, thereby gaining advantages over NGOs such as access to more plentiful funding sources or broader product offerings. The Private Finance Funds

(FFPs) of Bolivia have already experienced these advantages (see Chapters 6 and 7). In Uganda, MFIs have convinced the government to create a similar category of regulated entity for themselves.

## Bundling and Barriers to Exit

Firms can reduce competitive pressure if they find ways to make it harder for customers to switch providers by increasing the cost of switching or linking products. Customers who buy a razor from the leading shaving-products company find that they must continue to buy blades from the same company in order to fit the razor. When Microsoft bundled its web browser in a package with Windows and demanded that computer manufacturers supply both, it created a barrier to switching browsers and put Microsoft at odds with U.S. antitrust law. Banks often use such bundling techniques to keep their customers by linking products or through special penalties or bonuses. The Grameen Bank methodology has long had a built-in barrier to exit as long as other providers use the same methodology. Customers who leave one Grameen provider start at the bottom of a second Grameen provider's loan ladder and may lose their group-fund contributions as well. Similarly, credit unions promise that good savers will eventually qualify for credit.

## Market Niche

Another strategy is to identify a protected corner of the market or a specialized service in which competition is less intense or in which a firm can develop a specific advantage. Niche strategies can be effective but are subject to the same forces that erode other forms of advantage, with the added limitation of smaller market size. In microfinance, which is already a market niche within the broader retail-banking market, it is a challenge to identify a genuinely unique niche that does not overlap substantially with other MFIs.

## Sustained Competitive Advantage

Beyond these specific strategies are a wide range of attributes firms develop to give them an advantage in competition. In microfinance, we see competitive advantage in areas such as funding costs, knowledge of markets, technologies, reputation, infrastructure, and legal status. Thinkers on business strategy often emphasize that the most effective and long-lasting advantages are those that are difficult for others to duplicate and that equip a firm to change with the market. For example, an attractive product may be a source of immediate advantage, but if it is easily copied, the advantage may be temporary. The more sustainable advantage could be internal capability to identify and implement product refinements.

### Competitive Strategies in the Mainstream Financial Sector

As a part of the broader financial-services industry, microfinance requires a greater understanding of the dynamics of competition among banks and other financial institutions. In finance, the barriers to entry of financial institutions can be substantial, for reasons ranging from infrastructure costs to customer relationships to licensing. However, it is just as important to note that among licensed financial institutions barriers to copying innovations are often low. If this is true for microfinance, one would expect competition to focus around proven market segments rather than new segments, where any entrant must bear the costs and risks of innovation. Indeed, we repeatedly observe MFIs clustering around prime clients all offering virtually the same product.

A general trend in the financial sector involves the increasing dominance of a few large institutions that provide a full range of services, a trend evident in the financial sectors of the majority of developed countries. This observation suggests that due to economies of scale in banking, microfinance could gradually be absorbed into the large-scale commercial banking world, as have other lines of financial business, such as consumer lending.

Another recent competitive move in the financial sector is for banks to pursue fee-based business, mainly fees for processing transactions (bill paying, money transfers, and so forth). Lender-only MFIs may have a hard time competing against banks with substantial fee-based businesses for both financial and customer-service reasons. It will be important for the microfinance field to learn more about the competitive forces in the mainstream financial sector and how they correspond to forces at work in microfinance.

### Comparative Advantages by Institutional Status

We look now at patterns of competitive advantage among MFIs of various types. Competitive strategies used by most institutions appear to be strongly linked to institutional type, history, and corporate culture. Each type of institution uses its status to create distinct advantages.

## Large, Well-Established Commercial Banks

Among the strongest institutional advantages are those associated with commercial banking, and particularly with large, well-established banks, including characteristics such as:

- *Public perception of safety.* The public perceives large, historic banks, often backed by the state, as safe places to keep money. This perception creates a daunting barrier to entry for competing savings mobilizers. Bank Rakyat Indonesia's public trust and image may have presented an important barrier, discouraging competitors even though it showed that savings mobilization from smaller communities was possible.[5]

- *Lower cost of funds.* Banks with a tradition of savings mobilization attract funds from depositors of all sizes. These funds are traditionally more stable and cheaper than the funds raised by smaller, specialized banks issuing certificates of deposit (CDs). Examples of competition in microfinance between big banks and specialized banks can be found in Chile and Ecuador. Banco de Estado (Chile) and Banco de Pichincha (Ecuador) are large, historic banks. They have far lower funding costs than the newer, specialized banks, Banco de Desarrollo (Chile) and Banco Solidario (Ecuador), which rely to a greater extent on CDs. Cost differences could be passed to consumers as lower interest rates, or they could allow large banks to overcome the startup costs of developing microfinance capacity.

- *Locational advantage through infrastructure.* Big, established banks typically have extensive branch-office networks that make it easier to reach clients. In countries where those networks are convenient to microfinance clients, they allow faster, cheaper scaling-up of operations. Banco do Nordeste in Brazil, Banco de Pichincha in Ecuador, and the Bank Rakyat Indonesia (BRI) units each expanded quickly and reached profitability in a short time in part because existing infrastructure reduced the cost of opening outlets far below the cost for a stand-alone microfinance operation.

- *Ability to spread fixed costs.* Commercial banks involved in a range of banking businesses may be able to spread some of their overhead costs widely, reducing the overhead charged to microfinance customers. These may include costs of senior management and major support functions such as accounting, reporting and audit, marketing, human resources, and information technology.

Taken together, this list shows large commercial banks with significant advantages in costs, access to funds, and access to clients. If they can marshal these advantages successfully, they can become formidable competitors in microfinance, as they already are in some countries, notably Chile and Indonesia. However, if they are to realize their potential, large commercial banks must overcome a series of primarily internal barriers—including corporate cultures antithetical to microfinance—that have until recently rendered most banks uninterested in microfinance and micro-level clients. These barriers are gradually falling, though not perhaps as fast as expected.

### Licensed MFIs: Specialized Banks and Finance Companies

Licensed MFIs, like EDPYMEs in Peru or FFPs in Bolivia, have access to sources of funds through capital markets and restricted lines of credit that are more plentiful and faster to obtain than funding available to their NGO cousins. However, these funding sources are generally not as cheap as those available to big banks. On the cost side, these specialized microlenders may be caught in the middle: they lack the deep pockets of the big banks, but at the same time, they have graduated from the subsidies NGOs use to start new product lines. They may therefore have a hard time garnering the resources needed to invest in new areas or products. FASSIL in Bolivia is an example of a specialized, non-subsidized lender that lacks the financial depth needed to weather Bolivia's economic recession and accompanying microfinance crisis (see Chapter 7).

Established MFIs like Prodem and Caja Los Andes in Bolivia have infrastructure and brand-name recognition that make it easier for them to connect with customers. Their smaller size and innovation-oriented corporate cultures may allow them to be more agile in trying new things than larger banks. Some of these lenders have chosen to base their competitive strategies on service quality and knowledge of the market. For example, Banco Solidario in Ecuador is focusing on offering clients an integrated package of services that will inspire loyalty—a bundling approach—in its head-on competition with the large, established Banco de Pichincha. Banco Solidario is betting that its greater understanding of and responsiveness to the clients will overcome some of the cost and position advantages of its larger competitor.

### NGOs

Competitive strategies for NGOs seem to revolve around market niche. NGOs may retain greater access to subsidies if they can convince donors that they serve a portion of the market that the commercial institutions will not serve. If they are reaching poorer, more rural, more disadvantaged clients, they can become cost-competitive by accessing subsidies even if they cannot access commercial sources of funds. In order for such a strategy to work, however, the NGOs must be able to distinguish their clients from those of mainstream MFIs. In competitive environments this has proven difficult. Consider the situation facing Pro Mujer and Crecer in Bolivia, two village-banking lenders. With their low-end strategies, first-time clients are probably distinct from the clients of the licensed MFIs. However, after a few loans those same clients qualify for loans from the larger MFIs. And given that the larger MFIs offer more flexible products (individual versus village-banking loans), many clients wish to move on. The village-banking NGOs have traditionally put up substantial barriers to exit around their clients, including loss of savings and loss of access to larger loans. In the context of heightened competition, such barriers may be inadequate.

### Credit Cooperatives and Credit Unions

Cooperatives have developed advantages for savings mobilization in various ways. They emphasize that as member-owned organizations, clients have a long-run stake and voice in their credit union. Market research in Bolivia shows that savers are attracted by this image of cooperatives as "mine." More generally, cooperatives have cultivated an image as the place to save. They were the first to enter this market, in the 1950s and 1960s in Latin America, and with first-mover advantage they established a brand that has survived in the public's mind despite many ups and downs of actual performance. Cooperatives also link savings with credit by making loan eligibility and size a function of amount saved. These linked products involve both an incentive to save and a barrier to exit.

### Summary

While each type of institution has its own natural advantages, all types are affected by the drive to provide better products and a better experience for clients as well as by the need to be efficient. All are working to respond to client preferences: faster turnaround, larger loans, new products, individual lending, new market segments, better treatment of clients, and use of automation.

In pursuing these strategies, the internal capabilities of the MFI matter greatly. The specialized MFIs are well-connected to the clients. They know a lot about them, understand how to relate to them, and are structured to reach them. These are traits most large banks lack. On the other hand, some of the older MFIs may have become rigid in their approach to products and clients, responding with difficulty to changes in the client relationship brought by competition. For example, institutions whose organizational structure was built around large-group lending are finding it difficult to add products such as individual lending or savings that require substantially different structures. This rigidity creates an atmosphere where newer entrants with bright ideas outperform the older entrants—a phenomenon apparent in microfinance from its beginnings. A young NGO oriented toward service quality, the Uganda Microfinance Union (UMU), has entered the market around Kampala. Although competitive, this market had been dominated by organizations using rigid methodologies. UMU, whose products are more convenient to clients, is shaking up the market. Bangladesh is also ripe for innovators. SafeSave and Buro Tangail are innovative, but, although successful, they have yet to pose a serious competitive threat to the established leaders—and their techniques have yet to be emulated by the leaders.

For existing MFIs the ideal strategy would be to combine the natural advantages of established institutions (lower costs, infrastructure, brand recognition, and access to funds) with those of the new (flexibility and client responsiveness). This combination could be developed through alliances between institutions, such as banks creating microfinance divisions using experienced providers. Alternatively, MFIs may create a core internal competency in market analysis and competitive strategy. In any event, MFIs faced with competition must develop a corporate culture that accommodates change.

## THE DYNAMICS OF OVERLENDING: AN INTRINSIC PROBLEM OF COMPETITIVE LENDING

In countries where competition for microfinance clients has become fiercest, notably Bolivia and Bangladesh and to some extent Uganda, evidence is emerging of a dangerous tendency: clients borrow more than they can handle and delinquency rises throughout the microfinance market. Overlending has led to a full-blown crisis in Bolivian microfinance (see Chapter 6). In Bangladesh, MFIs are increasingly concerned about the effect overlending may have on loan loss rates. A brief analysis suggests that overlending is an intrinsic tendency when the market for credit is competitive. Microfinance lenders need to understand the dynamics of overlending in order to protect against it.

The problem arises because when it comes to borrowing money, clients are not good judges of their own limits. In fact, market research from Bolivia has shown that many clients have counterproductive views. "If I borrow more, I earn more," is a frequently expressed axiom that microlenders undoubtedly encouraged prior to the crisis. Taking loans from multiple institutions can be a risk-diversification strategy or even a status symbol. In Uganda, small loan size was the most important reason (together with loan term) for clients changing lenders, as 12 percent of clients did in areas with competition over two years (Barnes, Gaile, and Kibombo 2001, 97–98). In AIMS studies of clients in Peru, nearly all clients had at some point taken loans from other institutions, sometimes simultaneously, including cooperatives, communal banks, banks, housing lenders, and NGOs. For many clients, taking multiple loans was associated with family financial crises. Even in countries with long histories of credit availability, portions of the population are chronically over-indebted, and the drive to borrow as much as possible is in evidence. We can take it as a trait of human nature that many people are susceptible to borrowing too much if a lender is willing to lend.

From the lender's perspective, it may appear foolish to lend customers too much money. However, in competitive conditions, when the game becomes attracting and keeping clients, lenders are pressed to offer clients the best possible deal. Offering a larger loan is an obvious strategy for attracting clients and seemingly easy to implement. In Bolivia, consumer lenders announced that they would lend to good customers of MFIs at larger loan sizes. They drew in tens of thousands of clients.

The incentive is strong to offer clients the largest loan possible. But what is the largest loan possible? Not all lenders assess this amount the same way. We look at two formulas, with the oversimplified but convenient labels *conservative* and *aggressive*. Conservative lending reflects a conservative policy regarding loan amount, as has characterized most microfinance. Assessment of client repayment capacity according to a set of proven norms is a fundamental technique of microfinance. Conservative lenders have a formula for profitability based on a relatively low loan amount, which the borrower can easily service, and a resulting very low loan-loss rate. The intensive assessment and follow-up required in this method lead to relatively high administrative costs. These variables can be combined with a competitive interest rate to produce a profitable operation.

Aggressive lenders achieve profitability by a different route. They give larger loans to the same clients, keeping administrative costs low by spending less time analyzing each client. With larger principal and lower costs, aggressive lenders can afford higher defaults, working the cost of default into a competitive interest rate. This is, in fact, the formula applied by consumer lenders.

If conservative and aggressive lenders compete for the same clients, it is clear that clients will prefer the lender offering a larger loan at the same interest rate. Other strategies to attract clients, like rapid turnaround or friendly service, may not count as much with clients as access to more money. When an aggressive lender is operating in a market, the conservative lender is pushed to follow.

This situation sets up a classic dilemma: if all parties were to engage in restrained behavior (lending within the clients' limits), the results would be good for everyone (low defaults). However, it would be foolhardy for a single lender to exercise restraint without knowing if others will follow. Therefore, no lender maintains a restrained manner and everyone is worse off (high defaults throughout the system).

This is exactly what has happened in Bolivia. Bolivia's overlending was driven by the entry of consumer lenders, who miscalculated their ability to serve microentrepreneurs with consumer-credit techniques and subsequently collapsed. Although no lender would deliberately enter a market to lose money, there is still room for miscalculation and lack of market knowledge, and cautious lenders will lose clients to overlenders even if those lenders are behaving in an uninformed or non-sustainable way. Moreover, in competitive markets some players may pursue non-sustainable strategies deliberately, as a way to gain a temporary advantage.

Similarly, it is difficult for lenders to agree to abide by norms that prevent overlending because there is significant incentive to cheat on such agreements in order to get more clients. Lenders lack sanctions with which to punish defectors.

What are the responses to this dilemma? It may well be that the dramatic overlending that has shaken Bolivia is associated with the newness of the competitive market in microfinance. When clients and lenders become familiar with the situation, more clients will know their limits and fewer lenders will enter recklessly. However, the incentives behind the overlending dynamic will persist.

Two possible regulatory responses combat this phenomenon. The first is the credit bureau. Availability of complete data about the indebtedness of clients allows lenders to avoid overlending. (It may also, however, allow competitors to select good clients of other lenders to pursue with more attractive offers.) The level of credit bureau sophistication needed to provide accurate and timely information is only available in the more developed of the countries where microfinance operates. Credit bureau information that is incomplete or out of date helps but does not eliminate the problem (see Chapter 13).

Another regulatory response is to establish clear norms regarding re-payment capacity so that lenders are penalized for exceeding the debt-service limits of their clients. For salaried clients, such a norm is easy to specify: debt service may not exceed some maximum percentage of monthly income. For microentrepreneurs, such a norm would be much more difficult to establish and enforce, given the difficulty of obtaining accurate income information about all the costs and revenues of a microenterprise and its associated household. Each microfinance lender has its own methods of making this assessment, and no one has attempted to codify these in a general regulation.

Taken together, the possible regulatory responses coupled with the growing experience base of microlenders and their clients may be suffi-cient to keep overlending from becoming a crisis in most countries. How-ever, the underlying incentives will continue to exert an influence. The days of very low delinquency among MFIs may disappear as competi-tion increases.

## CONCLUSION

This first attempt to analyze how competition will affect MFIs is far from providing answers, but some messages are exceedingly clear. Com-petition puts MFIs into a world in which they have less control than before and that will be characterized by continual change.

A number of specific challenges have surfaced, some of them extremely serious for the continued viability of various MFIs. The need for MFIs and governments to act collectively to avoid overlending is among the most salient. Another challenge is the threat to group lending and to the rigid, inconvenient methodologies that occur when customers have a choice of institutions. This threat compels every institution to rethink its relationship to customers. A third challenge is the recognition of the strong natural advantages available to formal financial institutions, especially large banks, once they become committed to the microfinance sector.

MFIs that wish to survive competition must learn to look outside themselves by adding externally focused competencies in the areas of market research and analysis of competitive advantage. MFIs should gain a deep understanding of their clients and of their own competitive advantages. They should focus their business strategies around enhancing their advantages, particularly those that will help them adapt to the continual change that competition is creating in the microfinance marketplace.

## NOTES

1. References throughout the chapter to the experience of clients of Mibanco, Peru, were provided directly to the author by Elizabeth Dunn of the AIMS project and are based on her extensive survey research, forthcoming from AIMS. The author is grateful to Elizabeth Dunn for her assistance.

2. Author's calculation based on ASOFIN, CIPAME, and FINRURAL, *Microfinanzas: Boletín Financiero* [La Paz] (June 2000).

3. AIMS papers are available on the AIMS section of www.mip.org; MicroSave-Africa papers are available at www.MicroSave-Africa.com.

4. According to William J. Baumol and Alan S. Blinder, a market is said to operate under perfect ompetition when the following four conditions are satisfied:

> 1. Numerous participants. Each seller and purchaser constitutes so small a portion of the market that his or her decisions have no effect on the price.
> 2. Homogeneity of product. The product offered by any seller is identical to that supplied by any other seller.
> 3. Freedom of entry and exit. New firms desiring to enter the market face no impediments that the existing firms can avoid. Similarly, if production and sale of the good proves unprofitable, there are no barriers preventing firms from leaving the market.
> 4. Perfect information. Each firm and each customer is well informed about the available prodcuts and their prices (William J. Baumol and Alan S. Blinder, *Economics: Principles and Policy*, 5th ed. [New York: Harcourt Brace Jovanovich, 1991]).

5. Many additional factors also contributed to BRI's success in savings mobilization, as documented in the writings of Marguerite S. Robinson, *The Microfinance Revolution: Sustainable Finance for the Poor* (Washington, D.C.: World Bank, 2001).

**11.**

# Governance and Ownership of Microfinance Institutions

**María Otero with Michael Chu**

## INTRODUCTION

Governance is the process by which a board of directors, through management, guides an institution in the fulfillment of its corporate mission and protects the institution's assets over the course of time. The board of directors provides oversight, gives direction to managers of the institution, and carries out its function on behalf of a third party. Shareholders constitute the third party in for-profit corporations; in nonprofits the third party is not as easily defined because there are no owners and can include clients, staff, and donors.

The interplay between board and management centers on the relationship between *strategy* and *operation*, with the board basing its discourse on the *strategy* it has jointly defined with management, and with management ensuring that *operations* are deployed effectively. Effective governance occurs when a board is able to provide guidance to management in strategic issues and is effective in being the ultimate arbiter of the performance of management. Management, in turn, assumes operational authority and ensures that the institution's program of activities achieves

This chapter draws heavily from Rachel Rock, María Otero, and Sonia Saltzman, *Principles and Practices of Microfinance Governance* (Bethesda, Md.: Development Alternatives, Microenterprise Best Practices Project, August 1998).

the objectives set forth by the board. Both sets of priorities are required to navigate an institution successfully through its short-term and long-term evolution. The challenge of governance, therefore, is to employ the perspectives and experiences of the board and management to maximize their overall contribution to the institution's performance.

In the case of microfinance, governance has assumed increasing importance for several reasons. First, as microfinance institutions (MFIs) grow in their outreach, the size of their assets, as reflected in their portfolio, also grows to considerable size. Ensuring effective management of this growth requires added input and involvement by a board. Additionally, an increasing number of microfinance institutions are becoming regulated and acquiring shareholders who in turn comprise the board. As regulated institutions, capturing deposits is perhaps their most important challenge and the one that requires the greatest oversight. Finally, microfinance institutions are operating in increasingly competitive markets. Maintaining or increasing market share also becomes an important component of the institution's strategic objective.

This chapter will provide a clear articulation of the function of microfinance boards for effective governance. After a brief discussion of the duties and functions of a board, we describe the key players in governance and set forth the conditions that must exist for effective governance. We then address the major issues that governance of microfinance institutions face, focusing on those that have become regulated and operate as commercial financial institutions. Finally, we provide a summary of ACCION International's experience as shareholding board member of eight microfinance institutions over the last ten years.[1]

## DUTIES OF A BOARD DIRECTOR

Standards of conduct and performance in governance apply to all boards and are framed in three concepts that establish the code of behavior for governance.[2]

- *Duty of Care.* Board members are informed on the data relevant to their decisions, are prudent in deliberations, exercise independent judgment, and are present at meetings.
- *Duty of Loyalty.* Directors place the interest of the corporation above their own or any other entity. This duty also relates to conflicts of interest, corporate opportunity, and confidentiality.

• *Duty of Obedience.* Board members commit to upholding the institution's mission. For nonprofit organizations, the duty of obedience grows, in part, out of the fact that such organizations rely heavily on the public's trust when soliciting donations and grants. In turn, the public has the right to be assured that such funds will be used for the purpose for which they are given (Leifer and Glomb 1992, 33). In for-profit organizations, the responsibility is to the investors (both equity and debt), especially if the funds are from public sources. In this context, being faithful to the institutional mission translates into maximization of returns to investors (and, in some cases, like microfinance, balancing profitability with social impact) in a manner that is consistent with the institution's mission.

## CONTINUUM OF BOARD INVOLVEMENT

There is a continuum of board involvement in the governance of an institution, characterized on one end by the *rubber stamp* board, and on the other end by the *hands-on* board. The *rubber stamp* board exercises too little oversight of management and tends to be ill prepared, short on knowledge, and unlikely to chart a strategic position for the organization. The *hands-on* board is strong in expertise, actively involved in defining the strategy and monitoring its implementation. However, in the extreme, a hands-on board may exercise too much oversight of management and interfere with its work. In the middle of the spectrum falls the *representational* board, which, while less involved than the hands-on board, contributes to the institution in establishing key linkages with the business, banking, and government sectors. The challenge facing a microfinance institution is to achieve the type of board—which here is termed *multi-type*—in which members actively provide guidance in strategic issues without interfering in management's operational responsibilities and assist the institution in establishing key linkages.

## ROLE AND RESPONSIBILITIES
## OF THE BOARD OF DIRECTORS

A board of directors is entrusted with the fiduciary affairs of the organization. The term *fiduciary* refers to a person or persons to whom property or power is entrusted for the benefit of another. Treating directors and managers as fiduciaries provides a mechanism for imposing sanctions if they fail to exercise their responsibilities to the corporation, without necessarily requiring that all of those responsibilities be spelled out in precise detail in advance.

### Legal Obligations of the Board

As a fiduciary, the board of directors has several legal obligations, including ensuring that the institution complies with its articles of incorporation and government rules and regulations, that it maintains its legal status, and that it understands the potential liability to its members.

### Relationship Between Board and Executive

While the relationship between a board and the executive director or CEO evolves over time, it must be grounded in a clear understanding of the respective roles of each. Management is intimately involved in daily operations, has an up-to-date and in-depth understanding of the immediate challenges and opportunities, and is obliged to react in an effective and timely fashion. An institution's executive will consult with senior management on key issues but is accountable on an individual basis to the board. Effective boards maintain operational distance from the institution, drawing on the institutional memory of the directors and making binding decisions as a group.

### Areas of Responsibility

Effective governance requires boards to focus on three major areas of responsibility:

#### Management Accountability

A board must define the process and mechanisms to identify a competent executive, set clear and measurable goals for management, monitor performance of the executive, and identify weaknesses and confront these when they adversely affect the institution. In other words, the board has the ultimate responsibility of hiring, retaining and firing the organization's CEO.

*Strategic Planning and Policy Setting*

The board should provide the following:

- *Direction.* Governance must deal with strategic issues not raised by daily operational priorities of the institution.
- *Institutional Policy.* A policy-centered approach allows a board to place all operational and administrative activities of the institution under the responsibility of management but within the framework of defined policies.
- *Solutions.* The board provides strategic thinking plus guidance, as well as technical skills in order to provide value-added input that may assist the CEO in reaching the institution's goals.

*Board Self-Assessment*

A board must be accountable for its own performance and ensure the quality of its directors while preventing the entrenchment of any director, especially the chair. A mechanism should be in place for self-evaluation and identification of weaknesses.

## THE CONTEXT THAT FRAMES GOVERNANCE

Boards govern in the context of a variety of external actors, which can be divided into three groups: providers of capital, regulatory bodies, and stakeholders. Each group demands different types and degrees of accountability from the institution, depending on the organizational structure of the MFI, as outlined in Table 11.1.

Each of the external actors sets the standards and objectives of accountability that are a condition for its participation. For example, a donor agency might require that an institution's customer base include a certain percentage of women. Regulators set legal limits on leverage for an MFI or procedural standards, such as the daily reporting of an institution's reserves.

The board of every MFI should assess its governance environment. To whom is the MFI externally accountable and in what way? Does the institution's governance adequately and appropriately respond to the expectations of relevant external actors? The relationship among the external actors, the board, and the internal operations as led by management

**Table 11.1: Actors in the Governance Environment by MFI Institution Type**

| | Nonprofit | Public | Mutual | Private/For-profit |
|---|---|---|---|---|
| **Providers of capital** | Donor institutions and individuals, commercial banks (lines of credit), providers of guarantees, NGO itself (through retained earnings) | Government, second-tier financial institutions | Savings deposits of owners/members and external sources of funding such as donors, liquidity funds organized by national and international federations | Providers of equity capital (shareholders) who exercise the responsibilities of ownership; and debt (who may require contractual terms and conditions). These may include profit-maximizing investors, socially responsible investors, NGO retained earnings, management, employees, savings deposits, and multilateral public sector development banks (IIC, IFC) |
| **Regulatory body** | No regulatory body for NGOs. Few regulations for NGOs in developing countries[1] | Superintendency of Banks, Central Bank, Finance Ministry | Where it exists, specialized credit union regulatory agency | Superintendency of Banks |
| **Other stakeholders** | Clients, employees, suppliers of outside expertise (e.g., legal counsel) Microfinance experts | Government officials, clients, employees, suppliers | Members as clients, employees, suppliers | Employees, clients, suppliers, industry |

[1]*Regulations governing nonprofit corporations in the United States are more extensive.*

is dynamic. The board demands internal accountability from management, yet at the same time is accountable to outside actors. The board must also constantly assess which of the external actors are most important for the institution. Figure 11.1 illustrates the context within which a board operates and its relationship to outside forces of accountability. Effective governance requires that board members understand the context in which they operate and respond to it appropriately.

**Figure 11.1: The Context that Frames Governance**

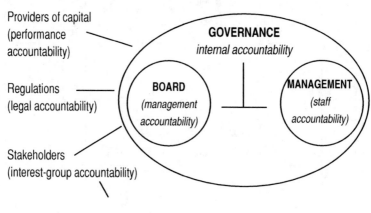

*External accountability*

Having defined the roles and responsibilities of boards, there are additional conditions to ensure effective governance. Individual directors must have the courage and the motivation to take positive action in guarding the best interests of the organization. This often requires an effective director to have something important at stake, which could be financial interests, personal reputation, relationship to a shareholding entity, and/or commitment to the institution itself.

## GOVERNANCE ISSUES IN MICROFINANCE

With the above discussion as a framework, this section addresses issues pertinent to governance for microfinance in particular.

### The Dual Mission:
### Balancing Social Impact with Financial Objectives

Most MFIs originated with a mission that combines social and financial objectives. The social mission—to provide financial services to as many of the lowest income population possible—is combined with a financial objective, which is to achieve financial self-sufficiency, enabling sustained service delivery without dependence on subsidies.

Because profits are a key ingredient in attracting private capital, for-profit MFIs face the difficult task of balancing social and financial objectives: reaching large numbers of very low-income microentrepreneurs while generating profits. Boards, through their own strategic decisions and policies, play a key role in assuring that the MFI responds adequately to both of these objectives.

## OWNERSHIP OF MICROFINANCE INSTITUTIONS

Closely linked to the issue of governance is ownership. The board of directors consists either of owners or of those who represent owners. Aligning the interests of each director with those of the institution is key to realizing effective governance. In regulated MFIs, creating this alignment is more complex because there are different types of owners who may have different priorities for the institution. Table 11.2 shows the predominant sources of equity capital provided for MFIs: NGOs, private investors, public entities, and specialized equity funds (Connell 1998). Each of these owners has a particular set of concerns at stake (Otero 1998). The discussion below considers each type of owner and reviews how its respective characteristics may strengthen or undermine a board's ability to fulfill its roles and responsibilities.

### Nonprofit NGOs

NGOs currently play a significant role as owners of microfinance institutions. The first column in Table 11.2 refers to NGOs that are investors in MFIs, such as Prodem, which currently owns 20 percent of BancoSol; K-Rep Holdings, which owns 25 percent of the K-Rep Bank;

**Table 11.2: What Is at Stake for Owners of Regulated Microfinance Institutions**

| NGO | Private Investors (Short-Term Capital) | Private Investors (Patient Capital) | Public Entities | Specialized Equity Funds |
|---|---|---|---|---|
| Institutional mission | Profit maximization | Return on Investment | Pursue development objectives | Return on investment |
| Return on investment | Dividends, sale of equity in shortest time possible | If necessary, build value through time | Interest in strengthening role in microfinance or entering this field | Institutional mission |
| Long-term concern | Short-term objectives; capacity for quick exit | Incorporates sense of social responsibility | Return on investment | Long-term investment, if necessary |
| Institutional credibility or image | Sacrifice mission to ensure highest profitability | Long-term investment | Political concern | Commitment to advancing microfinance field |

and Acción Comunitaria del Perú (ACP), which owns 60 percent of Mibanco. This shareholding pattern evolves from a predominant model for commercializing microfinance (see Chapter 2) in which an NGO creates a regulated institution and transfers its portfolio in exchange for shares and a board position. Because a growing number of NGOs currently are significant shareholders in regulated MFIs, identifying the strengths and weaknesses of the governance structure of an NGO itself informs our understanding of how these institutions perform the role of governance in a regulated MFI.

No real owners exist in nonprofit organizations. Donors provide the bulk of capital for NGOs, either as grants or concessionary loans. These donors may be private foundations, government foreign aid agencies, multilateral institutions, or individuals.[3] Well-developed NGOs also access commercially priced loans to grow their lending operation. For whom, then, do the boards of nonprofit institutions act as a fiduciary? To whom is the board accountable? While this discussion identifies various key stakeholders for NGOs, as shown in Table 11.2, the answer to the question of accountability is larger than any of the component parts identified in this table. An NGO board is accountable, first and foremost, to the *institutional mission*—as defined and approved by current and previous boards, and as understood by the various stakeholders, including donors and lenders.

Beyond commitment to the institutional mission, directors must have the *ability* to fulfill their duties responsibly, which is primarily a function of (1) their thoughtfulness and basic business sense—allowing board members to identify the warning signs of trouble, and (2) their willingness to pose difficult questions and face other board members and/or management with the problems they identify. Additionally, they must avoid situations that often lead to serious problems or failures. It is important, however, not to draw the conclusion that lack of real owners results necessarily in unstable and risky institutions. The experience of MFIs under this NGO model spans the spectrum from very weak to very successful. When the model has worked, it is because directors have assumed the commitment and responsibility characteristic of owners. For example, the NGO model has yielded successes within microfinance in those instances where individual board members have strongly identified with the institutional mission, possessed the ability to guide the MFI strategically, and held management accountable to performance objectives.

In fact, good governance is what successful NGOs have in common. Examples—among many others—include Compartamos in Mexico, ACP in Peru, ADEMI in the Dominican Republic, Kenya Rural Enterprise Program (K-Rep) in Kenya, ABA in Egypt, BRAC and the Association for Social Advancement (ASA) in Bangladesh, and SHARE in India. Indeed, it is the success of these institutions that has created the option to transform into regulated for-profit financial institutions, an option several of these have chosen.

NGOs have their institutional mission at stake when they assume an ownership role in a for-profit financial institution. Their investment serves as a means for the NGOs to further their mission. Therefore, their ownership role is to ensure that the MFIs do not lose sight of the need to balance profitability with client coverage. In ACCION's experience, the only effective way to do so on a sustained basis is for the NGO to assist actively in the continuous development of intellectual capital capable of producing the operational innovations successfully to serve socially important segments. In addition to expecting a social and financial return on their investment, NGO owners have a long-term concern for the institution. Since the NGO continues to work in the microenterprise development field in some capacity, it is committed to this investment for the long term.

When evaluating the effectiveness of the governance role that an NGO can play in a for-profit institution, it is important to highlight the level of expertise and effort this role will require. That is, the NGO must be able to deploy individuals to perform this function, which often entails high cost, both in cash and in foregone opportunities, at the expense of other priorities. The profile of the person deployed by the NGO—broad-based experience and adept in business, as well as ability to express opinions independently in a board setting—is also key in ensuring effective board representation. Not all NGOs have the in-house capacity to fulfill this role.

Additionally, careful review of reports, financial data, and projections requires an additional time commitment and is necessary for effective participation on a for-profit board. Finally, beyond human resources, the NGO must allocate financial resources to cover expenses related to travel for board representation. If an NGO is to play a significant role, for example as chair of the board or member of the executive committee of a for-profit board, it will incur a considerable investment in time and travel of executive-level staff.

### Private Investors: Short-Term Capital vs. Patient Capital

With few exceptions there is little to no pure private capital in these newly created MFIs (see the second and third columns in Table 11.2).

Such pure private capital is provided by private individuals, corporations, investment funds, and financial institutions, and is divided into two types of owners for MFIs. There are private investors who are short-term profit seekers and are interested solely in making a high return on their investment. They are attracted to MFIs by the impressive results some have achieved *as regulated institutions*—which is what gives potential investors confidence in the transparency and therefore replicability of these results. If there is a real or perceived possibility of earning higher levels of profits by abandoning the original mission of the institution, these owners may push in that direction, since institutional mission is not of particular concern to them. These private investors may be tempted to seek short-term profits, even if, for example, the distribution of dividends at a given point in time may not be the best decision for the institution's longer-term solid financial standing.

A second type of private investor (referred to in Table 11.2 as "patient capital"), motivated as well by return on investment, will also bring to the table a level of social responsibility that is reflected in support for the institution's mission regardless of earnings volatility. As such, patient capital maintains a longer-term perspective of the institution's operations and profit levels. To the extent that the private investors make an investment that is "significant" to them (independent of the absolute amount) in the MFI, they will bring to the board a sharpened interest in detecting early warning signs of potential problems and will seek solutions that do not force the institution to deviate from its mission.

Clearly, the second type of private investor is not only the preferred owner for regulated MFIs, but also the only type of private investor that will contribute in a significant way to the success of the institution, as defined by its client coverage and its profitability. Short-term profit maximizing investors can cause harm to any corporation, MFIs included, by subjugating the entity's longer-term viability to their own priorities, thereby ignoring the most basic responsibilities of governance discussed earlier in this chapter—duties of care, loyalty, and obedience to the institution.

### Public Entities

Public entities include two very different types of institutions—national governments and multilateral agencies, for example, the World Bank, the Inter-American Development Bank (IDB), the Asian Development Bank, and the Corporación Andina de Fomento (CAF). Both types

participate in the ownership of a microfinance institution, largely in response to their own policies and to "political" issues (using "political" in
the broadest sense of the word). Investment in microfinance by public
entities—both governments and multilaterals—is often motivated by the
expected social and economic benefits to microentrepreneurs, such as
increase in employment and income levels. Consequently, these owners
may be less concerned with financial return; their main motivation is
social.

Especially in the case of multilateral agencies, their internal structure
and operating procedures often impede their effective participation as
owners on a board. Staff that is responsible for a portfolio of loans or
projects generally cannot dedicate the necessary time to a board. In some
cases there may not be continuity in the institution's representation on a
given board, thereby decreasing the institution's ability to function effectively as an owner.

Nevertheless, there is interest on the part of some multilaterals in contributing financial expertise and rigor as board members to the institutions in which they invest. Several of them—most notably the IDB through
the Multilateral Investment Fund (MIF)—have invested in specialized
equity funds, which, as discussed below, can serve more effectively as
owners of MFIs.

## Specialized Equity Funds

Specialized equity funds for this sector, such as ProFund and
ACCION's Gateway Fund (discussed below) in Latin America, and the
newly formed AfriCap Microfinance Fund for Africa, have as their objectives first and foremost, preserving capital and obtaining a return on
their investment.[4] They are concerned with achieving a balanced portfolio in terms of country risk, for example, and of meeting the criteria
outlined by the fund's charter, such as the breakdown in investments
between microenterprise and small business. But these owners also have
an institutional mission at stake. For example, in the case of ProFund, in
which the founding shareholders are four NGOs that specialize in
microfinance—ACCION, Calmeadow, FUNDES, and SIDI—the fund
mirrors the long-term interest in the success of the field that is key to the
NGOs that established it. There are several additional equity funds—
Oikocredit, IMI AG (founded by IPC), and DMCF Blue Orchard—with
similar structures.

A specialized equity fund brings additional important elements to the governance of the NGO. Since the fund's main purpose is to realize a gain on its investment, it allocates experienced staff and resources to monitor the performance of the MFI and to provide input at key junctures through board participation. Also, a specialized equity fund brings with it the accumulated expertise in this field through exposure and equity or debt participation in other MFIs. Additionally, as compared to multilaterals, it is also key to highlight the agility with which a specialized fund can make decisions. For example, capital calls that require quick response, whether to respond to regulatory requirements, to bolster a weak institution, or to respond to local financial crises, can best be met by specialized equity funds, which can turn around their decisions very quickly. Indeed, the capability of dedicated and skilled focus in identifying the MFIs in which to invest, the ability to exercise the governance role more effectively, and the structure that allows timely response matched to the circumstances constitute the reasons why it makes sense for the multilaterals to act through specialized funds, as the MIF has determined.

Having defined what is generally at stake for each potential investor in an MFI and what each brings to the board of the institution, one should ask what the appropriate mix of these various investors might be. The response is that in designing the participation of various parties on a MFI board, one should not put "balance" ahead of the willingness and ability of these potential investors to execute their governance role. This is one of the more important lessons learned by ACCION—the pitfall of acting on the stereotypes of the potential classes of investors such as NGOs, multilaterals, governments, private sector, equity funds. The key lies in having clarity as to what constitutes effective governance (as outlined at the beginning of this chapter) and then, on a case-by-case basis, to determine the extent to which the various potential investors are willing and capable of performing these duties.

### Credit Unions

Credit unions, where owners are also the institution's clients, present another form of ownership structure and, because they provide financial services to the microenterprise sector, are briefly discussed here. Member-owners in a credit union are the clients who fall into two categories: net savers and net borrowers. Each group has its own interests and priorities regarding the functioning and financial standing of the credit union. Board directors are democratically elected by membership (one person, one vote), but they may remain beholden to individual members who have mobilized votes on their behalf. Because board positions are restricted to members, directors may not necessarily possess the skills and experience required to manage a financial institution. Additionally, credit unions face challenges in governance related to (1) board representation and (2) regulation and supervision.

### Board Representation of Owners

The tendency toward unequal representation of the interests of the two categories of clients—net savers and net borrowers—can lead to the domination of one type of owner over the other. For example, when net borrowers hold the majority of board positions, they tend to seek policies for cheap credit, prejudicing the net savers. Borrower domination can also result if international organizations channel subsidized lines of credit through the credit unions, thereby discouraging credit unions from mobilizing savings. If the consequences of defaulting on these external funds are minimal, they will encourage a culture of high loan delinquency. Not surprisingly, net savers will not be attracted to such financial institutions.

Effective governance is therefore greatly aided in those credit unions that balance the number of net savers and net borrowers. Net savers are better able to hold management accountable, because they have a vested interest in the institution's profitability as a means of preserving the long-term viability of the credit union. They are also more successful in holding management accountable because of the threat of withdrawal of their deposits. In contrast, net borrowers have a much shorter time frame and favor policies that undermine financial viability, such as low loan rates.

### Prudential Regulation and Supervision

Because credit unions do not raise capital in the financial markets, they are not subjected to fiscal controls, yet they capture savings from their members. When implemented effectively, prudential regulation and supervision act as a check against excessive risk taking on the part of the board and management, and thereby protect credit union members and their *savings*. Specific guidelines for credit union regulations should include rules enforcing the roles and responsibilities of the board of directors, external auditor requirements, controls on insider operations, rules enforcing prudential disciplines, and loan risk-control standards.

Ownership remains intrinsically linked to effective governance, and one cannot assert that any one type of owner is more effective in governance than another. The profile of good governance is not determined by the type of owner, but rather by the adherence to the terms and requirements for all board members outlined in this chapter.

## Fiduciary Responsibility of MFI Boards

In many respects the fiduciary responsibility of the board of a financial intermediary can be considered greater than for other corporate entities. Protecting financial institutions and hence the financial system is a high priority for governments. Without solvent financial institutions, business, commerce, and the economy would become dysfunctional. The financial intermediary's very business is to deploy funds obtained from the public, either through investments from institutions or directly from individuals, which are several times the amount of its equity. Moreover, the liquid nature of a financial institution's product—money—requires more stringent internal controls than those of nonfinancial entities. In the absence of deposit insurance, as is the case in many developing countries, there is an additional emphasis on the fiduciary responsibility of the board of financial institutions in regard to savers. In addition to the need to maintain the solvency of a financial institution, the boards of regulated MFIs have several additional issues to consider that amplify their conventional fiduciary responsibility.

### Access to Financial Services

Microentrepreneurs as *borrowers* have few, if any, viable alternative financial-service providers. An insolvent MFI usually means the end of a client's access to capital at commercial rates. Microentrepreneurs as *savers* are also at greater risk than other economic segments of the populations in the event of loss. They generally lack other pools of savings and the financial-support networks to assist them if their savings are lost.

### The Microfinance Field

In the case of large-scale MFIs, such as BRI in Indonesia, Grameen Bank in Bangladesh, BancoSol in Bolivia, or several other newer but noteworthy institutions, such as K-Rep Bank in Kenya, Mibanco in Peru, and Compartamos in Mexico, insolvency would materially affect both the national and the international microfinance sectors. Given this contagion potential, locally, many low-income people may lose access to financial services, and observers and regulators would raise important questions about the viability of MFIs in the country. Additionally, insolvency of any of the large, widely known MFIs would set the microfinance field back many years. It is likely that potential lenders and investors would express their concern with the viability of this field by withdrawing or curtailing financial resources to microfinance.

## Risk Assessment in Microfinance Institutions

The provision of financial services in general has an associated set of risks, which the board of directors must be able to assess in its role as corporate fiduciary. MFIs operating in developing countries add several layers of additional risk to these operations. The characteristics of microfinance—information gathered in a nontraditional and decentralized process, high mobility of clients, lack of widely accepted guarantees, and rapid portfolio growth that can disguise asset quality—are additional factors that make risk assessment important. Further, the growth experienced by MFIs, the significant increase in competition among MFIs in many settings, and the evolution of some MFIs into regulated institutions make effective risk assessment an essential component of good governance.

The above areas are particularly relevant to any discussion of governance for MFIs. They demonstrate that while this field can make use of the knowledge and experience accumulated on the topic of governance in general, it nevertheless displays unique characteristics that require special attention. For those MFIs that are in the process of establishing regulated institutions and therefore in the midst of designing capital and board structures, the governance issues outlined here provide the basis for addressing them in their own practice. The challenge for all MFIs—nonprofit NGOs, newly created regulated MFIs, and credit unions—is to emerge with strong and long-lasting governance structures that will help assure their long-term sustainability. Toward this end, the concluding section of this chapter expands the discussion to include lessons gleaned from ACCION's experience in the governance of regulated MFIs over the last ten years.

## GOVERNANCE OF REGULATED MICROFINANCE INSTITUTIONS: ACCION'S EXPERIENCE

In the early 1990s ACCION International (with Calmeadow Foundation of Canada) initiated the move toward formalizing MFIs in Latin America with the first transformation of a Bolivian NGO, Prodem, into a bank, BancoSol. As part of this strategy, ACCION created an investment fund that would ensure its shareholding position in newly formed regulated institutions, as well as a position on their board. ACCION's objective for assuming a governance role in these institutions was twofold: (1) to be a player in defining the strategic direction for these institutions; and (2) to ensure that these institutions retain their original mission of reaching poor microentrepreneurs.

### ACCION's Gateway Fund

The ACCION Gateway Fund is a limited liability company created in 1997. It invests directly in MFIs that are regulated or in nonprofits that are being transformed into regulated financial institutions. The fund, which was capitalized by grants made to ACCION, is managed by Gateway ACCION International Manager, Inc. (GAIM), a wholly owned for-profit subsidiary of ACCION International. The investment objective of the fund is to generate long-term capital gains and current income through investments in equity, quasi-equity, and medium-term debt securities issued by MFIs in Latin America and the Caribbean. The estimated life of the Gateway Fund is ten years, with two three-year extensions at the option of the manager.

Since its founding, the Gateway Fund has invested in eight MFIs in Latin America and the Caribbean that form part of the ACCION Network or are long-term partners of ACCION. These investments help support a combined loan portfolio of over US$200 million in institutions that reach some 280,000 active clients (as of December 31, 2001). The Gateway Fund has been a founding member in startup MFIs in Haiti, Ecuador, and Venezuela. In addition, the Gateway Fund has provided the capital required for nonprofit MFIs to become fully regulated entities in Mexico and Peru. In all cases Gateway invests as a minority shareholder and plays a role in bringing other investors to the table.

In its role as investor, ACCION has participated actively in the governance of these institutions, attending monthly board meetings held in most institutions and carrying out the roles described in this chapter of a responsible board director. From ACCION's nearly ten years of experience investing in MFIs, the following are the major areas in which it believes governance of regulated MFIs is of particular importance.

## Maintaining High-Quality Management

From ACCION's experience, the underlying philosophy of good governance is to work in a collaborative fashion with the institution's management, and so long as it is merited, to demonstrate full and continuously expressed support for its performance. In this context the board facilitates and helps good management perform in as superior a manner as possible, providing support, obtaining information, and opening doors when needed. There are many examples in which high-quality managers are leading MFIs very effectively and are working closely with their boards of directors in this regard.

However, when management's performance can hinder the institution, perhaps the most important responsibility of governance is to avoid its entrenchment. The board must remain alert to managerial shortcomings that could be adverse for the institution. Changes in management may be required for a variety of reasons:

- The skills of the general manager are not aligned with the conditions the institution is facing. In some cases highly competent managers may be very well suited to lead the institution only during certain period of its development. For example, a manager who is highly effective at the startup of operations may lack the core competence needed to take the institution through expansion. The manager who can perform when the macroeconomic environment is friendly may be unable to lead the institution through an economic recession or financial downturn. Conversely, a manager who can bring an institution out of a crisis situation may not be nearly as effective once the institution is back on its feet.
- The board loses confidence in the manager for reasons beyond poor institutional performance or dramatic instances of weak competence on the part of the manager. Erosion of trust can be gradual, fueled by justifiable concerns, such as small but repeated poor

judgment calls by the manager, as well as less tangible reasons, such as personality differences that over time hinder the effective collaboration between the manager and the board. Even in cases in which the institution is performing well, boards may choose to replace the manager to safeguard the future.

- Introduction of a new set of core competencies needed for the future performance of the institution may also lead to managerial changes. For example, when an institution transforms from an NGO to a bank, its board must decide if existing leadership can assume the new responsibilities of a commercial institution. Since there are examples of NGO managers performing very effectively as managers of commercial institutions, as well as ample cases of the opposite outcome, a board cannot base its decision solely on the previous experience of other institutions.

In exercising its governance role, ACCION has participated in a variety of situations in which the board had to make changes in management for one of the reasons listed above. Effective governance when carrying out this responsibility includes playing some or all of the following roles:

- *Taking the lead in replacing management.* Any one member or group of members on a board can initiate a discussion regarding the effectiveness of management. If board members are fulfilling their duties to the institution—and holding these above their individual interests, personal relationships, and other concerns—then all board members need to be prepared to play this role at any time they believe the institution's future could be compromised.
- *Creating and participating in an effective process to obtain board consensus on whether to retain or release management.* The process of achieving board consensus on management's performance is essential, regardless of whether it chooses to retain or to replace management. This consensus must be ratified repeatedly, especially when an institution is going through a difficult stretch and the management needs clarity about the board's backing. If there are board members who disagree with the decision the board makes, it will be very difficult for existing management to operate effectively, and even more difficult for new management to gain the needed support of the board.

- *Holding management to highest standards.* ACCION's long-term experience with a wide range of MFIs, both nonprofit and regulated, has enabled it to define the profile of what constitutes effective management in this field, and to address this issue from its board seat. Some of the ways a board helps define high-quality management is by helping set up reporting formats, defining success benchmarking, and, in some cases, broadening the perspective to a national strategy. These, among others, have served as measures for determining the quality of management and its continued tenure.
- *Bringing global expertise and performance standards.* ACCION's expertise in microfinance has made it particularly adept in addressing this area. It has ensured that the board be well informed and up to date on the latest developments in the field, and measured the institution against these. Board knowledge of advancements in the field, for example, in market research, operational efficiency, loan loss provisioning, and introduction of new products, has improved the board's own capacity to assess the quality of management.
- *Maintain close watch.* Maintaining close contact with management and asking the hard questions, both strategic and operational, has enabled ACCION to assess, on an ongoing basis, how management was proceeding in its work.

Quality of management is fundamental to a field that is still in its infancy and to institutions that are management led. Replacement of management and definition of an effective process to do so—including lessons about clarity of expected performance measures—constitute some of the most difficult decisions that a board must make. Part of a board's effectiveness comes from maintaining frequent communication with management to (1) define areas of weak performance and (2) ensure management of full board support when it exists.

### Ensuring Board and Shareholder Effectiveness

Shareholder composition in MFIs varies. In some cases there is no majority shareholder; in others, especially those that have transformed from NGOs, the NGO holds a majority share. In many cases there are also individuals, selected by the shareholders, who are part of the board. In all cases ensuring board effectiveness requires that shareholders assume certain responsibilities. A majority position is not required to ensure that the governance of the institution is effective. In ACCION's case, it has maintained a minority shareholding position in every institution in which it has an investment. Its expertise in the field and a clear design either to work actively toward consensus on the board or, when necessary, to form influential blocs with other like-minded investors have enabled it to maintain a strong governance voice in these institutions. In the process it is able to initiate or participate in addressing the following issues with the full board:

- Upholding shareholders' value.
- Shareholder composition, including attracting potentially good shareholders and addressing the structural weaknesses of having an NGO in a majority position.
- Shareholder responsibility to the microfinance industry—protecting the development of microfinance.
- Recognition that while keeping governments out of shareholding positions is an underlying principle based on decades of experience, there are exceptions, such as IFI's shareholding position in FINAMERICA. Shareholders should explore under what circumstances governments can be involved as shareholders.
- Definition of the ground rules for board operations, as well as emphasis on building consensus among its members.
- Alignment with other shareholders to build a strong position in which several minorities together can have a stronger voice.
- Addressing governance as a topic for board members to discuss as part of their own internal assessment.
- Playing the role of chair—as ACCION has done in the case of BancoSol for three years and currently in Banco Solidario in Ecuador.

### *Active Role in Advising and Being a Friendly Critic of the General Manager*

Evaluating performance is not the only role that a board member should play in relation to management. Under normal circumstances the board and management work together in moving the institution forward, each effectively playing its respective role and operating together in a trust relationship. Part of governance, especially for board members who are very knowledgeable about microfinance, is to assume the following responsibilities: (1) to serve as a sounding board for management for good ideas or resolution of problems, as well as a source of advice; and (2) to assist in developing the business plan by addressing strategic questions through conversations and meetings, thereby helping management define the plan it will present to the board.

## Addressing Major Country Financial Crises or Policy Reforms Adverse to Microfinance

MFIs in various countries have encountered national-level crises, disasters, or policies that have adversely affected their operations. In these circumstances the board must step in to assume the role of defining and implementing a solution. There are three widely known examples in the last few years. First, the financial meltdown in Ecuador in 1998, which seriously threatened the viability of Banco Solidario, among other things, because of the severe lack of liquidity in the system. For an MFI, suspending lending to current clients is tantamount to closing the bank's doors. The board, led by ProFund and ACCION, was able to mobilize additional capital from other sources to help the institution overcome the most critical period.

Second, in Colombia the government instituted an interest-rate ceiling that did not permit FINAMERICA to operate in a viable manner. Board members and management met with government officials, conducted workshops, and pressured for changes to this policy. The result was the creation of a fee structure that has allowed MFIs to operate viably.

Finally, in Bolivia the economic recession, a long period of political uncertainty, and banking-system deterioration combined with several factors specific to microfinance to create a very difficult environment for MFIs. The over-indebtedness of the microfinance sector as it reeled from the bad practices of consumer lenders combined with an increasingly negative ambience for MFIs fueled by public demonstrations demanding debt forgiveness have required a very active role on the part of the board to address these issues strategically and operationally in each institution.

## Lessons in Effective Governance of MFIs

The experience of governance of regulated MFIs draws from the lessons of effective governance for any organization or company but also brings with it factors that are particular to microfinance. The following summarizes the most important lessons of ACCION's experience in governance of the last ten years.

- The board needs to take risks and act sooner rather than later when there are serious misgivings regarding the management of an MFI. In one case, ACCION gave management the benefit of the doubt and did not move quickly enough to insist on its replacement when it had such serious misgivings. The outcome of this mistake, as in the Finansol case described in Chapter 8, can lead to a crisis that requires enormous resources to overcome. In Finansol, ACCION, a minority shareholder, had to spearhead a rescue operation, divert scarce human resources from other technical efforts, and scramble to bring additional capital into the weakened institution.
- If the board does not establish well-defined performance expectations of management, it is very difficult to measure performance. Under these circumstances, when the board is dissatisfied with management, even if its reasons are valid, it cannot hold management accountable based on agreed standards of performance. This can create a situation that will potentially damage the institution.
- Developing a trust relationship between board and management is essential. The board has to be vigilant that it does not take this trust relationship for granted or lightly, permitting its misuse by board members or management. If the trust between the board and management erodes, it is very hard to regain.
- Because most shareholders in MFIs lack quick access to additional sources of capital, shortness of additional investment capital at crucial moments will require a concerted, dedicated effort on the part of the board to mobilize this capital.
- Short-term, profit-maximizing investors should not invest in MFIs if they are only pursuing the returns usually associated with the high growth seen in the early stages. Optimal private investors are those whose objectives for return are balanced with an understanding that preserving outstanding returns in this field is not the result of a magic bullet or unique virtues of the poor, but a consequence of management talent in the face of continuously changing circumstances as a young industry matures. In this regard microfinance is no different from any other emerging industry. If, on top of this, the private investor has a sincere appreciation for the social impact of the MFI, this will sustain a real commitment to the long-term

strength of the institution and ensure its adherence to its original mission. It is interesting to note that purely commercial investors have not been key to maintaining the commercial orientation of microfinance. While microfinance has attracted private investors, mostly local, these have made small investments in relation to the capital needed to reach massive numbers. Therefore equity funds that specialize in microfinance, whether fully owned by an entity, as in the case of ACCION's Gateway Fund, or that combine investors from various sources, as is the case of ProFund, AfriCap, and IMI, are particularly important players at this stage of development of regulated MFIs.

- There is considerable time and cost associated with the governance role. Governance requires constant interaction with management, detailed review of financials, and personal presence at board meetings and other board-related meetings. No institution, equity fund, or individual should take on a governance role unless its demands are clearly understood from the outset.
- Board members must assume the responsibility of protecting the microfinance field so that it can operate effectively. This role requires that one engage in considerable education of policy officials, regulators, supervisors, and others to avoid the emergence of negative policies or regulatory frameworks.

In summary, boards in which shareholders can set aside their own specific priorities and work together on a common vision constitute the most effective boards. Board members may differ one from the other—for example, the issuance of dividends, rate of return, or exit strategies—and still operate with the spirit of reaching consensus on behalf of what is best for the institution. If board members pull in different directions or give mixed directives to managements, they ultimately become a hindrance to the proper functioning of the institution. Commitment to building consensus in the context of the established rules for good governance is perhaps the most essential characteristics of effective governance.

## NOTES

1. ACCION became a board member of a regulated microfinance institution in 1992, when BancoSol was converted from an NGO into a bank. Since then, ACCION has become a minority shareholder in seven other regulated MFIs and is a member of the board in each.

2. This section is drawn from George W. Overton, ed., *Guidebook for Directors of Nonprofit Corporations* (Chicago: American Bar Association, 1993).

3. In the early stages of an MFI's existence, this capital is used for both operations and lending. As the institution matures and achieves greater levels of self-sufficiency, the loan capital is often obtained from local financial institutions.

4. There are a growing number of specialized equity funds. A recent survey conducted by CGAP identifies nearly forty such funds operating in the developing world and Eastern Europe.

# 12

# The Experience
# of Microfinance Institutions
# with Regulation and Supervision
### Perspectives from Practitioners and a Supervisor

**Leslie Théodore with Jacques Trigo Loubière**

Regulation and supervision have been prevalent topics in the microfinance field for the past several years. As the financial systems approach gained popularity with the success of BancoSol in Bolivia as the first commercial bank dedicated solely to microfinance, other microfinance institutions (MFIs), particularly in Latin America, have sought to gain access to the benefits of being a licensed, regulated financial institution. Regulated microfinance has occurred in a variety of forms: NGOs transforming into commercial banks or specialized financial entities; commercial banks going "down-market" and introducing microfinance products; and regulated institutions created for the express purpose of microfinance. The regulations governing these entities vary by type of entity and country.

The primary purpose of regulation of financial institutions is to "protect the solvency of financial intermediaries, keeping two objectives in mind: on a macro level, to protect the stability of the payments system, and on the micro level, to offer protection to the depositor (particularly the small depositor) from losses."[1] Supervision is the oversight process of ensuring that regulations are adhered to, risk is minimized, and troubled institutions are improved or closed. These broad purposes must be applied practically in a way that is relevant to microfinance.

Microfinance literature thus far has treated the broad topic of regulation and supervision somewhat theoretically. Focus has been on understanding different types of regulatory frameworks and the appropriateness of their use in the microfinance environment. Now that regulated microfinance has existed in numerous places for several years, it is possible to examine how the ideals of prudential regulation and supervision have been translated *in practice* to microfinance.

This chapter examines the experience in Latin America of commercial MFIs with supervision. Do the benefits of supervision outweigh the costs? Does supervision hamper growth in any way? What changes, if any, would MFIs recommend to the supervising agencies in their countries? Credit unions and other regulated but noncommercial entities were not examined. Credit unions operate in ninety-one countries, serve 108 million people and are an important part of the complete picture of regulating and supervising microfinance. However, the history of their regulation and supervision is a story unto itself, distinct from that of commercial MFIs (see Chapter 5).

While it is beneficial to collect the views of MFIs based upon their experiences with supervision, these must be balanced by the realistic constraints and requirements of the supervisory authorities. Therefore, this chapter also presents insights from Jacques Trigo Loubière, former superintendent of banks and currently minister of finance of Bolivia, regarding the approaches that can be taken to address the concerns of MFIs.

## THE MFI EXPERIENCE OF SUPERVISION

> *In order to operate as a regulated entity, you must reconcile yourself to what is possible given the existing rules, while explaining to the regulatory agencies the realities of the microfinance market.*
>
> —Banco Solidario, Ecuador

To understand whether there is a "happily ever after" for regulated MFIs, interviews were conducted with seven MFIs in Latin America: BancoSol (Bolivia), Banco Solidario (Ecuador), Caja los Andes (Bolivia), Calpia (El Salvador), Compartamos (Mexico), Finsol (Honduras), and Mibanco (Peru). The goal was to examine *how* the institutions are being supervised, and *what* is being supervised, and *what changes* the practitioners would suggest to the content and implementation of supervision.

The seven institutions interviewed represent six different countries and three different types of regulated entities. Two are commercial banks dedicated to microfinance that transformed from NGOs (BancoSol and Mibanco). One is a commercial bank that opened with 100 percent private capital for microfinance (Banco Solidario). The remaining four are NGOs that transformed into non-bank regulated entities or *financieras,* which have lower capital requirements and a more limited range of permitted activities than commercial banks. A brief background on each institution is provided in Table 12.1. Interviews with the seven MFIs revealed various opinions and experiences regarding interest rates, costs versus benefits of supervision, licensing issues, ongoing issues, supervisors' expertise, discussed below.

### Interest Rate

None of the MFIs cited interest rate regulation as a concern, because most operate in countries in which they can determine rates according to their requirements for financial viability. In the case of Banco Solidario of Ecuador, however, the Central Bank imposed interest rate ceilings of 24 percent in 2000. Banco Solidario had established a break-even interest rate of 36 percent per annum. The deficit was overcome by negotiating with the Central Bank a capped fixed commission of no more than US$150 per loan. Legally, this can be applied to any loan (consumer, micro, or corporate), but in practice it is only relevant to smaller loans. It is worth noting, however, that calls for interest rate restrictions are increasing in several countries of the region and that this issue could surface as a central concern for MFIs in the near future.

### Costs vs. Benefits of Being Regulated

> *Supervision allows informal institutions to formalize completely. It also forces these institutions to face their real situation, helping them to identify their weaknesses and opportunities in the market.*
>
> —BancoSol, Bolivia

> *Supervision contributes to better management.*
> —Calpia, El Salvador

From the MFI perspective there are benefits to being regulated, including increased access to capital, ability to provide a broad product

Table 12.1: Background on MFIs Interviewed

| Institution | BancoSol | Banco Solidario | Caja los Andes | Calpia[1] | Compartamos | FINSOL | Mibanco |
|---|---|---|---|---|---|---|---|
| **Country** | Bolivia | Ecuador | Bolivia | El Salvador | Mexico | Honduras | Peru |
| **Founded** | 1986 | 1995 | 1991 | n/a | 1990 | 1985 | 1969 |
| **Original name/structure** | Prodem/NGO | n/a | Procrédito/ NGO | Ampes Servicio Crediticio/ NGO | Compartamo/ NGO | Funadeh/ NGO | ACP/NGO |
| **Regulated** | 1992 | 1995 | 1995 | 1995 | 2001 | 1999 | 1998 |
| **New structure** | Commercial bank | Commercial bank | Financiera (FFP)[2] | Financiera | Financiera (SOFOL)[3] | Financiera | Commercial bank |
| **Number of active clients** | 60,976 | 14,645 | 41,665 | 34,390 | 62,797 | 15,026 | 58,088 |
| **Portfolio (US$ million)** | 77.8 | 6.3 | 46.8 | 26.5 | 10.9 | 6.3 | 36.9 |

[1] All statistics as of December 31, 2000, except Calpia's, which are as of December 31, 1999.
[2] Fondo Financiero Privado (private financial fund) is a specific structure for regulated non-bank MFIs in Bolivia.
[3] Sociedad Financiera de Objeto Limitado (limited liability financial company) is a regulated private-finance company in Mexico.

mix (especially savings and payments), and improved credibility. These benefits, however, are accompanied by increased direct costs, such as adding and training staff, modifying or replacing management information systems and supervisory fees. Indirect costs may include decreased flexibility and increased workload for staff dealing with examiners (Valenzuela and Young 1999, 10). FINSOL, for example, noted that supervision takes away some flexibility in decision-making and implementation of activities.

The MFIs interviewed were unable to state definitively their costs related to regulation and supervision. Nevertheless, most believe that the benefits of being regulated outweigh the costs. In addition to the direct, anticipated benefits, MFIs cited increased profitability, better general understanding of their clients, and the ability to offer more innovative products. Compartamos noted that while it is heavily supervised, as an SOFOL it is legally unable to capture savings and, therefore, the benefits may not (yet) outweigh the costs.[2]

### Initial Hurdles: Licensing and Approval Process

> *The process was long and tedious (lasting more than two years). The principal obstacles were: (1) the low priority the authorities placed on this, given the fact that the regulatory staff has a high volume of other work, and (2) the supervisors' lack of knowledge of microfinance.*
>
> —Compartamos, Mexico

> *The whole process was slow and complicated by virtue of our being the first FFP in the country.*
>
> —Caja los Andes, Bolivia

Most of the institutions interviewed were the first MFIs to obtain licenses in their countries. For this reason their experiences may have been more difficult than that of subsequent MFIs.

MFIs mentioned two areas of difficulty during the process of licensing and approval: (1) creating a capital and ownership structure that would satisfy the regulatory requirements, and (2) adjusting internal operations to meet regulatory standards.

### Minimum Capital Requirements

Maintaining adequate capital provides protection to institutions against various risks, allows for absorption of losses and therefore instills confidence among investors, lenders, clients, and regulators. But what *is* an adequate level of capital for microfinance? Minimum capital requirements for the institutions interviewed ranged from US$1 million to US$8 million. In some cases the choice to become a *financiera* rather than a bank was influenced by the high requirements for obtaining a banking license. It is widely accepted that the minimum capital requirements for specialized MFIs need not be as high as those for full-service commercial banks because of the low total portfolio size and the fact that the portfolio is not concentrated in a few large loans. Levels that are too high may discourage MFIs from commercialization, while low levels may allow unqualified entrants and may not provide enough control incentive to owners. Most institutions interviewed did not have difficulty meeting the minimum capital requirements for their chosen form. For a list of the minimum captial requirements for the surveyed countries, see Table 12.2.

**Table 12.2: Minimum Capital Requirements for Commercialization (US$ in millions)**

| Country | *Financiera* | Commercial Bank |
|---|---|---|
| Bolivia | 1 | 5.6 |
| Ecuador | 1.3 | 2.6 |
| El Salvador | 1 | 2.5 |
| Honduras | 5 | 8 |
| Mexico | 2.2 | n/a |
| Peru | n/a | 5.6 |

Information gathered from MFIs and bank superintendency websites, December 31, 2000, using local currency/US$ exchange rate as of that date.

### Special Regulatory Windows

In some countries the authorities have responded to the need for lower minimum capital requirements for MFIs by creating *financieras,* such as the FFPs (private finance funds) in Bolivia and EDPYMEs (small business and microenterprise development institutions) in Peru. Usually, these structures have fewer barriers to entry than a commercial banking license (such as lower minimum capital requirements), and they often place limits on the intermediary capability of the institutions, restricting the ability to capture savings and participate in the payments system. In some countries *financieras* predate microfinance. In those cases transforming

MFIs have been able to take advantage of these preexisting frameworks, as was the case for Compartamos, FINSOL, and Calpia.

The principal proposed benefit of specialized regulatory categories for MFIs is the ability to attract more sustainable institutions into the market, ultimately allowing for greater outreach to the poor. Robert Peck Christen and Richard Rosenberg warn against premature creation of new regulatory categories for microfinance in countries lacking sufficient successful MFIs to take advantage of the specialization. They warn against assuming that successful examples of specialized regulatory forms, such as the FFP in Bolivia, will transfer to countries where the context and environment differ. Specifically, they are concerned about providing licenses to weak institutions or institutions that cannot be effectively supervised or both (Christen and Rosenberg 2000, 26–27). Robert C. Vogel, Arelis Gomez, and Thomas Fitzgerald state that a potential danger is "a possibly endless proliferation of different regulatory specializations according to the development of new specialized market niches" (Vogel et al. 1999, 6).

## Ownership

> *The supervisors could not understand how a nonprofit organization could be an owner of a financial institution.*
> —Compartamos, Mexico

A chief challenge for MFIs is to assemble a group of founders-owners that meets the requirements of the banking authorities. Ownership is a fundamental issue because, unlike the directors of an NGO, the shareholders of a financial institution have to place their capital at risk and the institution's directors have fiduciary responsibility for the institution's health. Unconventional ownership persists even with transformed MFIs, because shareholders are not the for-profit investors who normally launch banks but a mix of NGOs, multilaterals, and others.

As Christen and Rosenberg note:

> Most of today's MFIs do not have this kind of ownership: large chunks of money from private, profit-seeking pockets seldom account for much of their equity base. The problem derives not from the personal quality of MFI board members, but rather from the organic structure of their incentives. This ownership problem is not solved just by getting a banking license. It is solved only where the ownership moves more

into the hands of people who will lose large sums of money if the institution goes under (Christen and Rosenberg 2000, 6).

Banking authorities must apply rules to MFIs that were originally developed to ensure that traditional financial institutions have sound ownership structures. The authorities have often been reluctant to approve the unconventional ownership structures proposed by transforming NGOs and have been particularly reluctant to accept NGOs and foreign institutions as shareholders.

When Compartamos transformed into a SOFOL, the supervisors were heavily involved in the process of authorizing advisors and board members, even asking Compartamos to change the proposed president of the board before approving the license. In the case of FINSOL, the regulations allowed only for individual citizens to be founders of a financial institution. Therefore, the NGO, Funadeh, could not participate as a founder of the institution it was creating. However, after the founding of FINSOL, Funadeh was able to buy shares of FINSOL, becoming the principal owner of the new institution.

The process through which an NGO gains ownership is important. Experience has shown that it is easier to ensure transparency in the transfer if the new regulated institution does not receive a portfolio from the NGO as part of its capital contribution in the new entity.[3]

### Internal Operations

> *Supervision does support the business by strengthening internal controls.*
>
> —FINSOL, Honduras

> *Our advice in dealing with ongoing supervision would be as follows: First, define in a clear and precise form the norms and parameters required. Later, establish mechanisms of control that are supported by the information systems, and possibly most important, ensure that all staff of the organization understand that the work of supervision and control is a general responsibility.*
>
> —Mibanco, Peru

Internal controls are the policies and procedures established by MFIs to ensure that their operations are efficient, effective, and adhere to banking regulations, and that their financial statements are accurate. Internal control is one mechanism MFIs use to minimize risk.

Most MFIs interviewed noted that re-engineering operating procedures, particularly in the area of internal control, was required to obtain a license as a regulated institution. As NGOs, the pre-transformation MFIs had not been subject to rigorous requirements for developing internal-control systems. In BancoSol, for example, internal controls were almost non-existent in the institution at the start of the transformation process. The internal audit function had not been sufficiently developed, and various other operational changes were also required.

The decentralized nature of microlending has often meant that MFIs have had unconventional types of internal controls not considered legitimate by bank examiners. NGOs often handled internal controls more informally, or purposefully avoided cumbersome controls in order to streamline their systems. For example, decentralization of loan approvals may include the authority of loan officers to approve applications in the field without the input of branch managers or credit committees, while regulators may require loan approval by at least two levels within the institution.

FINSOL recommends that institutions in Honduras considering transformation analyze their operating structures in relation to the laws of the country and undertake a thorough re-engineering of their operating processes.

## Staffing

> *At the beginning, it was complicated for the authorities to accept the fact that the same management that operated the NGO was going to administer the* financiera. *However, when they better understood the operations and saw that, in fact, we were already operating as a large* financiera *with all the requirements, they accepted it. Also, it helped that many of the staff had been in commercial banking.*
> —Compartamos, Mexico

> *In our institutions we must have personnel with knowledge and experience with supervisory norms, because these personnel must be in charge of receiving the supervisors and accompanying them through the entire control process. In this way, we can guarantee that the supervisors will have what they need in less time and with better quality.*
> —BancoSol, Bolivia

Supervisors review management qualifications before licensing an MFI, particularly for NGOs transforming into regulated MFIs. During the licensing process the applicant must present proposed managers and board members, and regulators must be convinced that the proposed team has the requisite skills to operate a financial institution.

In BancoSol's experience, staffing was a major issue in its transformation to a commercial bank. BancoSol contracted new staff with banking experience particularly in the areas of operations, accounting, and cashiers. Some of the new staff performed new functions (such as asset-and-liability management, liaison with supervisors), while in other cases staff with banking experience were brought in to fill existing vacancies in mainline operations. Therefore, personnel expenses rose during the transition and remained higher than they had been for the NGO. Caja los Andes also found that it needed to assign additional personnel to certain areas, such as evaluation of credit risk.

### Ongoing Supervision Issues

The challenges discussed above are generally dealt with as part of an institution's process of qualifying for a financial institution license and are not major issues once suitable systems and structures are in place. We now turn to core issues that remain throughout the life of a regulated MFI and apply to all aspects of operations.

### Reporting Requirements

> *Licensing brings drastic, substantial change for the institution in terms of reporting requirements, but without doubt, it is a beneficial change. All of the operating areas have been organized so that we can send monthly reports to the supervisors within the first ten days of the month. In our organization this has been automated 100 percent.*
> —FINSOL, Honduras

> *To date, supervision of information systems has been the major problem in terms of managing growth in operations with maximum efficiency and reliability.*
> —Calpia, El Salvador

In mitigating credit risk, bank supervisors rely on frequent reporting, particularly of portfolio quality indicators. The adaptation of the management information system to accommodate reporting requirements has been one of the principal tasks of re-engineering for MFIs during transformation. The system must be able to provide data, such as liquidity levels and asset quality, while also focusing on aggregate analysis of the portfolio.

Reporting requirements vary by country. In Bolivia and Peru daily reporting is required, while in Mexico and Honduras there are monthly requirements. The method of submission also varies by country. In Bolivia all submissions are done electronically through a protected network, while in Peru the majority are printed and sent through the mail.

In all of the MFIs interviewed, adherence to supervisory reporting requirements was noted as a challenge during the initial phase of licensing and throughout the life of the regulated institution. MFIs report that the *frequency* of the reporting is more difficult than the *content* of the reports. Daily reporting does not allow for problems such as systems failures and communication difficulties associated with operating in rural areas. Calpia noted that some reports are required more frequently than necessary and place undue demands on MFIs.

## Capital Adequacy and Leverage

Because MFIs have portfolios with low sectoral diversification and somewhat volatile delinquency, there are often stricter regulations in terms of leverage, provisioning, and liquidity (Lapenu 2000, 31). The Basle Agreement, which defines banking standards for the traditional banking industry, allows lending institutions to leverage their capital by twelve times. Regulators and other experts suggest that this factor is too high for microfinance. A rule of thumb often used is that a leverage factor of six or seven times may be more appropriate for microfinance. However, no research yet exists on which to base sound policy recommendations.

## Risk Classification of Loans

> *There exists a prejudice within the Superintendency as well as within the credit bureaus that microfinance is riskier than traditional banking. This damages the image of MFIs.*
> —Caja los Andes, Bolivia

An MFI's portfolio is assessed and separated into risk categories in order to determine the amount of provisions that must be set aside to cover potential loan losses. At least three problems arise between supervisors and MFIs in this area:

- Supervisors may classify microfinance loans as risky because they are not secured in conventional ways. This is a major issue and occurs repeatedly.
- Supervisors may not know how to measure and monitor the risk of a microloan portfolio. Their supervision methods were developed for assessing portfolios of fewer, much larger loans. This, too, has been a significant issue.
- Supervisors may apply provisioning rules for delinquent loans that are not suited to microfinance. This has not often been a major issue, as most transforming MFIs have already adopted a strict aging of arrears schedule to set provisions.

Difficulty arises because microfinance loans differ from other types of loans, and, according to MFIs interviewed, supervisors do not yet understand the risk associated with microfinance loans. Supervisors accustomed to reviewing larger individual loans at other financial institutions may review many small individual loans at MFIs. In reality, the risk of each of these small loans individually is minimal. It would be more effective to review the history and trends of portfolio quality in the institution and delinquency control systems.

From the practitioner perspective, a lack of understanding of the loan terms, the associated risk, and risk mediation results in higher levels of provisioning and more restricted leverage than should be required. These restrictions can handicap profitability: provisions are taken directly out of income, reducing the annual bottom line, while restricted leverage reduces returns to equity by keeping the portfolio smaller for a given amount of equity.

At the heart of this problem is the question of whether microloans are adequately secured. By prioritizing collateral documentation over payment history in assessing credit quality, supervisors show a lack of confidence in the risk-control techniques of microfinance. Bank regulations place a limit on the level of unsecured loans within a portfolio. In fact, such restrictions are part of the Basle guidance. Thus, if supervisors insist upon traditional collateral, the MFI may be in noncompliance with regulations or restricted from expanding its services (Churchill and Berenbach 1997, 40).

For BancoSol, solidarity-group lending posed an ongoing difficulty. These loans were classified as unsecured because regulations did not recognize group guarantees as a legitimate form of security. If rules governing unsecured lending had been strictly enforced, BancoSol would have had to close, as the rules specified that only a small share of a bank's assets could be held in unsecured loans. This situation was only formally resolved after the Superintendency's regulations recognized the validity of the solidarity-group guarantee, some years after BancoSol began. Until then, BancoSol had been operating precariously under a waiver that could have been revoked at any time.

In Peru, the Superintendency classifies loans as either microenterprise or commercial credit. Mibanco, however, has found problems with the criteria used to make this distinction. Mibanco noted that "the SBS [Superintendency of Banking Supervision] has defined a business as micro only if, simultaneously, the volume of its assets—excluding fixed assets—is less than US$20,000 and its total accumulated debt also is less than US$20,000. Our experience has demonstrated that in many cases, for the growth of the client's business or for the need to modernize its production processes, these limits are insufficient and should be increased."

In Ecuador, the Superintendency does not recognize microenterprise loans as a separate classification. The loans are classified as consumer loans, which are not allowed to exceed US$20,000. Without a microloan classification, it is unclear what type of guarantee is required, and there is a potential for interest rate control. According to Banco Solidario, because its loans are classified as consumer loans, the supervisors do not recognize the microlending cost structure.

## Documentation Requirements

> *The required documentation for very small loans should be minimal, and that which should serve as assurance is the existence of the business and/or past credit.*
>
> —Mibanco, Peru

> *At the time of transformation we had to collect the documents to back up all the loans we had already made so that we could fulfill the norms.*
>
> —BancoSol, Bolivia

Loan documentation requirements for traditional credit do not transfer well to microcredit. Documentation such as financial statements, tax returns, registration, and licenses are generally not available for microbusinesses. For the microlenders, attempts to obtain such traditional documentation and to register collateral can be prohibitively expensive or not feasible. One of the MFIs interviewed also noted that no paper trail exists for illiterate applicants. Although loan officers do collect information directly from the borrowers and construct documentation such as cash-flow statements in analyzing borrowing potential, supervisors may not regard this internally generated documentation as sufficient. During the licensing process, for example, Compartamos was asked by regulators to modify its contracts and promissory notes.

### Microfinance Expertise of Supervisors

> *Some of the supervisors have knowledge of microfinance, a fact that facilitates mutual understanding and aids the supervision work. We believe that within the Superintendency there should be personnel specialized in the supervision of microfinance entities.*
>
> —Mibanco, Peru

> *Supervision is often too rigid or extreme in the use and application of norms, which sometimes do not fit the characteristics of the microfinance market. Thus, there is a need for more flexibility in the implementation of the rules. It is necessary to complete specialization and professional development of the people in charge of controlling and supervising MFIs.*
>
> —BancoSol, Bolivia

The Bolivian Superintendency has been a leader in the area of specialized supervision, creating a separate unit of supervisors to oversee microfinance. To increase their capacity, they have received technical assistance and adapted the ACCION CAMEL instrument as a method of supervision.[4] Despite these efforts, it is the view of the Bolivian MFIs interviewed that further training and adaptation of tools is required.

The key common denominator in all of the supervision challenges faced by MFIs mentioned above is the level of microfinance expertise of supervisors. In the eyes of the MFIs, it is the lack of knowledge of supervisors regarding microfinance that results in regulations and supervision that are not sufficiently adapted to the realities of microfinance. At

Compartamos in Mexico, for example, supervisory review of operating manuals was impeded, in the view of the MFI, by the fact that the supervisors did not really understand the nature of the loans or the related credit procedures.

Lack of microfinance experience and expertise by the supervisors is understandable in some countries, such as Honduras, that have only one or a handful of regulated MFIs. However, in countries with advanced microfinance, and particularly with specialized microfinance windows, it should follow that the supervision of these new financial entities should also be specialized. Mibanco suggests that in addition to adapted supervision, a specialized unit could "act as a prudent forecaster of the real or potential difficulties that affect the sector of microfinance in the country. Also, this unit could consolidate the information of all MFIs and make this information available to all those interested."

## A SUPERVISOR'S PERSPECTIVE—BASED ON INTERVIEWS WITH JACQUES TRIGO LOUBIÈRE

Many of the concerns of the microfinance practitioners revolve around the lack of knowledge of supervisory authorities about the microfinance sector and how this translates into practical supervision of microfinance activities. It is useful, therefore, to consider the perspective of the supervisors and why, in many cases, microfinance is low on their list of priorities. Two issues are paramount: the small size of microfinance relative to the challenges regulators face, and the inflexibility of supervisory systems when confronted with an unfamiliar form of financial service.

In most countries, 90 to 95 percent of all banking activities by monetary volume are in traditional banking. Microfinance is a small sector that carries little risk for the stability of the financial system as a whole. Supervisors can afford to ignore the microfinance sector without jeopardizing the health of the financial system they are entrusted to protect. This is especially true in times of systemic financial crisis. Most Latin American countries have experienced profound financial crises at some time during the last decade. The regulatory authorities have had to liquidate many banks and return deposits to the public. In such a setting, supervisors simply lack time for microfinance.

Because most supervisors don't know how microfinance works, they are very reluctant to accept modification of supervisory norms and even more unwilling to create new types of financial intermediaries specifically for microfinance. Supervisors tend to view any modification to norms as granted flexibility, which is not normally allowed. The culture, rules, and attitudes of supervisory authorities constitute an enormous barrier to changing the traditional norms.

## Supervisors' Concerns

It is important to understand how some supervisors perceive the microfinance sector. Two of their main concerns are the costs of supervision and the perceived volatility and risk of the market.

### Costs of Supervision

It is a common belief that the costs of regulating and supervising MFIs is prohibitively high due to the large number of operating MFIs and the small asset base under their control. It is important, however, to distinguish between startup and ongoing supervision costs. In the experience of Bolivia, the Superintendency initially incurred high costs to establish a good management information system with an internal private network allowing for real-time reporting from each MFI and to train supervisors about microfinance. Ongoing costs are lower, but data are not available to determine the specific costs of supervising MFIs, as costs are incurred in a variety of departments of the Superintendency.

### Risk Volatility

In general, financial intermediaries (banks and MFIs) are fragile and volatile because they operate with higher levels of leverage than private enterprises. The volatility of MFIs is compounded by the vulnerable nature of the clients, particularly subsistence farmers or small-scale vendors.

However, MFIs have several advantages over traditional banks. MFIs practice better borrower analysis (banks often rely on guarantees, which do not present the full picture of risk). Additionally, MFIs may prove to be somewhat less subject to systemic financial crisis, as experienced in Bolivia and Ecuador in recent years. In these cases the regulated MFIs performed better than traditional banks. In Bolivia in 2001, during a period of financial sector crisis, the capital adequacy indicator for MFIs was 19.2 percent, while for banks it was 13.9 percent.[5] Similarly, portfolio provisioning for MFIs was 11.5 percent, while for banks it was 7.4 percent. Better performance in the case of Bolivia clearly reflects the fact that MFIs were following more conservative capital adequacy and provisioning policies than mainstream banks.

## Monitoring Loan Portfolio Quality

It has been theorized that good supervisory tools do not exist to monitor microfinance portfolio loan quality reliably (Christen and Rosenberg 2000, 9). This is a case where adaptation of traditional finance tools to microfinance is necessary. In Bolivia, for example, the Superintendency does not attempt to supervise each individual loan, because it would be materially impossible to do so. The high number of loans between US$100 and US$1,000 prevents any such categorical review. Instead, a portfolio selection is used to give a broad picture of the situation of the overall portfolio. It should be noted that the most important aspect of monitoring portfolio quality and microfinance in general is to ensure that credit technology, policies, and procedures are complied with and that these correspond to the norms of the supervisory agencies. These policies and procedures are the first line of defense against risk.

## Credit Bureaus

An important tool to ensure that portfolio quality remains high throughout the retail lending system is a central credit-risk bureau that allows financial entities to obtain the debt level of their borrowers. It does not matter whether this is maintained by the state through the Superintendency of Banks or the Central Bank, or if it is administered by the private sector. It is critical that it function well, have the capacity to collect information in real time, and be able to transmit this information immediately to all institutions throughout the financial system (see Chapter 13).

## Regulating Activities vs. Institutions

Liza Valenzuela and Robin Young affirm that the focus of microfinance regulation should center on the *activity* of microfinance—lending to the self-employed sector—rather than on *institutions* (Valenzuela and Young 1999, ix). Attempts to channel all microfinance into specialized MFIs will not address institutions that provide a variety of services to a broad range of clients (such as banks that go "down-market" to serve the microentrepreneur while maintaining traditional banking activities). From a supervisor's perspective, an activity-based approach is preferable but can often be difficult, given the laws governing banking in various countries. In many countries there are laws that provide specialized regulations for each type of financial institution, such as commercial banks, investment banks, mortgage institutions, consumer institutions, MFIs, and cooperatives. The legal classification of these entities generates confusion and does not foster the establishment of entities that reach poor clients. General norms that regulate the financial intermediation activity are more comprehensible and facilitate the introduction of norms specialized to microfinance.

### Getting Microfinance onto the Supervisors' Agenda

> *Supervision must be handled with transparency and constant dialogue with the supervisors. It is very important that the dialogue is open from the side of the supervisors as well.*
>
> —Caja los Andes, Bolivia

Over time, training of supervisors will be the key to ensuring that microfinance is well understood and that supervision is appropriately adapted to the particularities of the field. In the interim, open communication between the MFI and the supervising entity can help identify mutually acceptable mechanisms of supervision. Dialogue will allow for increased cooperation and compromise to agree upon norms that achieve the supervisors' objectives while allowing MFIs to operate effectively. Understanding the perspective of the supervisors will help MFIs propose solutions that serve the purposes of both sides.

### Understanding the Importance of MFI Regulation and Supervision

To convince supervisors or government representatives of the importance of licensing and regulating MFIs, regulators must be educated on the benefits of supervised microfinance activity. The main benefits, from a supervisor's perspective are:

- *Opening the Banking Sector to the Poor.* The number of people with access to credit can be increased through microfinance. While this is the basic assumption for most practitioners in the field, it must be communicated to the supervisory agencies. In Bolivia, for example, the average microcredit loan is US$600, whereas the average outstanding loan in commercial banks is more than US$100,000. While two-thirds of the outstanding portfolio (by dollar volume) of the banking system is found in those loans of US$100,000 and up, loans of less than US$10,000 account for 85 percent of the number of borrowers.[6] Thus, from the point of view of monetary and financial system stability, it makes sense for supervisors to focus on mainstream banking, but in terms of the number of a country's citizens directly affected, the broad outreach of microfinance is more significant. In addition to expanded access to credit, the benefit of expanded access to a broad array of financial services, such as the transfer of funds and savings, should be emphasized.

- *Decreased Cost of Credit.* Regulation and supervision of MFIs may foster increased competition in the sector. While this may have some negative results that need to be closely monitored, such as client over-indebtedness, competition also leads to increased efficiency in MFIs and a greater focus on client satisfaction. The end result is often a decrease in the cost of credit for the microentrepreneur. In Bolivia, for example, the average annualized interest rate for MFIs prior to the introduction of the FFP law was 72 percent. This rate has now decreased to 36 percent.

- *Stable Sector of Financial System.* As has been seen in Ecuador and Bolivia, regulated MFIs fared better than traditional banks during periods of systemic financial crisis. This is directly opposed to many supervisors' belief that MFIs are highly volatile institutions with high levels of risk. These experiences should be better documented and used as illustrations to supervisors of the strength and stability of regulated MFIs.

## Autonomy of Superintendencies

A high level of autonomy is one of the hallmarks of an effective supervisory system. Many a banking crisis has resulted from the failure of governments to give supervisors the independence needed to sanction weak institutions or inappropriate behavior. This issue lies at the core of financial-sector development in general. Although it is not directly an issue for microfinance, nevertheless, it is likely that a more autonomous superintendency will be better positioned to support microfinance effectively. For example, in autonomous superintendencies it is possible to invest in the skills of staff who will not rotate with the change of political administration.

A sufficient budget, skilled personnel, and appropriate infrastructure must be in place for an autonomous superintendency to be effective.

- *Sufficient Budget.* Supervisors must have the authority and ability to collect supervision costs from the entities that they oversee. A sufficient budget enables them to hire and train specialized supervisors and focus significant attention on the microfinance sector.
- *Skilled Personnel.* Institutions that are autonomous need to establish norms to hire personnel with requisite financial skills independent of any political pressure. There should be objective examinations during the hiring process to determine the skill levels of potential hires. The salaries of this staff must be adequately high in order to diminish the loss of trained personnel to the private sector and decrease staff turnover.
- *Infrastructure.* The superintendency must obtain the resources to develop high quality management information systems to complete their function in an efficient, technically advanced manner.

### Training of Supervisors

Successful supervisor training will address many of the concerns of supervised MFIs in terms of lack of knowledge, adaptation, and flexibility. Often, a supervisor arrives at an MFI with a set of preconceptions about the type of information that will be available to conduct the review. Supervisors expect cash flows, financials, and other "typical" information in the loan files of the micro-borrowers. They expect loan documentation that may be unavailable or unrealistic in the microfinance setting. As is clear from the experience of practitioners, adaptation often does not take place, and supervisors apply unrealistic norms. Rather than adapt their preconceptions to the realities of the microfinance field, many supervisors instead expect practitioners to change their methodologies to conform to traditional banking.

Supervisors should undergo training to understand that one cannot apply the same norms to microfinance that are used for commercial loans or consumer credit. In Bolivia, the Superintendency has created a separate section of advisors (approximately four staff members overseeing eight institutions) specializing in the field of microfinance.[7] This is completely separate from the group of supervisors that audit traditional banking activity. Technical assistance was provided to the supervisors in the field of microfinance from several sources, such as Development Alternatives International (DAI), Consultative Group to Assist the Poorest (CGAP), and ACCION International.[8]

Training of supervisory staff should have both classroom and field components so that all knowledge gained in the classroom is given context in the realities of field implementation. Supervisor trainees should have the opportunity to visit the headquarters offices of MFIs as well as accompany loan officers into the field to visit branch offices and clients.

Critics of technical assistance argue that staff turnover within the supervisory agency can render such assistance virtually useless. Personnel turnover is very high because government agencies are politically associated and influenced in Latin America. For this reason it makes sense to target training efforts toward superintendencies that have a relatively high level of autonomy.

## Specialized Regulatory Windows: The Bolivian Experience

Despite the fact that there appears to be a lack of knowledge of microfinance among supervisory entities, there is a great deal of pressure to create specialized financial entities for microfinance, arising in part from government and donor desires to be seen as working to reduce poverty. NGOs also pressure regulators to create special mechanisms that will allow them to capture public deposits and investor money. Supervisors must balance this pressure with their own requirements for prudential regulation and supervision and their capacity to supervise new entities.

Recognizing the dramatic impact of BancoSol in opening the banking sector to an entirely new segment of the Bolivian population, the Superintendency of Banks created a regulatory structure especially designed to support other MFIs. In 1996, it developed the FFP (Fondo Financiero Privado) regulations, with charter requirements and supervisory structures specifically designed for microfinance institutions. FFPs were given a lower paid-in-capital threshold than banks, more appropriate for microfinance (from US$5.6 million for banks to US$1 million for FFPs), enabling institutions to enter more easily the commercial microfinance marketplace.

The Bolivian Superintendency still found that the feasibility studies of MFIs proposing formalization of their activities did not contain sufficient information in terms of a thorough technical, financial or economic analysis. It worked painstakingly with the applicants to address their areas of weakness. As a result, seven new institutions had been licensed by the end of 2000. Among these were four institutions created from or by successful microfinance NGOs (Caja los Andes, Prodem FFP, FIE, and Eco Futuro), one private venture set up to pursue both microfinance and consumer lending (FASSIL), and two other entities not focused on microfinance. Together, the microfinance FFPs plus BancoSol served about 200,000 poor entrepreneurs in 2000. Even in the face of a severe economic crisis that has shaken the Bolivian financial sector, the regulators have been able to work with institutions to contain losses and maintain the viability of the MFIs. MFIs have so far been successful in this difficult period compared with traditional banks: the three leading regulated MFIs registered profits in 2000, compared to losses totaling over US$30 million among traditional banks.

It is crucial to note, however, that the fundamental initiative that led to the creation of Bolivia's licensed microfinance "industry" came from the MFIs themselves. The Superintendency, with its FFP legislation, responded to this emerging initiative and therefore facilitated its maturing into a set of formal institutions.

## NEXT STEPS

If one agrees that the future of microfinance lies in regulated environments, it is clear that the critical next step in advancing regulation and supervision of microfinance is to work with regulators and bank superintendencies to better understand the sector. This should be accomplished through a mutual exchange of information, with the microfinance sector gaining better understanding of the goals, perspectives, and constraints of regulators. The microfinance sector should work with regulators and supervisors to increase their capacity in microfinance, giving them tools and training to establish and regulate norms for MFIs. Additionally, now that there is sufficient experience of regulated microfinance, there should be continued efforts to understand how regulation and supervision are implemented in practice and to disseminate this to interested parties. By effectively understanding institutions and managing risk in this sector, regulatory entities will increase stability, competition, and growth in microfinance, ultimately bringing many more individuals into the banking sector.

## NOTES

1. Claudio Gonzalez-Vega, in ACCION International, "Conference on Microenterprise Development: Regulation and Supervision of Microfinance Institutions, Summary of Proceedings" (November 27–28, 1995), 19.

2. Compartamos originated as a nonprofit *institución de asistencia privada* (IAP) and transformed into a regulated private finance company called an SOFOL in 2001. The SOFOL license does not currently allow for the capture of savings, but laws have been introduced that would change this restriction.

3. In the original BancoSol transformation, there was a direct exchange of portfolio held by the NGO for shares in the new institution. However, this method of purchase requires a costly and potentially contentious audit of the portfolio. More recent transformations have used a different method. In this method the nonprofit uses cash to purchase shares in the new entity, and the clients, rather than the portfolio, are transferred. On the day the new entity starts operating, the NGO ceases making new loans and operational staff moves to the new entity. As loans are repaid, the NGO accumulates cash, which it uses to purchase shares or places on deposit with the new entity. The new entity begins making new loans using funds supplied by the NGO (and other sources). In this way clients are transferred, but there is no transfer of portfolio. Over a transition period that is as long as the longest term loan, all loans of the NGO are retired (except bad debt still being collected). During the transition, the NGO may pay a fee to the new entity for management of its portfolio, since the NGO immediately gave up its credit-management staff. This process ensures that the new regulated entity starts its life with a clean portfolio. This also makes it easier for the NGO to split its contribution appropriately between debt and equity.

4. CAMEL stands for **C**apital adequacy, **A**sset quality, **M**anagement, **E**fficiency, and **L**iquidity.

5. Capital adequacy is the ratio of total capital to risk weighted assets. When measured in this way, the Basle Accords allow for a minimum capital adequacy ratio of 8 percent.

6. Financial data from the Superintendency of Banks and Financial Entities (SBEF) (March 2001).

7. The eight institutions are BancoSol, Caja los Andes, FIE, FASSIL, Fondo Eco Futuro, Fondo de la Comunidad, Financiera Acceso, and Prodem.

8. The Bolivian Superintendency employs three different diagnostic tools: (1) the ACCION CAMEL for FFPs and microfinance banks; (2) PEARLS (**P**rotections, **E**arnings, **A**sset quality, **R**ates of return and cost, **L**iquidity, and **S**igns of growth) from WOCCU for cooperatives; and (3) methodology developed by Aristóbulo de Juan of the World Bank during the 1980s.

## 13.

# Credit Bureaus
## A Necessity for Microfinance?

### Anita Campion and Liza Valenzuela

## CREDIT BUREAUS:
## A NECESSITY FOR MICROFINANCE?

Growing competition and the desire to avoid crises of over-indebtedness such as that experienced in Bolivia in 1999 have led to a serious interest in client information sharing. Microfinance institutions (MFIs) are increasingly exchanging client blacklists (lists of past clients who are no longer eligible to receive loans from an institution because of poor repayment histories), creating semiformal credit bureaus, or participating in private credit bureaus. Institutional survival is the most basic objective—sharing information on client histories will minimize risks and help maintain the healthy portfolio quality that has allowed MFIs to become sustainable. In competitive environments where other commercial players are offering small loans, a second objective is also becoming important: credit bureau consultation will help reduce transaction costs by weeding out clients with poor repayment histories, resulting in increased institutional efficiency.

This chapter provides a basic introduction to credit bureaus and their intersection with the world of microfinance. It argues that MFIs, particularly those in competitive markets, need to share information and will benefit from credit bureau consultation. However, a review of the information markets in five Latin American countries reveals that such markets are far from perfect and vary tremendously in terms of their levels of development.[1] The chapter then turns to questions of institutional and market structure. Should MFIs form their own credit bureaus, regardless of the state of development of the market, or should they participate in private or public credit bureaus, however imperfect they may be? Finally, the chapter discusses the roles of governments, MFIs, and donors, and how they can help promote healthy credit information markets.

### The Benefits of Client Information Sharing

Why should MFIs share information about clients? The benefits are multiple, and, at a minimum, occur on three levels: the institutional level, the client level, and the market level.

Institutional benefits are the most obvious. By knowing more about the credit histories of potential clients, financial institutions can choose whether or not to lend to certain clients. Clients with a track record of delinquent loans are probably not good credit subjects and will likely not receive loans. Similarly, a client with two or three other outstanding loans, with or without arrears, may be unable to handle another loan. Credit bureau reports can also reduce transaction costs for an institution. For example, the three banks lending to microenterprise clients in Chile consult a credit bureau as soon as a loan application is received. Clients with delinquent loans are automatically declined, freeing the loan officers' time for review of less risky clients.

Clients, particularly good clients, benefit from credit bureau reports as well. Clients with a good record are able to get quicker, preferential service or access to lotteries or other products. Additionally, savings from reduced transaction costs could eventually be passed on to borrowers through lower interest rates. Increased efficiency in the evaluation of loan applications may result in faster loan processing. For instance, a manager of INFOCORP, a credit bureau in Peru, claims that the use of credit bureaus has reduced the waiting time for loan applicants from a week to twenty-four hours in some cases (Guillamon et al. 2000, 9). While default-prone clients are not enthused about credit bureau reports, their desire for a good record (and increased access to goods and services) tends to encourage payment of past due debts.

Markets for goods and services also benefit from a healthy flow of information. Without a large defaulting clientele, financial institutions are more profitable and can expand their services. A fair, transparent information system helps promote confidence among vendors and consumers, resulting in greater volumes of transactions.

### What Information Is Shared?

Most credit bureaus collect both positive and negative information—positive information includes outstanding and previous loans, in addition to past-due payments, while negative information pertains only to loan delinquencies. If a client has missed one or more loan payments, a consultation on that individual will turn up the client's past-due record. The negative information is useful to financial institutions because it indicates the potential client's willingness to repay. Positive information is more useful, however, because it gives a broader picture of the client. Armed with this information, the institution can verify the level of indebtedness of the client and be in a better position to measure the client's repayment capacity. Some credit bureaus also include other data, such as tax information, bounced checks, and legal suits.

MFIs might seek to obtain the following client information from other financial institutions:

- *Current and past delinquencies or defaults.* Knowing a client's credit history facilitates credit risk assessment.
- *Current outstanding balances, including information on guarantees and collateral.* With complete information about the client's current level of indebtedness, the MFI can more easily assess repayment capacity. Information on guarantees or collateral pledged against existing loans will help the MFI protect itself from accepting the same guarantee to secure a new loan.
- *Credit histories of guarantors and co-signers.* Some MFIs authorize loans based on guarantors or co-signers. The MFI might refuse to accept a certain guarantor or co-signer who has a poor credit history with another financial institution.

Depending on the macroeconomic environment and needs of the MFI, additional information might be useful, such as business and home addresses of the client, previous businesses owned, assets, and marital status. By examining such client-related information at the time of the loan application, the MFI can quickly eliminate potentially bad borrowers from the review process, thus reducing overall transaction costs.

### Types of Credit Bureaus: Mechanisms Through Which MFIs Can Share Client Information

As environments become more competitive, MFIs have begun to participate in systems for sharing clients' credit information. Such systems include public credit bureaus, private credit bureaus, public-record information agencies, specialized credit bureaus, and informal sharing of blacklists.

Table 13.1 presents different types of credit bureaus found in Bolivia, Chile, El Salvador, Peru, and Uruguay.

### Public Credit Risk Bureaus

Many Latin American countries have a central credit risk bureau operated by the country's Central Bank or Superintendency of Banking Supervision (SBS), whose objective is to monitor the general health of the economy and the financial sector. By managing a central database of information from financial institutions, the SBS can closely monitor the financial risk of the banking sector and the overall economy.

The four examples of public credit bureaus in Table 13.1 are maintained within each country's SBS, which uses the information to supervise regulated financial institutions. In Chile, the Chamber of Commerce has also been designated as the collection point for past-due and related information from all sources (financial, commercial, and educational institutions), which it then disseminates in a weekly bulletin.

---

**Box 13.1: Bolivia's Public Credit Bureau**

Until recently, the SBS in Bolivia operated the only legal credit bureau in the country, with information from thirteen banks, thirteen credit unions, eleven savings and loans, and seven FFPs. Its database contains information on approximately one million clients (some of these clients may be repeated in the database) and is accessible 24 hours a day, 365 days a year through an intranet. The credit bureau receives an average of five thousand inquiries each day.

The database, which tracks 140 different variables on clients and guarantors, is used to review the overall state of the economy and the health of local financial institutions, and as a credit bureau. Approximately thirty of the variables are used in the credit bureau.

The Superintendency requires financial institutions to use the credit bureau when making loan decisions. This requirement applies to new loans and renewals, individual loans, and loans made to solidarity-group members. Financial institutions are required to obtain written permission from clients to check credit histories. If the Superintendency finds a violation of this restriction, the institution may receive a written letter of warning or be fined.

Table 13.1: Summary Data from Five Credit Bureau Country Case Studies

| | Bolivia | Chile | El Salvador | Peru | Uruguay |
|---|---|---|---|---|---|
| Population (in 2000) | 8.3 million | 15.2 million | 6.3 million | 25.7 million | 3.3 million |
| **Credit Bureaus** | | | | | |
| Public | Superintendency | Superintendency and Chamber of Commerce | Superintendency | Superintendency (two parallel systems) | None |
| Private credit bureaus | None | DICOM SINACOFI DataBusiness SIISA Others | DICOM Pro-Crédito | CERTICOM DICOM INFOCORP Others | Clearing de Informes |
| Public information vendors (private) | SIPROTEC Datos | All private bureaus sell public data | All private bureaus sell public data | All private bureaus sell public data | n/a |
| Private specialized credit bureaus (microfinance) | FINRURAL (NGO) | None | INFORED (private/NGO) | None | None |
| Informal blacklists | Group of NGOs | None | None | None | None |

In the four countries with public credit bureaus, banks are required to provide specific data on the quality of their loan portfolios. In most cases this information is shared only with regulated institutions that report to the Superintendency, because of bank secrecy laws. In many Latin American countries this poses a serious access problem for unregulated MFIs, credit unions, and other unsupervised institutions that lend to micro-entrepreneurs.

Public credit bureaus most commonly track information on loan delinquencies or past defaults (negative information). More complete credit bureaus, such as that maintained by the Chilean SBS, also track positive information, such as clients' available credit lines and active outstanding loan balances. With access to positive information, financial institutions can better determine the full credit risk of issuing a new loan and can avoid client over-indebtedness. The Salvadoran public credit bureau provides both negative and positive information, but only on active loans.

By and large, public credit risk agencies have not been particularly useful to MFIs because many are still unregulated and cannot participate in the risk bureaus or access the databases online. In Chile, however, with client authorization a microcredit NGO can request an individual credit report from the Superintendency.

In Peru, prior to late 1997, even regulated microfinance and consumer-lending institutions were not benefiting from the credit risk agency, as loans under US$4,500 were not listed. Text box 13.2 describes the sweeping changes made to Peru's public credit risk agency and the resulting benefits for both regulated and unregulated MFIs

### Private Credit Bureaus

A key difference between public and private credit bureaus is that private credit bureaus derive information from voluntary sources. Private credit bureaus sign subscription agreements with information providers that, in turn, gain access to the information provided by other subscribers. A second important difference is that while public credit bureaus usually collect only a standard set of data for government authorities to assess risk, private credit bureaus collect a variety of data in response to customer demand.

In many countries private credit bureaus have emerged in response to increased consumer lending. The entry of private credit bureaus in Chile in the mid 1990s, for example, was buttressed by the growth of consumer

---

### Box 13.2: Peru's Public Credit Bureau for Microloans

Until November 1997 the Peruvian SBS's credit bureau collected, processed, and distributed information only on clients with loan amounts exceeding US$4,500. This limit was imposed to minimize delays in the manual processing of information. With the introduction of new technology, however, the capacity of the credit bureau to manage large amounts of information expanded. As Peru's microfinance and consumer-lending sectors grew, the government felt pressure to include microloans in its database. So, with support from the IDB, a system of dual credit bureaus was created: one for loans over US$4,500 and one for loans under this amount, which includes information from cooperatives and microfinance NGOs. The SBS retains control of the credit bureau for loans exceeding US$4,500 and outsources the management of the database of the smaller loans to a data-processing firm.

The SBS's information exchange revealed that many small-loan clients had up to eight loans secured by the same collateral without adequate repayment capacity, fueling the demand for more information services. This pushed the Superintendency to make information from both databases available on the Internet, accessible with a code and password. The database of larger loans contains 170,000 registries, versus two million in that of smaller loans.

---

lending. Consumer lenders, which make their profits based on a high volume of small loans with high interest rates, depend on credit bureau data to reduce transaction costs and assist with credit scoring.

Private credit bureaus have also emerged in response to an unmet demand for credit information services. Technological advances have allowed private credit bureaus to become highly adept at assessing information needs of different financial and commercial players. By merging data from different sources, private credit bureaus can create customized reports that respond to specific needs of different information users.

Private credit bureaus tend to be responsive to the diverse needs of financial institutions and do not limit their services to information management. Some private credit bureaus, such as Pro-Crédito in El Salvador, offer collections services and even training in credit analysis and collections for their members. Others, such as SIISA in Chile, offer database consulting, portfolio management, and credit-scoring services to help financial institutions better use and manage client data.

## Public Information Vendors

In addition to traditional public and private credit bureaus, some countries have information agencies that collect, consolidate, and/or disseminate public-record information. These vendors of public information typically manage large databases of information collected from many sources, including public records, legal announcements, and newspapers. This information, which might not appear in credit bureaus, can be helpful to financial institutions attempting to assess credit risk. For example, a private broker of public information will often have records of people whose businesses have failed, which is helpful when assessing the risk of lending to someone for a new business venture.

Until recently, although the Bolivian government considered client credit-history information too sensitive and confidential to entrust to a private firm, private vendors were allowed to collect and disseminate publicly available information. SIPROTEC, part of the Bolivian Chamber of Commerce, provides records of publicly available data, including penal and civil judgments. SIPROTEC's database has more than two million names, including both individuals and corporate entities. Eighty percent of all regulated financial institutions in Bolivia use this service, including BancoSol and Caja Los Andes. BancoSol also uses a similar regional private company called Datos. BancoSol uses SIPROTEC and Datos only for information pertaining to small-business clients (loans greater than US$30,000). Caja Los Andes uses SIPROTEC's database for large microfinance clients requesting loans over US$5,000.

## Specialized Credit Bureaus

There are many examples of specialized credit bureaus in Latin America, created by business associations in response to specific information needs of their members. In the case of Chile, banks and commercial houses don't have access to very timely data about each other's clients. Information available to the public through the Chamber of Commerce is over a month old. Hence, two "sectorial" credit bureaus have emerged, one created by the banking sector and another created by the nine largest department stores, as both sectors considered it useful to develop a more timely and presumably less costly source of information for members.

The case for specialized microfinance-sector bureaus is somewhat less clear. Unregulated microcredit NGOs have wanted to create specialized credit bureaus because they usually believe that traditional credit bureaus and public information vendors are not useful to them. There are at least five reasons behind this belief:

1. Public credit bureaus are unavailable to NGOs. Unregulated institutions cannot access the databases of superintendencies or central banks, although, in some countries, such as Chile, an NGO with client authorization can get a report on a particular client. This public-sector database, however, excludes lending activities of unregulated institutions.

2. In countries where private credit bureaus exist, microcredit NGOs believe their clients will not be listed, as the clients generally have not had access to loans from formal financial institutions or consumer lenders.

3. In some countries, microcredit NGOs, believing they serve a different market niche, have wrongly assumed they are not allowed to participate in private credit bureaus. In Mexico, for example, a group of NGOs was considering creating its own credit bureau because the group thought it could not access the local private credit bureau. In fact, NGOs were just as eligible as any other business to become subscribers.

4. There is concern over the possibility that good clients might be "stolen" by banks if positive repayment data were shared in a credit bureau. These NGOs may be unaware that institutions accessing a private or public credit bureau must have client authorization.

5. Microcredit NGOs complain that private bureaus are too costly.

For these and other reasons, in countries as diverse as Nicaragua, Benin, and the Philippines, microcredit NGOs and their associations have been considering the feasibility of creating specialized credit bureaus that are more formal than informal blacklists. El Salvador is the first example of a country in which such a formal specialized credit bureau has been created. In 1996 USAID funded a project informally to collect and disseminate names of bad debtors from six MFIs. This project led to the eventual creation of INFORED, a specialized for-profit credit bureau for the microfinance industry. Launched in 1999, it received funds from USAID for the purchase of computer equipment and software development, as well as investments from six MFIs. INFORED currently has affiliate agreements with fifteen institutions: thirteen microfinance NGOs, one cooperatively owned finance company, and a commercial enterprise. INFORED's database remains small in relation to other credit bureaus and to the total microfinance market. INFORED's business plan targets all institutions that lend to low-income individuals, and its core challenge is to increase the breadth of its database to be more useful and cost effective.

In Bolivia, an association of MFIs (FINRURAL) has created a database that tracks delinquent loans with information primarily from and for its affiliates. Originally the system was limited, only providing information on microfinance NGO clients with loans over ninety days past due, and the service was discontinued. The system was improved, however, and FINRURAL has applied for a license to establish a full-service private credit bureau for MFIs. FINRURAL is also attempting to overcome past limitations by linking to the public credit bureau in order to create a system similar to Peru's dual credit bureau. The objective is for FINRURAL to provide NGOs with access to the public credit bureau and to include NGO information in the Superintendency's credit bureau.

It should be noted that many group-lending NGOs around the world, usually those in less-competitive environments, believe that credit bureaus, whether specialized or open to all, are not useful to them. One NGO director in El Salvador argued that in the case of a community bank with thirty women, for example, it would be impractical and costly to get a credit report on each member. Because the women guarantee each other's loans, it is up to them, not the NGO, to assess an individual member's willingness to repay.

### Informal Blacklists

In many countries unregulated MFIs have created informal systems to track and share client information. These systems usually begin with the MFI compiling its own internal blacklist; as defaults and over-indebtedness have become chronic in highly competitive markets, NGOs are exchanging these internal blacklists to avoid lending to known bad borrowers.

In Bolivia, MFIs share blacklists informally each month on a quid pro quo basis. Lists contain only names and identification numbers of past delinquent loan clients. In the late 1990s in Nicaragua, unregulated MFIs also developed a voluntary system of information sharing in which MFIs took turns being the consolidators and distributors. Because it was a voluntary system, however, some MFIs were often late in reporting the data, and without timely information, the system became less useful and MFIs began to lose interest.

## Advantages and Limitations
## of the Various Credit Bureau Types

Unfortunately, none of the countries studied exhibits a perfect credit bureau market in which all parties needing information have full access to timely data. Each country, perhaps with the exception of Uruguay, excludes certain institutions or lacks full positive information on clients. As countries begin to consider structures for credit information sharing, it is useful to analyze the strengths and weaknesses of the different credit bureau types, as each has advantages and disadvantages.

### Public vs. Private

The main advantage of a public credit bureau is that the government can mandate the participation of regulated institutions. Legally required participation facilitates the rapid development of a large database that includes the majority of active loan clients in the country. In addition, the government can set reporting standards, which facilitates the compilation of information into the database. By including all clients of regulated financial institutions, a public credit bureau can offer a one-stop source of credit history information, but public credit bureaus rarely include data from unregulated financial institutions. Regulators usually cannot justify the additional cost of including these institutions, because they perceive their relative potential impact on the overall economy to be small. Given that superintendencies or central banks already collect financial information from regulated financial institutions for supervision purposes, it is probably cost efficient for them to utilize the data in a national credit risk bureau, or better yet, to make data available to licensed private credit bureaus.

Private credit bureaus tend to be more customer service oriented than public credit bureaus, because, to make a profit, they must focus on satisfying the needs of participating institutions. This orientation often results in the development of more customized products and services. The downside of private credit bureaus is that they generate concerns about privacy in environments that lack adequate laws and regulations to protect clients. In countries where private credit bureaus have demonstrated ethical management of private data, this has not been a concern. For example, ethical management of the privacy issue has facilitated the success of the private credit bureau in Uruguay, Clearing de Informes, allowing it to become the country's key source of information for financial institutions.

Table 13.2 summarizes the advantages and disadvantages of public and private credit bureaus.

**Table 13.2: Comparison of Public and Private Credit Bureaus**

| Public Credit Bureaus | | Private Credit Bureaus | |
|---|---|---|---|
| Pros | Cons | Pros | Cons |
| • Mandate participation of all regulated MFIs<br><br>• Regulators already collect information from regulated MFIs to monitor the economy | • Not necessarily responsive to information needs of MFIs<br><br>• Not likely to include unregulated MFIs | • Responsive to information needs of MFIs<br><br>• Wide range of products and services | • Rarely include all key financial institutions<br><br>• Concerns about client privacy |

### *Specialized* vs. *Nonspecialized*

The advantages of specialized credit bureaus are clear: they are more apt to be tailored to the specific needs, capacities, and concerns of subscribing members than nonspecialized bureaus. In the case of a microfinance credit bureau, for example, information on defaults within a group-borrowing setting could be included, something not normally included in a nonspecialized credit bureau report. Given that member institutions are similar, there might also be fewer issues pertaining to report design, data transmission, troubleshooting, and database updating.

Based on the experience of INFORED in El Salvador, there are at least three major disadvantages of the specialized market model. First, these specialized bureaus, because they are by nature exclusive to members, do not capture the full range of potential clients or of useful data on listed clients. Although common wisdom has been that microentrepreneurs take loans only with microcredit lenders, these clients often also have loans outstanding with consumer lenders or stores, and such data would not appear in microfinance credit bureau databases. Additionally, the files of clients who are listed in the database will only include data pertaining to loans taken with the database's subscribing microlenders; the files will not indicate whether a client is delinquent on a utility bill, for example, or whether the client has a judicial action pending. Second, because these bureaus are less able than more generic bureaus to attract a broad spectrum of institutions, their databases remain quite small, making it difficult for them to reach the volume of business necessary to achieve sustainability. Third, because membership in the bureau is voluntary, some institutions may decide not to report for a particular month or to provide information late. In such cases, although the organization may be excluded from accessing the database, all subscribers suffer.

FINRURAL in Bolivia has faced some of the above problems. For example, it has not met all the needs of microfinance NGOs for client-history information because it has not included clients of institutions other than regulated MFIs. Additionally, inconsistencies have occurred in the level of participation of member NGOs. There has also been concern over whether less-sophisticated microcredit NGO have adequate information systems to ensure accurate and timely data transmission to the database. Some NGOs report up to three months late, which at one point led Prodem, an MFI with a good management information system, to report only clients with loans past due over ninety days.

Nonspecialized credit bureaus, on the other hand, tend to be larger and more cost effective than their specialized counterparts. In seeking larger, more-profitable clients, nonspecialized credit bureaus rarely market their services to small, unregulated MFIs. Consequently, they lack data on MFI clients. Moreover, unless the nonspecialized credit bureau is highly sophisticated, large databases can be less flexible and responsive to the development of reports customized to the needs of a small group of MFI subscribers. (There is a case, however, of one large, private credit bureau in El Salvador that created a "microcredit report" overnight when it saw a market opportunity.)

Table 13.3 summarizes the key advantages and disadvantages of specialized and nonspecialized credit bureaus.

### Developing an Effective Credit Information System

In most countries, it is possible to develop a cost-effective credit information system that meets the majority of information needs within the financial/commercial system and safeguards consumers' right to privacy. However, this effort entails far more than the simple choice of institutional type. An overall policy framework is also required to ensure proper functioning of the system.

**Table 13.3: Comparison of Private Specialized and Nonspecialized Credit Bureaus**

| Specialized Credit Bureaus | | Nonspecialized Credit Bureaus | |
|---|---|---|---|
| **Pros** | **Cons** | **Pros** | **Cons** |
| • Respond to specific needs of MFIs. | • Hard to attract non-MFIs.<br><br>• Small database makes it difficult to reach scale and sustainability.<br><br>• Unregulated MFIs tend to have less sophisticated reporting systems and MIS. Data may be less reliable. | • Can include all potential clients.<br><br>• Larger databases are more cost effective. | • Often exclude clients of unregulated MFIs.<br><br>• Large databases may be less able to generate customized reports.<br><br>• Costs of consulting the bureau may be high for a low-volume MFI. |

## Background Conditions for an Effective Credit Information System

For a credit information system to be effective, the following conditions must be in place in the country:

- Reliable national identification system
- Adequate policy/regulatory structure
- System to protect clients' privacy and channels to dispute information

Reliable identification system. One of the most important conditions for an effective, accurate credit information market is having a unique identification number for each individual and business. In some countries the number is associated with a national identity card, whereas in others it is a tax-related number. Although the source of the number is irrelevant, it is critical that the number be unique, that all individuals have one, and that it be used by all sources. For example, although in many countries regulated financial institutions are required to collect the borrower's tax identification number, few microcredit borrowers possess a tax identification number.

El Salvador lacks a universal and unique personal identification number system, greatly complicating the task of sorting out identities. As a result, many MFIs operate with various identification numbers. This contributes to a higher effective cost for consulting credit information on microfinance clients, as MFIs often request up to three searches per individual—by name, electoral card number, and tax identification number—and may need to investigate further to interpret the results.

*Adequate regulatory structure.* Legislation authorizing the existence of private bureaus must be accompanied by mechanisms for registering or licensing the bureaus. Given that bureaus handle sensitive information, only those with high ethical standards should be allowed to operate. Barriers to entry should be reasonable enough to permit the emergence of various competing credit bureaus. Processes such as spot checks or effective mechanisms for consumer complaints should be in place to ensure that credit bureaus that do not abide by standards are fined or, in extreme situations, have their operating licenses revoked. In many countries the role of monitoring credit bureau compliance with privacy laws is delegated to the courts. An effective judicial system is a condition for such a policy choice.

Bank secrecy laws, present in most Latin American countries, have also wreaked havoc on credit information markets. El Salvador, Chile, and Bolivia have highly fragmented credit information systems, accessible to some financial service providers and not to others, largely because of antiquated bank secrecy laws. As the financial sector has broadened and brought in new, non-bank players, it has become urgent to modernize these laws. Fairness is also an issue. Because banks are beginning to compete with unregulated MFIs, this asymmetric access provides an unfair advantage to the banks and discourages unregulated institutions from sharing their data. This results in a particularly fragmented credit information system even within the microfinance sector, because the industry comprises both regulated and unregulated financial institutions.

El Salvador has made some efforts to address these concerns, though its solution remains far from perfect. Private credit bureaus must receive authorization from the Superintendency before collecting information from banks. The Superintendency also has the right to inspect credit bureaus to

ensure that appropriate safeguards on access and use of banking information are respected. The Superintendency states that it has no objection
to banks sharing client information with credit bureaus that meet professional conduct criteria and agree to open their operations and premises to
inspection as needed.

While El Salvador clearly allows banks to share information with approved credit bureaus, it is also clear that the purpose of information
sharing is only to promote the efficient transmission of credit information between banks and other regulated financial institutions. The Superintendency prohibits credit bureaus from disseminating client information received from regulated institutions to unregulated users.

*Protection of clients' privacy and channels to dispute information.*
Most countries in Latin America refer to privacy issues in their legislation, often in their founding constitutions. Few countries, however, have
approved specific laws to protect consumers' right to privacy regarding
financial information, incorporating principles espoused in international
conventions of the Organisation for Economic Co-operation and Development and the United Nations. These conventions are, however, the
basis of recent legislation in Chile and Argentina.

In setting consumer protection laws, authorities usually aim to strike a
balance between adequate consumer protection and the promotion of efficient markets. Approved in August of 1999, Law 19628 in Chile, *The
Protection of Private Life,* focuses specifically on how personal information is handled in response to the rapid growth of personal and business
information databases in the 1990s. The law protects consumers from
unscrupulous practices by database holders and provides a maximum
time for which information should be kept. The provisions most relevant
to credit bureaus and financial institutions are as follows:

- *Use of personal information.* The borrower must authorize the dis-
  semination of the information, which can only be collected and
  used for specified purposes. Information in public records, however, is openly available and can be used without the individual's
  authorization.
- *Rights of individuals.* An individual has the right to request his or
  her record at no charge. If information is incorrect, the individual
  can demand that it be corrected or eliminated. Information bureaus
  must communicate changes to parties who received the information.
  Should there be a dispute over the information, the law provides a

legal procedure for resolution. Individuals may also request to be withdrawn from lists used for commercial marketing purposes.

- *Data collected and time frame.* The law lists the types of economic, banking, financial, and commercial information that may be disseminated through credit bureaus, such as unpaid installments, bounced checks, and loan arrears from all types of institutions (including commercial houses). Such information may be held in databases for seven years from the time an obligation was due. Once the obligation is repaid, the information can remain for three years. The creditor must report payment of past-due obligations to the data bureaus within seven working days.
- *Treatment of public-record information.* Public-sector institutions such as the judiciary, the labor ministry, and the taxation department collect information pertaining to their areas of interest. They are not required to seek the consent of individuals to collect or use this type of personal information. The Civil Registry and Identification Bureau is responsible for maintaining a register of public information bureaus.

## Traits of an Effective Private Credit Information System

Assuming that appropriate policy conditions are in place, a credit information market in a country with a relatively dynamic economy should begin to see the emergence of private credit bureaus. In recent years, as many countries in Latin America have experienced a surge in consumer lending and thousands of new clients have become indebted, private credit bureaus have become a necessity.

Credit information markets ideally should be competitive and offer reasonable prices; be responsive to information needs of different economic sectors; and offer complete, accurate, and timely data. Such characteristics will not only inspire providers of information to report and use the data but also encourage consumers to maintain good credit records that will provide future benefits.

*Competitive, reasonable pricing.* The fundamental competitive challenge for private credit bureaus is to sign affiliate agreements with as many institutions as possible in their targeted market niche. Only in this way will the credit bureaus reach a large enough scale to be an attractive source of credit referencing. In reality, startup credit bureaus in competitive markets need to sign up major creditor institutions more than these institutions need the credit bureau's services. In El Salvador, INFORED is now facing this critical challenge.

Although a recent entrant, DICOM has quickly been able to capture important market share in El Salvador and Chile. Its success is due to four factors: (1) it is nonspecialized (open to all); (2) it is technologically advanced, making it easy for institutions to supply information and consult the database; (3) it has instant credibility because it is associated with one of the world's largest credit bureaus (Equifax); and (4) it uses sophisticated, client-oriented marketing. By designing a customized product and pricing schedule specifically for MFIs, DICOM/El Salvador has demonstrated that it can also service the microfinance market.

Prices for credit information are still high according to many MFIs, such as in El Salvador and Peru. For others, particularly regulated MFIs and other commercial institutions, the benefits to the institution exceed the per-consultation cost. As competition among credit bureaus increases, it is hoped that prices will be reduced and become more attractive to unregulated institutions.

*Complete, accurate, and timely data.* For the data to be most useful to lenders or other commercial institutions, the information should be as complete, accurate, and timely as possible. In markets with significant information fragmentation by sector, client data are usually incomplete. Accuracy is another issue, particularly in countries without a system of single national identity cards. Ensuring that functioning mechanisms are in place to correct inaccuracies is a critical principle of consumer rights. It is also common for there to be substantial time lags in the information. At DICOM/Chile, for example, a client's late payment to a local bank will not appear in the DICOM database until at least thirty to forty-five days after the payment was due, as the information is reported to the Chamber of Commerce and then downloaded by DICOM.

### Integrating Microfinance into Credit Information Markets

As microfinance moves into the mainstream of the financial system in many countries and MFIs begin to compete for clients, credit bureaus will play an increasingly important role in stabilizing the market and discouraging client over-indebtedness. While increased competition encourages MFIs to offer competitive products and leads to greater outreach, it can also create an incentive to provide more debt than clients can handle. With information from credit bureaus, microlenders can make better lending decisions and reduce risks to the institution and to clients.

In environments where there is little competition and minimal consumer lending activity, MFIs have little need for a credit bureau. However, when clients begin to access loans from multiple sources, MFIs will find value in having access to a database of client credit information. At that point, MFIs will at least be willing to share information in return for information from others, and will possibly pay for that access. For countries that are approaching or have reached this level of competition, the following may be needed to ensure meaningful integration of microfinance into the credit information system:

1. National initiatives to promote links between large unregulated MFIs and public credit bureaus
2. A willingness on the part of MFIs to share information and develop standard reporting systems
3. Technical-assistance providers to help set up information systems and develop MFI capacity to fulfill information-reporting requirements
4. Donor support to encourage a legal framework for public and/or private credit bureaus

### National Initiatives

Several initiatives can be taken to ensure the participation of MFIs in a credit information system. Governments can make bank secrecy laws more flexible to avoid fragmentation of the credit information market. This could entail making key information (such as arrears) available to all financial institutions, whether regulated or not. Furthermore, public credit bureaus could require universal and standard reporting to encourage completeness and accuracy in information sharing.

Although allowing MFIs to participate in public credit bureaus would encourage the most complete data, the bureaus would have to grapple with how to recover costs. In Bolivia, the Superintendency's credit bureau is examining ways to include unregulated institutions. At present, the overall regulatory fees charged by the Bolivian SBS include participation in the public credit bureau. Because these fees are assessed based on asset value, traditional finance institutions tend to pay a larger amount than MFIs. In a sense, non-MFIs are subsidizing the participation of regulated MFIs. It would be difficult to develop a cost-effective mechanism to include microfinance NGOs without placing an additional burden on traditional finance institutions. One possible solution would be to use the approach of the Peruvian SBS, which subcontracts with a private credit bureau that can also make money on providing additional information services, effectively cross-subsidizing credit reports for small MFIs.

## MFIs' Role and Participation

To participate in formal credit information-sharing mechanisms, MFIs need to be willing to share information, pay for the service, and conform to common reporting standards. The microcredit movement has emerged somewhat chaotically, which has led to an industry without standard accounting and reporting systems. Efforts such as those by the *MicroBanking Bulletin* and MicroRate to create and standardize performance indicators for microfinance have helped address some of the differences in accounting, reporting, and ratio analysis. For unregulated MFIs to participate in a credit information system, many will need to adopt standard charts of accounts, and revise and update management information systems.

In addition, effective participation in a credit information market often requires a minimal level of technology to handle the information-transfer process. Beyond a reliable Internet connection, no expensive, specialized equipment is required. However, even this requirement can be prohibitive for MFIs operating in rural areas or for small unregulated MFIs with manual accounting systems.

A recent survey of twenty Mexican MFIs concluded that those with computerized systems, Internet access, and frequent information flows between branches and headquarters would be able to subscribe to a private credit bureau with only minor software adjustments. On the other hand, those institutions with limited computer usage or with weak or highly centralized information flows would require investments in systems to be able to participate in a credit bureau (Hamilton 2001).

## Technical Assistance

In some cases technical assistance may be needed to overcome the accounting and technology barriers to full MFI participation. Although credit bureau staff are, by necessity, skilled in helping institutions develop links to transfer information from their portfolio management systems into a credit bureau's database, additional, outside assistance may still be necessary, depending on the MFI's level of sophistication.

## Donor Support

Responding to interest in credit information sharing from MFIs, donors are increasingly being called upon to support the creation and expansion of credit bureaus. As noted earlier, El Salvador's INFORED marks the first case of a for-profit credit bureau created by NGOs and supported by a donor agency. In Peru, donors helped create the parallel public credit bureau for small loans. These types of efforts require careful planning and a good understanding of the local market and its laws.

As a general principle, donors should make sure that efforts to support the development of credit information markets do not compete with or undermine private-sector initiatives. After all, like any private business, credit bureaus have emerged without the support of donors in many countries around the globe. Donors should also be aware that specialized credit bureaus may create further market fragmentation in some countries, which would, in the end, defeat the purpose of promoting credit information sharing. As financial markets develop, public and private credit bureaus will emerge. It is helpful to have donor support to establish a flexible policy framework for credit information, so that when credit bureaus do emerge, key parameters are in place, such as licensing standards, a national identity card system, privacy laws, communications infrastructure, and accounting and reporting standards.

Donors can influence local governments, credit bureaus, financial institutions, and clients by:

- Supporting laws that encourage reporting of arrears and indebtedness data for all important lenders, as well as legislation that provides reasonable protection of clients' rights to privacy and protection from abuses of credit information bureaus.
- Assisting individual lenders to improve infrastructure, for example, by updating management information systems and technological capabilities.
- Supporting public information campaigns or the establishment of consumer protection agencies that will help increase clients' awareness of their privacy rights and the importance of building a credit record.

## Conclusion

As financial sectors deepen and become more competitive, credit information sharing will increasingly become a necessity for the healthy functioning of markets. In many countries in Latin America, MFIs are beginning to compete with one another and with other commercial players that offer similar products, such as consumer loans. Like the consumer lenders before them, MFIs are beginning to see the value of sharing information.

The country case studies reviewed in this chapter lead to the preliminary conclusion that it is unwise to develop very specialized credit bureaus that by their nature fragment the credit information market. Whether in El Salvador or Bolivia, the specialized bureaus cater to their institutional subscribers, but their databases miss a wealth of information on clients who have not yet fallen under the purview of that particular sector. Efforts to create specialized MFI credit bureaus have been based on the assumption that the market niche of MFIs is completely separate from the market niche of other lenders. This assumption is proving to be false, at least in many Latin American countries, where microfinance clients access a variety of sources of financing, including the corner store.

Pursuing quick-fix solutions, such as endowing an MFI association with equipment, software, technical assistance, and operating expenses to run a small MFI credit bureau, is tempting for donors. As has been illustrated by the cases of INFORED and FINRURAL, however, setting up a credit bureau is not a simple matter. It requires superior technology, business marketing sophistication, and the ability to attract large and multiple subscribers. With a large subscriber base a bureau can have something useful to offer, in addition to securing its financial sustainability. Absent any other existing options, however, a specialized MFI bureau could be viewed as a temporary bridging strategy until such time as the public and private credit bureaus make their way into the sector.

Where available, linking to a private credit bureau would appear to be a good alternative for both regulated and unregulated MFIs. Unregulated MFIs with limited accounting and reporting capabilities would need to make adjustments, but there is nothing preventing them from becoming institutional subscribers. Cost is a real issue, particularly for small MFIs that lack the volume of transactions to negotiate better deals with credit bureaus. An idea that should be explored is the possibility of negotiating a "bulk" price with a private credit bureau through an association of MFIs.

Without the burden of bank secrecy laws, public credit-risk agencies could hold considerable potential, particularly if the management of the credit reporting aspects were subcontracted to a private firm, as in Peru. This model combines the power of mandatory reporting and responsiveness to client information needs with universal access for those who require positive and negative information for making business decisions.

A variant of this approach is the Chilean model, in which all arrears data, bounced checks, bankruptcies, and so on must be reported to the Chamber of Commerce, which in turn disseminates the information to the public through a weekly bulletin. Although this mechanism provides only negative information, it does feed private credit bureaus with rich, nationwide information in addition to information derived through subscriber agreements.

As markets become more complex, the development community must be prepared to respond. Government authorities, donors, technical-assistance providers, microfinance networks, banking-and-commerce associations, and large institutional users must work together to develop an effective policy and institutional framework for client-information sharing. Providers of goods and services and consumers alike will benefit. In the end, this will also help the microfinance world, which is no longer the marginal sector it once was.

## NOTE

1. Three studies were conducted under USAID's Microenterprise Best Practices Project (Bolivia, Chile, El Salvador) and two (Peru and Uruguay) under the auspices of the Inter-American Development Bank (IDB). For the Bolivia study, see Anita Campion, *Client Information Sharing in Bolivia,* monograph (July 2000). For Chile, see Liza Valenzuela, *Credit Bureaus and Microfinance in Chile,* monograph (September 2000). For El Salvador, see Thomas Lenaghan, *Microfinance Institutions and the Market for Credit Information in El Salvador,* monograph. Microenterprise Best Practices Project (2000). For Peru and Uruguay, see Bernardo Guillamón, Kevin Murphy, and Saul Abreu, *Risk Mitigation as a Cost-Effective Micro-Finance Strategy,* case study, Inter-American Development Bank, Peru Global Microenterprise Credit Program (March 2000).

# Bibliography

ACCION International. 1995. "Conference on Microenterprise Development: Regulation and Supervision of Microfinance Institutions, Summary of Proceedings." Washington, D.C. (November 27–28).

Almeyda, Gloria. 2000. *"Cual es el Perfil Socio-económico de los Asociados de las Cooperativas de Ahorro y Crédito de El Salvador."* Revisión Institucional Interna, World Council of Credit Unions (July).

Aryettey, Ernest, Hemamala Hettige, Machiko Nissanke, and William Steel. 1997. *Financial Market Fragmentation and Reforms in Sub-Saharan Africa.* World Bank Technical Paper No. 356. Washington, D.C.: World Bank.

Barnes, Carolyn, Gary Gaile, and Richard Kibombo. 2001. "The Impact of Three Microfinance Programs in Uganda." AIMS Project Paper. Washington, D.C.: Management Systems International.

Baumol, William J., and Alan S. Blinder. 1991. *Economic Principles and Policies.* 5th ed. New York: Harcourt Brace Jovanovich.

Baydas, Mayada, Douglas Graham, Liza Valenzuela. 1997. *Commercial Banks in Microfinance: New Actors in the Microfinance World.* Bethesda, Md.: Development Alternatives, Microenterprise Best Practices Project.

Benjamin, McDonald, and Joanna Ledgerwood. 1998. *The Association for the Development of Microenterprises (ADEMI): Democratising Credit in the Dominican Republic.* A Case Study for the World Bank's Project on Sustainable Banking with the Poor. Washington, D.C.: World Bank (January).

Blair, Margaret. 1995. *Ownership and Control.* Washington, D.C.: The Brookings Institution.

Bolivian Superintendency of Banks and Financial Entities. 2000. "Recopilación de Normas para Bancos y Entidades Financieras" (November).

Bowen, William G. 1994. *Inside the Boardroom.* New York: John Wiley & Sons.

Branch, Brian, and Christopher Baker. 1998a. "Credit Unions: Overcoming Governance Problems—What Does It Take?" Washington, D.C.: IDB.

———. 1998b. "Overcoming Governance Problems: What Does It Take?" Paper presented at the Inter-American Development Bank Conference on Credit Unions, March 2, 1998. Washington, D.C.: IDB.

Brownbridge, Martin, and Colin Kirkpatrick. 2000. *Financial Regulation in Developing Countries.* Working Paper Series, Paper No. 12. Manchester: University of Manchester, Institute for Development Policy and Management.

Campion, Anita. 1998. *Current Governance Practices of Microfinance Institutions.* Washington, D.C.: The Microfinance Network (October).

————. 2000. *Client Information Sharing in Bolivia.* Monograph (July).

Campion, Anita, and Cheryl Frankiewicz. 1999. *Guidelines for the Effective Governance of Microfinance Institutions.* Occasional Paper No. 3. Washington, D.C.: The Microfinance Network.

Campion, Anita, and Sahra S. Halpern. 2001. *Automating Microfinance: Experience from Latin America, Asia, and Africa.* The Microfinance Network, Occasional Paper No. 5. Washington D.C.: The Microfinance Network.

Campion, Anita, and Victoria White. 2000. *Institutional Metamorphosis: Transformation of Microfinance NGOs into Regulated Financial Institutions.* Occasional Paper No. 4. Washington, D.C.: The Microfinance Network.

Campos, S., and M. Wenner. 1998. *Lessons in Microfinance Downscaling: The Case of Banco de la Empresa, S.A.* Washington, D.C.: Sustainable Development Department, IDB.

Carpenter, Janny, Kimanthi Mutua, and Henry Oloo Oketch. 1997. "Kenya" Case Study. In *Regulation and Supervision of Microfinance Institutions*, edited by Craig Churchill. Occasional Paper No. 2. Washington, D.C.: The Microfinance Network.

Carver, John. 1990. *Boards That Make a Difference.* San Francisco: Jossey-Bass Publishers.

Charitonenko, Stephanie, Richard H. Patten, and Jacob Yaron. 1998. *Indonesia, Bank Rakyat Indonesia—Unit Desa 1970-1996.* Sustainable Banking with the Poor, Case Studies in Microfinance. Washington D.C.: World Bank (June).

Christen, Robert Peck. 1997. *Banking Services for the Poor: Managing for Financial Success—An Expanded and Revised Guidebook for Microfinance Institutions.* Washington D.C.: ACCION International.

————. 2000. *Commercialization and Mission Drift, The Transformation of Microfinance in Latin America.* CGAP Occasional Paper No. 5. Washington D.C.: CGAP (December).

Christen, Robert Peck, and Richard Rosenberg. 2000. *Rush to Regulate: Legal Frameworks for Microfinance.* CGAP Occasional Paper No. 5. Washington D.C.: CGAP.

Chu, Michael. 1998. "Private Sector Incentives for Senior Management." In *Moving Microfinance Forward: Ownership, Competition and Control of Microfinance Institutions (1997 Microfinance Network Conference Summary)*, edited by Craig Churchill. Washington, D.C.: The Microfinance Network.

Churchill, Craig. 1997. *Managing Growth: The Organizational Architecture of Microfinance Institutions.* Bethesda, Md.: Development Alternatives, Microenterprise Best Practices Project (May).

————. 1998. *Individual Microlending Case Studies.* Toronto: Calmeadow Foundation.

————. 1999. *Client-Focused Lending: The Art of Individual Lending.* Toronto: Calmeadow Foundation.

Churchill, Craig, ed. 1996. *An Introduction to Key Issues in Microfinance: Supervision and Regulation, Financing Sources, Expansion of Microfinance Institutions.* Washington, D.C.: The Microfinance Network (February).

————. 1997a. *Establishing a Microfinance Industry: Governance Best Practices and Access to Capital Markets.* Washington, D.C.: The Microfinance Network.

———. 1997b. *Regulation and Supervision of Microfinance Institutions: Case Studies.* Occasional Paper No. 2. Washington, D.C.: The Microfinance Network.

———. 1998. *Moving Microfinance Forward: Ownership, Competition and Control.* Washington, D.C.: The Microfinance Network.

Churchill, Craig, and Shari Berenbach. 1997. *Regulation and Supervision of Microfinance Institutions: Experience from Latin America, Asia and Africa.* Occasional Paper No. 1. Washington, D.C.: The Microfinance Network.

Churchill, Craig, and Sahra Halpern. 2001. *Building Customer Loyalty.* Washington, D.C.: The Microfinance Network.

Connell, Martin. 1998. "Private Equity Capital in the Microfinance Industry." In *Moving Microfinance Forward: Ownership, Competition, and Control of Microfinance Institutions (1997 Microfinance Network Conference Summary)*, edited by Craig Churchill. Washington, D.C.: The Microfinance Network.

Consultative Group to Assist the Poorest (CGAP). 1997. "The Challenge of Growth of Microfinance Institutions: The BancoSol Experience." CGAP Focus Note No. 6. Washington D.C.: CGAP (March).

Cuevas, Carlos E. 1996. *Enabling Environment and Microfinance Institutions: Lessons from Latin America.* Washington, D.C.: Sustainable Banking with the Poor, World Bank.

Del Villar, Rafael, Alejandro Díaz de Leon, and Johanna Gil Hubert. 2001. "Regulation of Personal Data Protection and of Reporting Agencies: A Comparison of Selected Countries in Latin America, the United States, and European Union Countries." Paper presented at a World Bank seminar (February).

DeSoto, Hernando. 1989. *The Other Path: The Invisible Revolution in the Third World.* New York: Harper & Row.

Demb, Ada, and Friedrich Neubauer. 1992. *The Corporate Board.* New York: Oxford University Press.

Dhumale, Rahul, Amela Sapcanin, and William Tucker. 1998. *Commercial Banking and Microfinance in Egypt: National Bank for Development, Case Study.* New York: United Nations Development Program.

Dichter, Thomas W. 1999. "NGOs in Microfinance: Past, Present, Future." In *Microfinance in Africa,* edited by Steven A. Breth. Mexico City: Sasakawa Africa Association.

Drake, Deborah, and Maria Otero. 1992. *Alchemists for the Poor: NGOs as Financial Institutions.* Monograph Series No. 6. Washington, D.C.: ACCION International.

Duca, Diane. 1996. *Nonprofit Boards: Roles, Responsibilities, and Performance.* New York: John Wiley & Sons.

Dunford, C. 1998. "The Role of International NGOs in Microfinance." paper presented at the First Annual Rocky Mountain Microcredit Conference.

Dunn, Elizabeth. 1999. "Microfinance Clients in Lima, Peru: Baseline Report for AIMS Core Impact Assessment." AIMS Project Report. Washington, D.C.: USAID/ G/EG/MD, Management Systems International.

Dunn, Elizabeth, and J. Gordon Arbuckle Jr. 2001. "The Impacts of Microcredit: A Case Study from Peru." AIMS Project Report. Washington, D.C.: USAID/G/EG/ MD, Management Systems International.

Edgcomb, Elaine, and James Crawley, eds. 1993. *An Institutional Guide for Enterprise Development Organizations.* New York: The Small Enterprise Education and Promotion Network.

Foundation for Development Cooperation on Behalf of The Banking with the Poor Network. N.d. *The Policy and Regulatory Environment for Microfinance in Asia.* Brisbane, Australia: Foundation for Development Cooperation on Behalf of The Banking with the Poor Network.

Frankiewicz, Cheryl. 2001. *Building Institutional Capacity: The Story of PRODEM, 1987-1999.* Toronto: Calmeadow Foundation.

Gallardo, J. S., Bikki K. Randhawa, Orlando J. Sacay. 1997. *A Commercial Bank's Microfinance Program: The Case of Hatton National Bank in Sri Lanka.* World Bank Discussion Paper No. 369. Washington, D.C.: World Bank.

Glosser, Amy. 1994. "The Creation of BancoSol in Bolivia." In *The New World of Microenterprise Finance: Building Healthy Financial Institutions for the Poor,* edited by Maria Otero and Elisabeth Rhyne. West Hartford, Conn.: Kumarian Press.

Gomez, Arelis, German Tabares, and Robert Vogel. 1999. *Microfinance, Bank Regulation, and Supervision: The Bolivian Case Study.* Bethesda, Md.: Development Alternatives, Microenterprise Best Practices Project.

Gonzalez-Vega, Claudio, and Douglas Graham. 1995. *Public Agricultural Banks: Lessons and Opportunities for Microfinance.* Paper presented at Seminar on Agricultural Development Banks and Microenterprises, Washington D.C. (June).

Gonzalez-Vega, Claudio, Mark Schreiner, Richard L. Meyer, Jorge Rodriguez Meza, and Sergio Navajas. 1996. "BancoSol: The Challenge of Growth of Microfinance Organizations." Economics and Sociology Occasional Paper No. 2345. Columbus, Ohio: Ohio State University (May).

González-Vega, Claudio, Mark Schreiner, Sergio Navajas, Jorge Rodriguez Meza, and Richard L. Meyer. N.d. "A Primer on Bolivian Experiences in Microfinance: An Ohio State Perspective." Columbus, Ohio: Rural Finance Program, Ohio State University.

Goodwin-Groen, Ruth. 1998. *The Role of Commercial Banks in Microfinance: Asia Pacific Region.* Brisbane, Australia: The Foundation for Development Cooperation.

Gregorio, Simon Peter. 1998. "Managing Exponential Growth and Transformation: The Case of CARD Rural Development Bank, Inc." Asian Institute of Management Center for Entrepreneurship. Written in collaboration with the Coalition for Microfinance Standards and TSPI Development Corporation.

Guillamón, Bernardo, Kevin Murphy, and Saul Abreu. 2000. *Risk Mitigation as a Cost-Effective Micro-Finance Strategy.* Case Study, Inter-American Development Bank, Peru Global Microenterprise Credit Program (March).

Hamilton, Eve. 2001. "Estudio de Factibilidad: La Afiliación de las Organizaciones de Finanzas Populares a un Buró de Crédito." ProDesarrollo (June).

Hannig, Alfred, and Edward Katimbo-Mugwaya, eds. 2000. "How to Regulate and Supervise Microfinance?—Key Issues in an International Perspective." Kampala: GTZ and Bank of Uganda.

Helms, Brigit. 1998. "CGAP Appraisal Report on CARD." Washington, D.C.: World Bank (April).

Houle, Cyril O. 1989. *Governing Boards: Their Nature and Nurture.* San Francisco: Jossey-Bass Publishers.

Inter-American Development Bank (IDB). 1995. "Micro 2001: Expanding Economic Opportunity Through Enterprise Development." Program Outline for Consultation with IDP Partners. Washington, D.C.: IDB.

Jansson, Tor, with Mark D. Wenner. 1997. "Financial Regulation and Its Significance for Microfinance in Latin America and the Caribbean." Washington, D.C.: IDB (December).

Katsuma, Yasushi. 1996. "Transforming an NGO into a Commercial Bank to Expand Financial Services for the Microenterprises of Low-Income People—PRODEM and Banco Solidario (BancoSol) in Bolivia." *Kokusai Kyoryoku Kenkyu* 12/1 [Japan] (April).

Lapenu, Cécile. 2000. *The Role of the State in Promoting Microfinance Institutions.* FCND Discussion Paper No. 89. Washington, D.C.: International Food Policy Research Institute (June).

Law No. 19628 of the Republic of Chile. 1999. *Ley de Protección de la Vida Privada* (August).

Ledgerwood, Joanna. 1999. *Microfinance Handbook: An Institutional and Financial Perspective.* Washington, D.C.: World Bank.

Leifer, Jacqueline Covey, and Michael B. Glomb. 1992. *The Legal Obligations of Nonprofit Boards.* Washington, D.C.: National Center for Nonprofit Boards.

Lenaghan, Thomas. 2000. *Microfinance Institutions and the Market for Credit Information in El Salvador.* Monograph. Bethesda, Md.: Development Alternatives, Microenterprise Best Practices Project.

Lepp, Anja. 1996. "Financial Products for MSEs—The Municipal Savings and Loan Banks of Peru." In *Small Enterprise Development* 7/2, 103-5. Southampton Row, London: Intermediate Technology Publications Ltd. (June).

"A Lesson from National Bank of Kenya." 1999. *Market Intelligence* (January 14).

Lewis, Edward M. 1993. *An Introduction to Credit Scoring.* San Rafael, Calif.: Fair, Isaac and Co.

Llanto, Gilberto. 1998. "Policy and Regulatory Issues Facing Microfinance in the Philippines." Paper presented at the Coalition for Microfinance Standards, National Summit. Asian Development Bank (August).

Luang, Eduardo C., and Malena Vasquez. 1997. "Philippines" Case Study, Occasional Paper No. 2. In *Regulation and Supervision of Microfinance Institutions,* edited by Craig Churchill. Washington, D.C.: The Microfinance Network.

Lubière, Jacques Trigo. 1996. "Supervising and Regulating Microfinance—The Bolivian Experience." *Small Enterprise Development* 7/3, 103-5. Southampton Row, London: Intermediate Technology Publications (September).

Matin, Imran. Forthcoming. "Overlapping in Microfinance: A micro study from Bangladesh." *Small Enterprise Development Journal.*

Morduch, J. 1999. "The Microfinance Promise." In *Journal of Economic Literature* 37/4.

Navajas, Sergio, Jonathan Conning, and Claudio Gonzalez-Vega. 1999. "Lending Technologies, Competition, and Consolidation in the Market for Microfinance in Bolivia." Columbus, Ohio: Ohio State University.

Neuhauss, W. 2002. "Refinancing Banks in an Unstable Financial Environment— The KfW Experience." In *Banking and Monetary Policy in Eastern Europe: The First Ten Years*, edited by Adalbert Winkler. New York: Palgrave/Macmillan.

Oberdorf, Charles, ed. 1999. *Microfinance: Conversations with the Experts*. Boston, Mass.: ACCION International and Calmeadow Foundation.

Otero, Maria. 1986. *The Solidarity Group Concept: Its Characteristics and Significance for Urban Informal Sector Activities*. ACCION Monograph Series No. 1. New York: PACT.

———. 1989. *Breaking Through: The Expansion of Microenterprise Programs as a Challenge for Non-Profit Institutions*. Monograph Series No. 4. Boston, Mass.: ACCION International (October).

———. 1998. "Types of Owners for Microfinance Institutions." In *Moving Microfinance Forward: Ownership, Competition and Control of Microfinance Institutions (1997 Microfinance Network Conference Summary)*, edited by Craig Churchill. Washington, D.C.: The Microfinance Network.

Otero, Maria, and Elisabeth Rhyne, eds. 1994. *The New World of Microenterprise Finance: Building Healthy Financial Institutions for the Poor*. West Hartford, Conn.: Kumarian Press.

Overton, George W., ed. 1993. *Guidebook for Directors of Nonprofit Corporations*. Chicago: American Bar Association.

Paxton, Julia. 1999. *Colombia, Banco Caja Social*. Sustainable Banking with the Poor, Case Studies in Microfinance. Washington, D.C.: World Bank (March).

Pederson, Glenn D., and Washington K. Kiiru. 1997. "Kenya Rural Enterprise Program: A Case Study of a Microfinance Scheme." Africa Region/World Bank No. 3. Washington, D.C.: World Bank (December).

Poyo, Jeffrey, and Robin Young. 1999a. *Commercialization of Microfinance: Cases of Banco Económico and Fondo Financiero Privado FA$$IL, Bolivia*. Bethesda, Md.: Development Alternatives, Microenterprise Best Practices Project.

———. 1999b. *Commercialization of Microfinance: A Framework for Latin America*. Bethesda, Md.: Development Alternatives, Microenterprise Best Practices Project (February).

Poyo, Jeffrey, Robin Young, and Jean Steege. 1999. *Commercialization of Microfinance: Case of Multicredit Bank, Panama*. Bethesda, Md.: Development Alternatives, Microenterprise Best Practices Project.

Reille, Xavier, and Dominique Gallmann. 1998. "The Indonesia People's Credit Banks (BPRs) and the Financial Crisis." Second Annual Seminar on New Development Finance, Goethe University of Frankfurt (September).

Rhyne, Elisabeth. 1996. "Major Issues in Supervision and Regulation." In *Key Issues in Microfinance*, edited by Craig Churchill. Washington, D.C.: The Microfinance Network (February).

———. 2001. *Mainstreaming Microfinance: How Lending to the Poor Began, Grew, and Came of Age in Bolivia*. West Hartford, Conn.: Kumarian Press.

Rhyne, Elisabeth, and Robert Peck Christen. 1999. *Microfinance Enters the Market-place.* Washington, D.C.: United States Agency for International Development.

Robinson, Marguerite S. 1994a. "Financial Intermediation at the Local Level: Lessons from Indonesia: Part II, A Theoretical Perspective." Development Discussion Paper No. 482. Cambridge, Mass.: Harvard Institute for International Development.

———. 1994b. "Savings Mobilization and Microenterprise Finance: The Indonesian Experience." In *The New World of Microenterprise Finance,* edited by Maria Otero and Elisabeth Rhyne. Westport, Conn.: Kumarian Press.

———. 1994c. *The Framework and Development of the Bank Rakyat Indonesia Unit Banking System, 1970-1994.* 2 vols. Jakarta: Center for Policy and Implementation Studies.

———. 1995. *Where the Microfinance Revolution Began: The First Twenty-five Years of the Bank Dagang Bali, 1970-1995.* Gemini Working Paper No. 53. Washington, D.C.: United States Agency for International Development.

———. 1998. "Microfinance: The Paradigm Shift from Credit Delivery to Sustainable Financial Intermediation. In *Strategic Issues in Microfinance,* edited by M. S. Kimenyi, R. C. Wieland, and J. D. von Pischke. Aldershot, England: Ashgate Publishing Company.

———. 2001. *The Microfinance Revolution, Sustainable Finance for the Poor, Lessons from Indonesia, the Emerging Industry.* Washington, D.C.: World Bank.

Rock, Rachel. 1997. "Peru." In *Regulation and Supervision of Microfinance Institutions, Case Studies,* edited by Craig Churchill. Occasional Paper No. 2. Toronto: The Microfinance Network.

Rock, Rachel, and Maria Otero, eds. 1997. *From Margin to Mainstream: The Regulation and Supervision of Microfinance.* Monograph Series No. 11. Washington, D.C.: ACCION International.

Rock, Rachel, Maria Otero, and Sonia Saltzman. 1998. *Principles and Practices of Microfinance Governance.* Bethesda, Md.: Development Alternatives, Microenterprise Best Practices Project (August).

Rosenberg, Richard. 1994. "Beyond Self-Sufficiency: Licensed Leverage and Microfinance Strategy." CGAP Discussion Paper. Washington, D.C.: CGAP (April).

Rulianti. *Managing Through Crisis or Disaster (BRI Experience).* 2001. Presentation at Challenges to Microfinance Commercialization Conference, June 5-6, Washington, D.C.

Rutherford, Stuart. 2000. *The Poor and Their Money.* New Delhi: Oxford University Press.

Schmidt, Reinhard, and C. P. Zeitinger. 1994. "Critical Issues in Small and Microbusiness Finance." Frankfurt, Germany: Interdisziplinare Projekt Consult.

———. 1996. "The Efficiency of Credit-Granting NGOs in Latin America." In *Savings and Development* 20, 353-84.

———. 2001. "Building New Development Finance Institutions Instead of Remodeling Existing Ones." *Small Business Development* 3.

Schmidt, R. H., and A. Winkler. 2000. "Financial Institution Building in Developing Countries." *Journal für Entwicklungspolitik* 16/4.

Schonberger, Steven, and Robert Christen. 2001. *A Multilateral Donor Triumphs over Disbursement Pressure: The Story of Microfinance at Banco do Nordeste in Brazil*. CGAP Focus Note No. 23. Washington D.C.: CGAP.

Schor, Gabriel. 1997. *Commercial Financial Institutions as Microlending Partners, Some lessons of the MicroProgram in Paraguay*. Draft version. IPC Working Paper No. 15. Frankfurt.

Seibel, Hans Deiter. 2000. *Agricultural Development Reform*. Rural Finance Working Paper No. 7a. IFAD (November).

Stack, Kathleen, and Didier Thys. 2000. "A Business Model for Going Down Market: Combining Village Banking and Credit Unions." *The MicroBanking Bulletin* 5 (September).

Staschen, Stefan. 1999. *Regulation and Supervision of Microfinance Institutions: State of Knowledge*. Eschborn: GTZ (August).

Steege, Jean. 1998. "The Rise and Fall of Corposol: Lessons Learned from the Challenges of Managing Growth." Bethesda, Md.: Development Alternatives, Microfinance Best Practices Project.

Steinwand, Dirk. 2001. *The Alchemy of Microfinance: The Evolution of the Indonesia Peoples Credit Banks (BPR) from 1895 to 1999 and a Contemporary Analysis*. Berlin: Verlag fur Wissenschaft und Forschung (VWF).

Superintendencia de Bancos e Instituciones Financieras de Bolivia. 1996–2000. *Anuarios Estadisticos*.

USAID. 1998a. *Informe de Conferencia: "Instituciones Bancarias: Proporcionando Servicios en Microfinanzas."* Santiago, Chile (April).

———. 1998b. *Proceedings: The Commercialization of Microfinance Conference*, Nairobi, Kenya, May 11-14.

———. 2000. "Regulated Institutions Providing Microfinance Services." Salvador, Brazil.

Valenzuela, Liza. 2000. *Credit Bureaus and Microfinance in Chile*. Monograph (September).

Valenzuela, Liza, and Robin Young. 1999. *Consultation on Regulation and Supervision of Microfinance: A Workshop Report*. Bethesda, Md.: Development Alternatives, Microenterprise Best Practices Project (December).

van Greuning, Hennie, Joselito Gallardo, and Bikki Randhawa. 1998. *A Framework for Regulating Microfinance Institutions*. Washington, D.C.: World Bank (December).

Vogel, Robert C., Arelis Gomez, and Thomas Fitzgerald. 1999. *Microfinance Regulation and Supervision Concept Paper*. Bethesda, Md.: Development Alternatives, Microenterprise Best Practices Project.

Wallace, E. 1996. "Financial Institutional Development—The Case of the Russia Small Business Fund." In *Small Business in Transition Economies*, edited by J. Levitsky, 76-84. London: Intermediate Technology Publications.

Wasmus, Koen. 1999. *The Rehabilitation of Centenary Rural Development Bank LTD.: Lessons Learnt*. 2d draft. Frankfurt (June).

Webster, L. M., R. Riopelle, and A.-M. Chidzero. 1996. "World Bank Lending for Small Enterprises 1989–1993," World Bank Technical Paper No. 311. Washington D.C.: World Bank.

Wenner, Mark D., and Sergio Campos. 1998. *Lessons in Microfinance Downscaling: The Case of Banco de la Empresa S.A.* Washington D.C.: IDB.

Westley, Glenn, and Sherrill Shaffer. 1999. "Credit Union Policies and Performance in Latin America." *Journal of Banking and Finance* 23: 1303-29.

Zeitinger, C. P. 2002. "Financial Institution Building: Only a Drop in the Ocean?" In *Banking and Monetary Policy in Eastern Europe: The First Ten Years*, edited by Adalbert Winkler. New York: Palgrave/Macmillan.

# Contributors

**Deborah Drake** has worked with ACCION International since 1990 and currently serves as vice president and special assistant to the president. Upon joining ACCION, Ms. Drake served as director of new financial instruments, exploring and implementing new mechanisms for financing microenterprise programs, and later as director of ACCION's U.S. and Latin America Bridge Funds. In 1995 she was promoted to senior director of special projects, where she developed and managed financial initiatives to facilitate the access to capital markets by ACCION's lending affiliates. Before joining ACCION, Ms. Drake worked as a banking specialist in the Financial Policy and Systems Division of the World Bank and as assistant vice president at the American Security Bank in Washington D.C. Ms. Drake holds a B.S. in foreign service from Georgetown University.

**Elisabeth Rhyne** joined ACCION International as senior vice president in October 2000, managing its Research, Development and Policy Department and leading ACCION's Africa initiatives. Ms. Rhyne has published numerous articles and four books on microfinance. She is co-editor of *The New World of Microenterprise Finance* and authored *Mainstreaming Microfinance: How Lending to the Poor Began, Grew, and Came of Age in Bolivia,* published by Kumarian Press in May 2001. Prior to joining ACCION, Ms. Rhyne worked as an independent microfinance consultant based in Mozambique. From 1994 to 1998, she was the director of the Office of Microenterprise Development at USAID. From 1989 to 1993 she designed and coordinated USAID's GEMINI project. Ms. Rhyne earned a master's and the Ph.D. in public policy from Harvard University. She holds a bachelor's degree in history and humanities from Stanford University.

**J. Gordon Arbuckle Jr.** is a research associate in the Department of Agricultural Economics at the University of Missouri, with research interests in economic development, poverty alleviation, and microfinance. He has worked with the AIMS project since 1997. As co-author of the

Peru Core Impact Assessment, he supervised the field-data collection and participated in the data analysis. His other AIMS research has centered on the nexus between impact assessment and market research and on client-focused new product development. Prior to working at the University of Missouri, Mr. Arbuckle worked as a consultant on community-based environmental management and economic-development projects in Latin America and the Caribbean, including long-term assignments in Guatemala and Jamaica.

**Anita Campion** is the banking and enterprise development manager for Chemonics International, a development consulting firm based in Washington D.C. Formerly, Ms. Campion was the director of the MicroFinance Network, a global association of advanced microfinance institutions. Her chapters for this book were written during her tenure at the MicroFinance Network. She has fifteen years of combined experience in formal and informal finance. Ms. Campion spent three years in Mali as the small enterprise development program director for the Peace Corps and was regional manager for Asia and Latin America for Global Volunteers. She also served on the board of ProMujer in Bolivia from 1994 to 1995. Ms. Campion has worked as a pension specialist and as a senior financial advisor for formal financial institutions in the United States. Her international development career was initiated in Costa Rica, where she worked as a small business consultant from 1988 to 1990.

**Robert Peck Christen** is senior advisor to the Consultative Group to Assist the Poorest and is the director of Naropa University's Microfinance Training Program. Mr. Christen edits the *Microbanking Bulletin,* an industry wide publication devoted to financial sustainability. As an international consultant, Mr. Christen has advised commercial banks interested in microfinance, central banks, and banking superintendencies interested in the regulatory framework for microfinance, and donor agencies interested in performance standards. Prior to his work as an independent consultant, Mr. Christen worked for ACCION International, where he established microcredit NGOs in Costa Rica and Chile. In addition, Mr. Christen is the author of several publications related to sustainable microfinance.

**Michael Chu** is the managing director and founding partner of Pegasus Venture Capital, an investment firm dedicated to the deployment of venture capital in the Latin marketplace. Previously, Mr. Chu served as president and CEO of ACCION International during a six-year period of innovation and expansion of services. Mr. Chu joined the staff of ACCION International in August 1993 upon his early retirement from the investment firm of Kohlberg Kravis Roberts & Co. (KKR), where he was an executive and limited partner in the New York office. Mr. Chu, a native of Kunming, China, grew up in Montevideo, Uruguay. He holds a B.A. degree with honors from Dartmouth College and an M.B.A. with high distinction from the Harvard Business School.

**Lynne Curran** is senior director of Latin American Operations at ACCION International, where she is responsible for the financial analysis and performance monitoring of the ACCION Network of microfinance institutions, as well as CAMEL evaluations of MFIs and the transfer of the ACCION CAMEL to other institutions. Previously, Ms. Curran worked in the Capital Markets Department of ACCION International, where she was involved in ACCION's efforts to link microfinance to the world's capital markets, including the establishment of the Gateway Fund, ACCION's equity fund. Ms. Curran holds a B.A. degree from Tufts University and an M.A. from Lesley University.

**Elizabeth Dunn** is an applied economist and faculty member in the Department of Agricultural Economics at the University of Missouri. Her research focuses on low-income households, their economic decisions, and their responses to poverty-alleviation programs and policies. She is a specialist in the collection and analysis of primary data, including both quantitative and qualitative data, and has recently been working on longitudinal impact evaluations in Peru, Bosnia-Herzegovina, and Missouri. She received the Ph.D. in agricultural economics at the University of Wisconsin-Madison in 1991. As a consultant, she has provided research and training services to a number of organizations, including USAID, the World Bank, CARE International, and the Monsanto Company. In recent years Dr. Dunn's work has focused on the collection and use of client-level information for impact evaluation and program improvement in microfinance.

**Patricia Lee** is a director of Communications at ACCION International. She is responsible for writing journal articles, researching microfinance issues, and producing institutional publications. Previous to working at ACCION, Ms. Lee worked for Cambridge Energy Research Associates, an energy consulting firm and as a marine policy researcher at Woods Hole Oceanographic Institution. She received a B.A. in international studies from Colby College in 1995.

**Barry Lennon** is a senior financial advisor in USAID's Microenterprise Development Office. He manages the Implementation Grant Program (IGP), an annual grant window that makes financial investments into microfinance institutions worldwide. Over the past seven years Mr. Lennon has completed field appraisals and market assessments in thirty-five countries in Africa, Asia, Latin America, Eastern Europe, and the Newly Independent States. Prior to joining the Microenterprise Office, Mr. Lennon spent fourteen years in Central America with USAID developing financial service programs for low-income people through government-owned and private commercial banks, and a wide range of non-bank financial institutions such as credit unions and agricultural marketing and supply cooperatives.

**Rochus Mommartz**, who works for IPC, has concerned himself with microfinance issues at both a practical and a theoretical level since 1991. His work has focused on aspects associated with the regulation of microfinance institutions and with analysis of their efficiency, as well as on the implementation of management systems. He co-authored the book *Analyzing the Efficiency of Credit Granting NGOs.*

**María Otero** was named president and CEO of ACCION International in January 2000, where she had been executive vice president since 1992. She joined ACCION in 1986 as director of its microfinance program in Honduras. Ms. Otero has published several monographs on micro-enterprise and co-edited *The New World of Microenterprise Finance*, published by Kumarian Press in 1994. Ms. Otero serves as chair of the MicroFinance Network and has served in an advisory capacity to the World Bank's Consultative Group to Assist the Poorest (CGAP). Since 1997 Ms. Otero has been an adjunct professor at Johns Hopkins School for Advanced International Studies. Ms. Otero was born and raised in La Paz, Bolivia, and resides in Washington, D.C.

**David C. Richardson** is the senior manager of technical development for the World Council of Credit Unions (WOCCU) and has worked in the International Credit Union Movement for the past fifteen years. He is responsible for the development and integration of new technical products and services to improve credit union financial performance and expand the market share of credit unions around the world. For nine years prior to joining WOCCU, Mr. Richardson managed a $200 million agricultural investment loan portfolio for the Mutual Life Insurance Company of New York (MONY). He holds a master's degree in agri-business management from Texas A&M University and currently resides in Colorado Springs, Colorado.

**Gabriel Schor** has been one of IPC's managing directors since 1990, with overall responsibility for Latin America. In this capacity he focuses on the design and implementation of projects that promote financial market development through institution building. Dr. Schor and his team seek to create practical incentives for commercial banks to develop innovative products for microentrepreneurs and small farmers and to increase the supply of low-income housing. After completing his studies, Dr. Schor worked as a research associate at the University of Trier.

**Leslie Théodore** is an independent consultant who until 2001 was a senior director at ACCION International, where she managed grants and contracts from multilateral institutions as well as from the U.S. and foreign governments. Before joining ACCION, Ms. Théodore worked as a development officer at EARTH, a sustainable agriculture university based in Costa Rica, and as a trust administrator at Boston Private Bank and Trust Company. She holds a master's of international management from the American Graduate School of International Management (Thunderbird) in Glendale, Arizona.

**Jacques Trigo Loubière** is currently the minister of finance of Bolivia. Previous to this appointment, Mr. Trigo served for six years as Bolivia's superintendent of banks and financial entities. During that time he established a special regulatory framework for microfinance institutions within Bolivia, which has since been adopted in many other countries. Outside of Bolivia, Mr. Trigo spent ten years in various positions at the Inter-American Development Bank, including those of principal economist and executive director. He has held the positions of executive director and president of the Central Bank of Bolivia and has worked internationally as an independent financial consultant. Mr. Trigo, fluent in English, Spanish, Portuguese, and French, received his undergraduate degree in economics from Mackenzie University in São Paulo, Brazil, and holds a master's degree in economics from the Sorbonne University in Paris, France.

**Liza Valenzuela** is a deputy director of USAID's Office of Microenterprise Development in Washington, D.C., where she manages the office's grant programs; provides technical support to programs in selected countries in Latin America, Africa, and the Middle East; and follows emerging trends such as commercialization and regulation and supervision. She worked with USAID microenterprise programs in Bolivia and Honduras from 1988 to 1996. Prior to USAID, she worked with NGOs engaged in microlending activities.

**Victoria White** has been senior director of Africa Operations for ACCION International since April 2001. From 1998 to 2001 Ms. White worked with Calmeadow on advisory assignments for several microfinance institutions. Prior to joining Calmeadow, she was a project officer with USAID, where she managed the Microenterprise Best Practices project. From 1991 to 1993, Ms. White was a bank examiner with the Federal Reserve Bank of New York, where she used financial tools and models to analyze asset quality, capital adequacy, liquidity, and earnings of foreign and domestic banks. Ms. White has a B.A. from Wellesley College and a master's in international economics and international affairs from Johns Hopkins School for Advanced International Studies.

# Index

# Also from Kumarian Press...

## Microfinance

**Defying the Odds:** Banking for the Poor
Eugene Versluysen

**Mainstreaming Microfinance**
How Lending to the Poor Began, Grew, and Came of Age in Bolivia
Elisabeth Rhyne

**The New World of Microfinance**
Building Healthy Financial Institutions for the Poor
Edited by María Otero and Elisabeth Rhyne

## Conflict Resolution, Environment, Gender Studies, Global Issues, Globalization, International Development, Political Economy

**Advocacy for Social Justice:** A Global Action and Reflection Guide
David Cohen, Rosa de la Vega, Gabrielle Watson

**Bringing the Food Economy Home:** Local Alternatives to Global Agribusiness
Helena Norberg-Hodge, Todd Merrifield, Steven Gorelick

**The Humanitarian Enterprise:** Dilemmas and Discoveries
Larry Minear

**Going Global:** Transforming Relief and Development NGOs
Marc Lindenberg and Coralie Bryant

**Managing Policy Reform:** Concepts and Tools for Decision-Makers in Developing and Transitioning Countries
Derick W. Brinkerhoff and Benjamin L. Crosby

**Running Out of Control:** Dilemmas of Globalization
R. Alan Hedley

**Shifting Burdens:** Gender and Agrarian Change under Neoliberalism
Edited by Shahra Razavi

**The Spaces of Neoliberalism:** Land, Place, and Family in Latin America
Edited by Jacquelyn Chase

**War's Offensive on Women**
The Humanitarian Challenge in Bosnia, Kosovo, and Afghanistan
Julie A. Mertus

**Where Corruption Lives**
Edited by Gerald Caiden, O.P. Dwivedi and Joseph Jabbra

Visit Kumarian Press at **www.kpbooks.com** or call **toll-free 800.289.2664** for a complete catalog.

*Kumarian Press, located in Bloomfield, Connecticut, is a forward-looking, scholarly press that promotes active international engagement and an awareness of global connectedness*